D0065479

Gods and Heroes

Gods and Heroes:

A Quick Guide to the Occupations,

Associations and Experiences

of the

Greek and Roman Gods and Heroes

by

Caroline Thomas Harnsberger

BL
727
.H35

The Whitston Publishing Company

Troy, New York

1977

Copyright 1977
Caroline Harnsberger
ISBN 0-87875-125-4
Library of Congress Catalog Card No. 76-21470
Printed in the United States of America

INDIANA
PURDUE
LIBRARY
NOV 1980

FORT WAYNE

WITHDRAWN

TB 11/17/80

Preface

In our modern life, in our conversation, in our reading and in all the news media, we are constantly associating ourselves, however unconsciously, with the gods, goddesses and heroes in the Greek and Roman myths. We go to *Palladiums* to see *Hellenic* games; we construct *Nike* missiles, send *Apollo* space-ships to *Lunar* regions, and make *Mercury* explorations to *Venus* and *Mars.* We exert *Herculean* effort; design *Cyclopean* architecture; suffer from *Insomnia* or *Somnambulism* or *Hypnotic* effects; we used to *Vulcanize* tires; take some derivitives of *Morphine* in our drugs. We cannot escape the mythical gods.

But despite this involvement and interest we are unable to find quickly and satisfactorily information about gods and goddesses through the subject with which the character is associated. If we do not already know their names, our search can be complicated and endless.

For instance, how can we locate the various names of the goddesses of the moon without going through a complicated process of cross-reference? How can we find the names of the many gods who bore wings, or rode in chariots, and how do we locate those kings of the winds who were so colorful? The books of mythology to date do not simplify this effort.

My purpose is to make this information easily available by supplying a quick guide to the associations, and relation of the gods to, for example: dew, madness, music, prophecy, ridicule, the sea, shepherds, sleep, serpents, trees, unrequited love, etc. to name but a few subjects.

To further exemplify: under *River,* we find that Acheloüs

was a river-god who could change form; under *Stone,* we learn that Sisyphus was in the Under World, and as punishment had to roll a stone endlessly uphill.

Under another subject heading, we see that Acheloüs had an association with the *Cornucopia,* that it was his horn that Hercules tore away to present to the Naiads, who made a Cornucopia out of it.

Under *Indiscretion,* we find out more about Sisyphus, that he was indiscreet enough to disclose his witnessing the intrigue of Jupiter with Aegina.

Stories evolve as we pursue the occupations and associations which most interest us. And at last, we can find what we want to know about a god without being sure of his name.

The characters are listed under both their Greek and Roman identities, and their names are used interchangeably.

Caroline Thomas Harnsberger

TABLE OF CONTENTS

ABDUCTION *See also* CARRIED OFF

Antenor (Gr.)--The Trojan who advised the return of Helen to her husband, King Menelaüs of Sparta, after she ahd been abducted by Paris.

Antiope (Gr.)--In a campaign against the Amazons, Theseus carried off their queen, Antiope, and married her.

Helen (Gr.)--Her abduction started the Trojan War, which lasted nine years.

Paris (Gr.)--Aphrodite, the goddess of love, aided him in his abduction of Helen.

Pirithoüs (Gr.)--He went to the Under World to abduct Pluto's wife, Proserpina. There Pluto seized him and chained him to an enchanted rock at his palace gate.

Theseus (Gr.)--At one time he abducted Helen, but returned her. Then he assisted his friend, Pirithoüs, to kidnap Proserpina, and was seized with him by Pluto. When Hercules arrived, he liberated Theseus, but left Pirithoüs to his fate.

ADOPTION *See also* SHEPHERDS

Laiüs (Gr.)--King of Thebes; married to his cousin, Jocasta; father of Oedipus. Because an oracle had told him he would be killed by his son, he sent the infant off to the mountains with a herdsman. A shepherd took him to King Polybus.

Oceanus (Gr.)--He and his wife, Tethys, adopted Juno, and brought her up in their palace in the remote west beyond the sea.

Oedipus (Gr.)--Because his feet had been pierced and tied with thongs, they were swollen when he was taken to King Polybus and his queen at Corinth, and after adopting him they dubbed him Oedipus, meaning Swollen-Foot.

Polybus (Gr.)--King of Corinth. *See* Oedipus.

ADVENTURE *See also* EXPEDITION

Aeneas (Gr.)--After escaping from the burning city of Troy, he built several ships, and embarked for Italy, where he was to found the Roman race. Along the way, he had nearly as many adventures as Ulysses.

Cadmus (Gr.)--During his search for his sister, Europa, he was met by Apollo, who told him to find a cow in a field and to follow her wherever she might wander. When she stopped, he was to build a city on the spot and to call it Thebes. During these adventures, he killed a dragon sacred to Mars.

Hercules (Ro.); Alcides (Gr.)--He had many hair-raising adventures during his Twelve Labors, performed at the command of Juno for his cousin, King Eurystheus.

Ulysses (Gr.)--After taking part in the Trojan War for nine years, he outfitted several ships, and sailed from Troy for his own kingdom of Itaca, encountering unbelievable adventures during the ten years, with long stop-overs at various islands, and a visit to the Under World, to ask the prophet, Tiresias, there how to proceed home across the oceans.

ADVISOR *See also* COUNSELOR

Antenor (Gr.)-- *See same under* ABDUCTION

AEGIS *See* SHIELD; SYMBOL

AFFECTION

Anteros (Gr.)--He was a symbol of reciprocal affection.

AGE, OLD *See also* YOUTH

Aeson (Gr.)--After he had reached old age, the sorceress, Medea, restored him to the vigor of youth.

Ascanius (Gr.); Iulus (Ro.)--Son of Aeneas, who, during the Trojan War, promised to take care of Euryalus's aging mother.

2

Baucis (Gr.)--An old Phrygian peasant woman, wife of Philemon, who entertained Mercury and Jupiter in disguise, in their modest cottage.

Celeus (Gr.)--An old man who asked Ceres to cure his son, Triptolemus, of a fever.

Cumaean Sibyl (Gr.)--A young prophetess, who lived in a deep cavern at Cumae, Italy. Apollo offered her any gift and she asked to live forever, forgetting to add eternal youth. She had to look forward to centuries of bearing the burdens of old age.

Furies, The three (Gr.)--Goddesses of vengeance, they often visited earth to punish irreverence to old age.

Nereus (Gr.)--A genial old man of the sea, distinguished for his knowledge, and love of truth and justice. Husband of Doris; father of fifty daughters.

Phaon (Gr.)--In the guise of an ugly old crone, Aphrodite begged passage on his ferry boat, then gave him a salve possessing magical qualities of youth and beauty.

Philemon (Gr.)-- *See* Baucis.

Proteus (Gr.)--A prophetic sea-god, who could assume different shapes. He was similar to Nereus, in being a genial little old man of the sea.

Sarpedon (Gr.)--Zeus permitted him to live three generations.

Silvanus (Ro.)--A rural deity. *See same under* SYMBOLS.

Tithonus (Gr.)--Aurora stole him away and asked Jupiter to grant him immortality, but forgot to have youth joined in the gift. He grew old, and when he could no longer walk, she changed him into a grasshopper.

Vertumnus (Gr.)--He came to Pomona disguised as an old woman, to advise her to choose a youth such as Vertumnus to love.

AGRICULTURE *See also* SOWING

Athena (Gr.); Minerva (Ro.)--The virgin goddess; she presided over agriculture and navigation.

3

Ceres (Ro.); Demeter (Gr.)--Goddess of sowing, reaping and of agriculture in general.

Iasion (Gr.)--A hero or deity of agriculture.

Triptolemus (Gr.)--After she cured him of a fever, Ceres taught him the use of the plow, and the rewards which labor can win from the soil. Later, she took him in her chariot drawn by winged dragons. through all the countries of the earth, and under her guidance, he imparted to mankind valuable grains, and the knowledge of agriculture.

ALLIES

Aeneas (Gr.)--During his adventures, he met Pallas, who led him to his father, the Arcadian chief, Evander, and his little commonwealth, where they became allies against the Rutulians.

Mezentius (Gr.)--King of the Etruscans, and Turnus, Chief of the Italian tribe, the Rutulis, became allies during the Trojan War.

Seven against Thebes (Gr.)--This expedition of seven heroes was led by Adrastus, to aid Polynices to recover his kingship from his usurping brother, Eteocles.

ALPHABET

Cadmus (Gr.)--He introduced the alphabet from Phoenicia into Greece, and invented many useful arts.

ALTAR

Consus (Ro.)--An early Italian god of the earth. His altar is said to have been discovered underground by Romulus.

Proteus (Gr.)--He instructed Aristaeus to select four bulls and four cows, and to build four altars on which to sacrifice them, to appease the nymphs after he caused the death of Eurydice.

Pylades (Gr.)--Son of King Strophis of Phocis. *See same under* TEMPLE.

ALTAR (cont.)

Vesta (Ro.); Hestia (Gr.)--Goddess of the hearth and its fire. From her altars those of the other gods obtained their fires.

AMAZON

Antiope (Gr.); Hippolyta (Gr.)--Queen of the Amazons; later the wife of Theseus.

Hippolyta (Gr.)-- *Same as* Antiope. It was she who had been given a girdle by Ares, which was coveted by Eurstheus's daughter, Admeta.

Penethesilea (Gr.)--A queen of the Amazons, who brought momentary success to the sinking cause of Troy.

Theseua (Gr.)--He was a leader in the campaign against the Amazons, carrying off their queen, Antiope, and marrying her.

ANCESTOR

Epaphus (Gr.)--Son of Io, by Zeus; born in Egypt after the wanderings of his mother. He was King of Egypt, and ancestor of a famous line, including Danaüs and Cadmus.

Cadmus (Gr.)-- *See same under* ARMY.

Harmonia (Gr.)--Daughter of Mars and Aphrodite; ancestress of the unquiet dynasty of Thebes.

Hellen (Gr.)--Son of King Deucalion of Thessaly, and Pyrrha. Father of Aeolus, Dorus and Xuthus. Hellen became founder of the Hellenic race. His son, Aeolus became an ancestor of the Aeolians, and Dorus, an ancestor of the Dorians.

Lares (Ro.)--These were spirits of ancestors, who watched over and protected their descendants.

Xuthus (Gr.)--Son of Ducalion and Pyrrha; brother of Aeolus and Dorus. The Achaeans and the Ionians derived from him.

ANGER

Bellerophon (Gr.)-- *See same under* GADFLY

Coronis (Gr.)--A raven told Apollo she was unfaithful to him; in his anger he killed her, and changed the color of the raven from white to black.

Demeter (Gr.); Ceres (Ro.)--She and Persephone were worshipped in Greece as the "Great Goddesses." When Pluto took Persephone to be queen of Hades, Demeter, in her anger and despair made the earth barren.

Furies, The (Gr.)--The three goddesses of vengeance: Alecto, Magaera and Tisiphone, sometimes called the Erinnyes, the persecutors, or angered ones.

Pegasus (Gr.)--The anger of the gods caused him to be stung by a gadfly and to throw his rider, Bellerophon.

ANIMAL *See also* BEAR; BEAST; BOAR; BULL; CHANGE IN FORM; COW; DEER; DOG; FAUN; GOAT; HEIFER; HORSE; LION; MINOTAUR; OXEN; RAM; SATYR; SHEEP; STAG.

Admetus (Gr.)--He won the hand of Alcestis by coming for her in a chariot drawn by lions and boars.

Amalthea (Gr.)-- *See same under* GOAT.

Aphrodite (Gr.); Venus (Ro.)--Sacred to her were rams, hares, dolphins, and tortoises.

Apollo (Gr.)-- *See same under* MOUSE.

Arcadia (Gr.)-- *See same under* BOAR.

Arcas (Gr.)--His mother, Callisto, had been changed into a bear by Juno. When Arcas tried to spear the bear, Jupiter stopped him, and placed both Arcas and Callisto in the heavens as the Great and the Little Bears.

Ares (Gr.); Mars (Ro.)--He sometimes fought from his chariot drawn by four horses, attended by his sons, Terror, Trembling, Panic and Fear.

Argus (3), (Gr.)-- *See same under* DOG.

Aristaeus (Gr.)--An Arcadian deity; guardian of herds and flocks. Proteus once restored a hive of bees for him.

ANIMAL (cont.)

Artemis (Gr.); Diana (Ro.)--The virgin goddess, also known as Agrotera, the huntress. But she was at the same time, guardian of wild beasts and domestic brutes.

Augeas (Gr.)--King of Elis. He owned a herd of 3000 oxen, whose stalls had not been cleaned our in thirty years. It was Hercules' sixth Labor to purify the stables in one day.

Bacchus (Gr.); Dionysus (Gr.)--The god of wine. He rode on the tiger, the panther or the lynx.

Battus (Gr.)--He broke a promise of secrecy by informing Apollo that Mercury had robbed the god of his cattle.

Callisto (Gr.)-- *See* Arcas.

Centaurs (Gr.)--Intelligent creatures, half—horse, half—man.

Cercopes (Gr.)--Thievish gnomes whom Jupiter had changed into apes for because they deceived him.

Ceres (Ro.); Demeter (Gr.)--Among animals, cows, sheep, and pigs were acceptable to her.

Chimaera (Gr.)--A fire-breathing monster. *See same under* MONSTER.

Circe (Gr.)--A sorceress who lived in her own palace on the island of Aeaea, surrounded by lions, tigers, and wolves which had been tamed by her art. She feasted any persons who came there, then turned them by magic into beasts.

Diana (Ro.); Artemis (Gr.)--Her favorite animals were the bear, the boar, dogs, goats and especially the hind.

Epimetheus (Gr.)--He bestowed on man and other animals, faculties for their preservation; courage, strength, swiftness, sagacity; claws to some; wings and shells to others.

Faunus (Ro.); Pan (Gr.)--A rural deity, worshipped as a god of animal life. He was a patron of husbandry, hunting, herding and the secret lore of nature.

Gryphons (Gr.)--Guardians of gold. *See same under* LION.

ANIMAL (cont.)

Helle (Gr.)--She fell from the back of the vaulting ram with the golden fleece into the strait between Europe and Asia; afterward called the Hellespont; now the Dardanelles.

Hercules (Ro.)--His first Labor was to kill the lion which infested the valley of Nemea. He strangled it, and afterwards always wore the lion's skin' *See* Augeas.

Iacchus (Gr.); Bacchus (Gr.)--The god of wine, and especially the god of animal life.

Io (Gr.)--Because of Juno's jealousy, Jupiter had to disguise his love for Io by changing her into a heifer.

Mars (Ro.); Ares (Gr.)--His chosen animals were haunters of the battle-field—the vulture and the dog.

Midas (Gr.)--Apollo gave him ass's ears when he judged against him in a music contest.

Nemean Lion (Gr.)--An animal of great strength which roamed dangerously through the valley of Nemea. Hercules stangled it, and carried the entire carcass back to King Eurystheus.

Orthia (Gr.); Diana (Ro.)--Mistress of brute creation. It was she who punished Agamemnon for killing a stag sacred to her. When Oeneus failed to pay her due honor, she sent an enormous boar to ravage the fields of Calydon, thus bringing about the Calydonian Hunt.

Pelias (Gr.)--The unsurping King of Iolcus; father of Alcestis, whose hand he had promised to the suitor who should come for her in a chariot drawn by lions and boars. Admetus won her.

Proserpina (Ro.); Persephone (Gr.)--Cows, sheep and pigs were sacred to her.

Ulysses (Gr.)--Pretending madness, he plowed with an ass and an ox yoked together, then sowed salt.

ANKLE

Achilles (Gr.)--His mother, Thetis, tried to make him invulnerable by holding him around the ankles and dipping him into the river Styx. This is one account, *see same under* HEEL.

Marpessa (Gr.)--Called the "fair-ankled," she declined the attention of Apollo, but was carried off by the strong man, Idas.

ANT *See also* COMPANION

Daedalus (Gr.)--In his search for the artificer, Daedalus, the Cretan King, Minos, sailed to many ports, demanding of each local ruler that he thread a spiral sea shell. When Cocalis in Sicily returned the shell the next day completely threaded, minos knew that Daedalus had found haven there, for no one else was clever enough to solve the problem. The inventor had tied one end of a thread to an ant and it had made its way through the windings of the shell.

APE *See* ANIMAL

APPLE, GOLDEN

Atlas (Gr.)--He possessed an orchard of trees bearing apples of gold, so precious that he had them guarded not only by his daughters, the Hesperides, but by a fierce dragon, Ladon, whose eyes never closed in sleep.

Eirs (Gr.)--Goddess of discord. She threw a golden apple, inscribed "for the fairest," into an assembly of gods to cause contention. Three goddesses claimed it, and when the decision was put to Paris of Troy, he awarded the apple to Aphrodite.

Gaea (Gr.)--Mother Earth. She gave the tree of the golden apples to Hera for a wedding present.

Hercules (Ro.); Alcides (Gr.)--The most difficult of his Twelve Labors was the robbery of the golden apples of the Hesperides. To perform this, he had the cooperation of Atlas, for whom he held up the world while Atlas picked some for him.

Hesperides (Gr.)--These were the four nymph daughters of Atlas and Hesperis: Aegle, Arethusa, Erytheia and Hestia; guardians of the golden apple orchard.

Hippomenes (Gr.)--Atalanta was so fleet of foot that she felt safe in offering herself as a prize to the one who could beat her in a race. Hippomenes appealed to Venus for help, and she gave him three

APPLES, GOLDEN (cont.)

golden apples, telling him to drop them in Atalanta's path as they ran. Because the virgin stopped to pick them up, Hippomens won the race and her hand.

Landon (Gr.)–He was the dragon, or serpent, who helped the Hesperides to guard the golden apples.

Paris (Gr.)–Sone of King Priam and Hecuba. *See* Eris.

ARCHER *See also* ARROWS

Diomede (Gr.)–He was struck by an arrow shot by Pandarus, but felled the archer with his spear.

Iole (Gr.)–Her father, King Eurytus, promised her hand to the suitor most successful in an archery contest. Hercules won, but the King refused to fulfill his agreement. *See same under* INSANE.

Teucer (Gr.)–The best archer of the Greeks.

ARGONAUTS

Atalanta (Gr.)–This famous and beautiful heroine-huntress took part in the Argonautic expedition.

Calaïs (Gr.)--He was a winged warrior who, with his brother, Zetes, went on the Argonautic expedition and served well in an encounter with the monstrous birds, the Harpies.

Cepheus (Gr.)–King of Aethiopia; one of the Argonauts. At his death, he was changed into a constellation.

Coronus (1), (Gr.)–A leader of the Lapithae in Thessaly; one of the Argonauts.

Hylas (Gr.)–A lad who attended Hercules during the Argonautic expedition. Once Hercules deserted the expedition to try to recover him from the Naiads, who had pulled him down into the depths of a spring. The nymphs kept him captive, and he became a numbered among the blessed.

Idas (Gr.)–A hero who, with his inseparable brother, Lynceus, took part in the Argonautic expedition.

Jason (Gr.)--At the suggestion of his uncle, the usurping Pelias, King of
    Iolcus, Jason assembled fifty famous heroes, including Hercules, Or-
    pheus, Castor and Pollus, Meleager, Peleus and Telamon, and engag-
    ed Argus to build a large vessel to cross the seas to the kingdom of
    Colchis. There they were to go in quest of the Golden Fleece, kept
    by King Aeëtes. This was known as the Argonautic expedition.

Lynceus (Gr.)-- *See* Idas.

Menoetius (Gr.)--Father of Patroclus; one of the Argonauts.

Orpheus (Gr.)--He contributed to the Argonautic expedition with his
    song.

Telamon (Gr.)--Son of Aeacus; one of the most steadfast of the Argo-
    nauts.

Theseus (Gr.)--One of the older heroes; like Hercules, he joined every ex-
    pedition and hunt.

Zetes (Gr.)-- *See* Calaïs.

ARM

Andromache (Gr.)--Noblest of women in the *Iliad;* known as the "White-
    armed."

Enceladus (Gr.)--One of the mightym hundred—armed giants who warred
    against the gods and were overthrown by Athena.

Hecate (Gr.)--A three-headed goddess with six arms, which carried a
    torch, or a spear and torch.

ARMY *See also* COMBAT; SOLDIER; WARRIOR

Agamemnon (Gr.)--King of Mycenae; a Greek general in the war against
    Troy.

Agenor (Gr.)--One of the bravest of the Trojan warriors.

Ajax, the Great (Gr.)--One of the most valiant of the Greek heroes at
    Troy.

ARMY (cont.)

Alcmaeon (Gr.)--Leader of the Epigoni against Thebes. After destroying the city, he returned to Argos and put his mother to death for her intrigue with Polynices.

Cadmus (Gr.)--Minerva ordered him to take the teeth of a dragon he had killed and sow them in the earth. They sprouted into armed men who fought one another until only five were left. These five became the ancestors of the Thebans.

Eteocles (Gr.)--His refusal to share the kingship of Thebes with his brother, Polynices, led to expedition of the Seven against Thebes. The siege lasted so long that the leaders decided to let the brothers settle their quarrel by single combat. They fought and felled each other.

Myrmidons (Gr.)--The soldiers of Achilles; and army that was created for his grandfather, Aeacus, by Jupiter.

Odysseus (Gr.); Ulysses (Gr.)--One of the leaders of the Greek army during the Trojan War; the hero of the *Odyssey,* which narrates his many adventures.

Polynices (Gr.)--He was given an army by King Adrastus of Argos, to help enforce his claim against his brother, Eteocles.

ARROW *See also* AVENGE; WOUND

Achilles (Gr.)--He was struck in the heel by a poisoned arrow shot by Paris.

Alphenor (Gr.)-- *See same under* AVENGE.

Apollo (Gr.)--Resenting Jupiter's striking his son, Aesculapias, dead with a thunderbolt, he shot his arrows with vengeance at Jupiter's workmen, the Cyclopes. The god became so incensed he condemned Apollo to pasturing flocks in the service of the king.

Artemis (Gr.); Diana (Ro.)--Identified with the chaste brilliance of the moon; her symbols were the bow and arrow.

Aruns (Gr.)-- *See same under* WARRIOR.

Cupid (Ro.); Eros (Gr.)--To inspire love he pierced hearts with gold-tipped arrows; to produce the opposite, he used arrows tipped with lead.

ARROW (cont.)

Daphne (Gr.)--Since her heart had been pierced with a lead-tipped arrow, she rejected Leucippus, as well as the advances of Apollo.

Diana (Ro.)-- *See* Aruns.

Diomede (Gr.)--In the Trojan War, he was struck by an arrow of Pandarus, but he felled the archer with his spear.

Eros (Gr.); Cupid (Ro.)--The small powerful god of love; with his bow and arrows he shot darts of desire into the bosoms of men and gods.

Hercules (Ro.)--He shot Nessus, a centaur, with one of his famous poisoned arrows, for trying to ravish his wife.

Iloneus (Gr.)--Son of Niobe and Amphion; struck dead by an arrow of Apollo.

Machaon (Gr.)--In the Trojan War he was wounded by an arrow shot from the bow of Paris.

Nessus (Gr.)-- *See* Hercules.

Niobe (Gr.)--Thirteen of her fourteen children were slain by the arrows of Apollo and Artemis, to punish her.

Paris (Gr.)--He was wounded by an arrow of Hercules; and finally killed by an arrow of Philoctetes.

Philoctetes (Gr.)--He accidentally wounded himself in the foot with one of Hercules' poisoned arrows, and had to be carried to the Isle of Lemnos to recover.

Phoebus (Gr.); Apollo (Gr.)--He punished by slaying with the arrows of his sunlight.

Selene (Gr.)--An ancient goddess of the moon, whose weapons were the bow and arrow.

Telemachus (Gr.)--Son of Penelope and Ulysses, who helped his father dispatch his mother's many suitors, with a bow and arrow.

ART

Athena (Gr.); Minerva (Ro.)--The virgin goddess, who presided over the useful and ornamental arts.

13

ART (cont.)

Cadmus (Gr.)--He invented many useful arts, and introduced the alphabet from Phoenicia into Greece.

Ergane, Athena (Gr.)--Patroness of the arts, especially of weaving.

Prometheus (Gr.)--He stole fire from heaven, for the use of man to develop the arts.

ARTIFICER

Daedalus (Gr.)--A famous artificer who built a labyrinth to contain the monster, the Minotaur. Later, in prison, he constructed wings of feathers fastened on with wax, and flew over the walls.

Vulcan (Ro.); Hephaestus (Gr.)--A blacksmith for the gods, and the finest artificer of metal among them.

ASS

Midas (Gr.)--*See same under* EARS.

ASTRONOMER

Mercury (Ro.); Hermes (Gr.)--Skilled in invention, he was the forerunner of mathematicians and astronomers.

Urania (Gr.)--The Muse of astronomy; her symbols, a celestial globe and a compass.

ATHLETICS *See also* WRESTLER

Acheloüs (Gr.)--Although he could change form, he was no match for Hercules. *See same under* HORN.

Apollo (Gr.)--Patron of athletes.

Hecate (Gr.)--A three-headed goddess, who gave aid in war and athletic contests.

Mercury (Ro.); Hermes (Gr.)--His agility and strength made him easily prince in athletic pursuits.

14

ATHLETICS (cont.)

Perseus (Gr.)--In an athletic contest, he threw a discus which bounded the wrong way and hit a spectator, his grandfather, Acrisius. The injury caused his death, and fulfilled a prophecy.

ATONEMENT *See* PUNISHMENT; TORMENT

ATTENDANT

Ares (Gr.); Mars (Ro.)--His four sons: Terror, Trembling, Panic and Fear, were his attendants.

Bacchus (Gr.)--The god of wine; attended by Satyrs, Sileni and the Maenades. ·

Corybantes (Gr.)--These were wild attendants of Cybele, who accompanied her to mountains and forests to indulge in rites and revelries.

Cybele (Ro.)--Mother of the gods, who haunted mountain and forest fastnesses, accompanied by a train of wild attendants: Curetes and Dactyls, as well as the Corybantes, to celebrate with orgiastic rites in honor of her and her god lover, Attis.

Deimos (Gr.)--The personification of terror, or dread. A son and attendant of Mars.

Dike (Gr.)--The personification of justice; an attendant of Nemesis.

Echo (Gr.)--A talkative nymph; a favorite of Diana, whom she attended in the chase.

Furies, The (Gr.)--The three goddesses of vengeance; attendants of Proserpina, Queen of Hades.

Graces, The (Gr.)--Three graceful and beautiful goddesses; attendants of Venus, and intimate with the Muses.

Himeros (Gr.)--A personification of the longing of love; an attendant of Aphrodite.

Horae, The (Gr.)--Three goddesses; attendants of Venus, who assisted the Graces by twining odorous garlands and weaving robes for Venus.

ATTENDANT (cont.)

Hyale (Gr.)--A nymph; attendant to the chaste Diana.

Maenades (Gr.)--Women who danced and sang, and waved a staff in the air, in attending Bacchus with the Satyrs and the Sileni.

Phobos (Gr.)--The personification of Fear; a son and attendant of Mars (Ares).

Poena (Gr.)--With Dike and the Furies, she also attended Nemesis.

Proserpina (Gr.); Persephone (Ro.)--As the goddess of spring, she was pleasant and dear to mankind, but as the goddess of death, sitting beside Pluto, she was cruel and unyielding and gave harsh orders to her attendants, the Furies.

Satyrs (Gr.)--Deities of the woods and fields, they appeared as bearded creatures with snub noses, goat's ears and horse's tails. Their chief occupation was attending Bacchus.

Semnae (Gr.)--Another name for the three Furies; attendants of Prosperpina, the Queen of Hades.

Venus (Ro.); Aphrodite (Gr.)--This goddess of love and beauty conquered every heart. The Horae (Hours), the Graces and her winged son, Cupid, attended her.

AVENGE

Alphenor (Gr.)--One of the many children of Niobe and Amphion who were slain by the arrows of Apollo and Artemis, sons of Latona, to avenge Niobe's insult to the goddess.

Anteros (Gr.)--A god who avenged unrequited love.

Aruns (Gr.)--Slain by a secret arrow; launched by one of Diana's nymphs to avenge his killing the virgin warrior, Camilla.

Electra (Gr.)--She avenged her father, Agamemnon, by killing his murderers, her mother, Clytemnestra, and her mother's paramour, Aegisthus.

Erinnyes, The (Gr.)--These were the three Furies, Alecto, Megaera and Tisiphone, avenging spirits who brought retribution upon those who violated certain laws.

AVENGE (cont.)

Furies, The (Gr.)--The three goddesses of vengeance. *Same as* Erinnyes.

Orestes (Gr.)--Brother of Electra (Laodice), who helped her avenge their father, Agamemnon, by killing their mother for her perfidy.

Polyphontes (Gr.)--Slain by his brother, Aepytus, to avenge his father, Cresphontes, whose throne Polyphontes had assumed.

Semnae (Gr.)--The three Furies, who avenged the ghosts of those who had died violent deaths, and had no law or kin to avenge them.

Teucer (Gr.)--Although he was the best archer of the Greeks, he failed to avenge the death of his stepbrother, Ajax. For this, his father, Telamon, refused to receive him on his return from Troy.

Tisiphone (Gr.)--The avenging goddess of the three Furies. She applied a whip of scorpions to her victim, and passed him along to her sisters, Alecto and Megaera.

AX

Erysichthon (Gr.)--He violated with an ax an oak sacred to Ceres. *See same under* BLOOD, TRANSFORMED.

Vulcan (Ro.); Hephaestus (Gr.)--He assisted at the birth of Minerva, by splitting open Jupiter's head with an ax to facilitate the delivery.

B

BACCHUS

Bachantes (Bacchae), (Gr.)--Women worshippers of Bacchus, who followed in his train, filled with religious frenzy and indulging in wild orgies.

Bacchus (Gr.); Dionysus (Gr.)--The god of wine. He represented the vital strength of everything that grows; a promoter of civilization, a lawgiver, lover of peace, and King of Phrygia.

Lycurgus (Gr.)--King of the Edones, who, like Pentheus, resisted the worship of Bacchus.

BACCHUS (cont.)

Maenades (Gr.)--Women attendants of Bacchus, who danced and sang and waved in the air a staff (the *thyrsus*), entwined with ivy and topped with a pine cone.

Pentheus (Gr.)--He had no respect for the new worship of his cousin, Bacchus, and forbade rites to be performed. But cries of the Bacchanals could be heard everywhere. Once he happened on an orgy in the woods, and the revelers mistook him for a boar, and tore him to pieces. From then on, the worship of Bacchus was free to be established in Greece.

Satyrs (Gr.)--Goat—legged deities of the woods and fields; attendants of Bacchus.

Sileni (Gr.)--These were also attendants of Bacchus, deriving their name from the satyr Silenus, the jovial tutor of Bacchus.

BANQUET

Charites (Gr.)--The Graces, who presided over the banquet, the dance and all social pleasures.

Damocles (Gr.)--A flatterer in the court of Dionysius I, of Syracuse, who was seated at a royal banquet with a sword hung over his head by a hair, to rebuke his constant praise of the happiness of Kings.

Graces, The Three (Gr.)--They were Aglaia (brilliance), Euphrosyne (joy), and Thalia (bloom); attendants of Venus presiding over banquets, the dance and polite accomplishments.

BASKET

Erechtheus (Gr.)--King of Athens. He could take the form of a serpent. When he was carried from Athens in a basket by the three daughters of Cecrops, they discovered with such fright that he was a serpent that they jumped off the rock of the Acropolis.

BATHING

Arethusa (Gr.)--A woodland nymph of Elis. While bathing, she heard the voice of Alpheüs, god of the stream. Frightened, she ran into a cleft fashioned for her by Diana. A cold sweat changed her into a fountain, which plunged into the abyss, to come out in Sicily, with Alpheüs still in pursuit.

Artemis (Gr.); Diana (Ro.)--The ideal of grace and maidenly vigor; accustomed to bathing in springs and woodland brooks.

Tiresias (Gr.)--Early in his youth he had happened upon Minerva bathing in a stream. For this he was deprived of his sight, but afterwards he obtained from her knowledge of future events.

BATTLE

Eurytion (Gr.)--A Centaur, who became intoxicated at the marriage feast of Hippodamia and Pirithoüs. When he threatened violence to the bride, he started a battle which involved all the Centaurs, and the Lapithae people of Thessaly.

Mezentius (Gr.)--During the war between the Trojans and the Etruscans, he and Aeneas had a personal encounter, during which Aeneas hurled his lance, and finally dealt Mezentius a fatal blow with his sword.

Pandarus (Gr.)--A Trojan who broke a truce with the Greeks. In the two-day battle which followed, Pandarus wounded Diomede, and he in turn felled Pandarus with his spear.

Pirithoüs (Gr.)--A famous friendship between him and Theseus developed during a battle. Late Theseus took his part in the battle between the Centaurs and the Lapithaw (of which Pirithoüs was king). *See* Eurytion.

BEAR

Arcas (Gr.)--Jupiter arrested him from spearing a bear. *See* Callisto.

Callisto (Gr.)--To appease the jealousy of Juno, she had been changed into a bear. Her son was hunting and almost threw a spear at her, but Jupiter snatched them both away and placed them in the heavens as the Great and Little Bears.

Oceanus (Gr.)--He and his wife, Tethys, asked Juno not to allow the Great and Little Bears to dip into their waters. Consequently, these two constellations move around the pole, but never sink beneath the ocean.

BEAST

Artemis (Gr.); Diana (Ro.)--She was not only a huntress, but a guardian of wild beasts, as well as domestic brutes.

Cephalus (Gr.)--A young hunter, married to Procris. *See same under* HUNTER.

Circe (Gr.)-- *See same under* ANIMAL.

Diana (Ro.)-- *See* Artemis.

Eurylochus (Gr.)--From Ulysses' ship, he helped rescue the men who had been changed into beasts by Circe on Aeaea.

Icelus (Gr.)--He personated birds, beasts, and serpents.

Proteus (Gr.)--A prophetic sea-god who could assume the forms of horrible wild beasts.

BEAUTY *See also* LOVELINESS

Aphrodite (Gr.); Venus (Ro.)--The sweetly smiling goddess of beauty, love and fruitfulness.

Cassiopeia (Gr.)--She offended Neptune by boasting she was more beautiful than his attendants, the mermaids. To avenge the insult, he sent a monster to ravage the land. It was killed by Perseus.

Charis of Aglaia (Gr.)--Youngest of the three Graces; wife of Vulcan; the personification of beauty and grace.

Charites (Gr.)--The three Graces; Aglaia, Euphrosyne and Thalia; daugters of Jupiter by Eurynome; goddesses of beauty and grace.

Echo (Gr.)--One of the beautiful Oreads.

Graces, The three (Gr.)-- *See* Charites.

Hermes (Gr.); Mercury (Ro.)--A messenger of the gods; handsome, beardless, and ever in the prime of young vigor.

Hyperion (Gr.)--In later myth, he is identified with Apollo, god fo manly beauty.

Juno (Ro'); Hera (Gr.)--The Trojans were nearly shipwrecked by her after Paris selected Helen as the fairest in the land, instead of her.

Medusa (Gr.)--She dared to vie in beauty with Minerva. *See same under* HAIR.

Paris (Gr.)--He had to award a golden apple to "the fairest." His choice was to be made among three goddesses: Hera, who promised him power; Athena, glory, and Aphrodite, the fairest woman in the world. He gave an apple to Aphrodite, and she fulfilled her promise by enabling him to kidnap the most beautiful woman in the land, Helen, from her husband, Menelaüs. Menelaüs pursuit of them brought about the Trojan War.

Penelope (Gr.)--She showed beauty of character in remaining faithful to Ulysses through his twenty years' absence.

Phaon (Gr.)--Aphrodite gave him a salve which had magical properties of youth and beauty. *See same under* SALVE.

Psyche (Gr.)--She was so beautiful that when she passes, people sang her praises and strewed her way with chaplets and flowers.

Semiramis (Gr.)--Queen of Babylonia; noted for her great wisdom, beauty and voluptuousness.

Thetis (Gr.)--Her beauty was so great that even Jupiter sought her in marriage.

Venus (Ro.); Aphrodite (Gr.)--She was the goddess of love and beauty that conquered every heart.

BED

Procrustes (Gr.)--Called "The Stretcher." When travelers came by, he tied them to his iron bedstead. If they were shorter than the bed, he stretched them until they fit; if they were too long, he lopped off their limbs.

BEE

Aristaeus (Gr.)--A keeper of bees. *See also* Proteus.

Priapus (Gr.)--Protector of vineyards, gardens, bees, as well as herds and fish.

BEE (cont.)

Proteus (Gr.)--This prophetic sea-god told Aristaeus his bees had died to avenge his causing the death of Eurydice. He instructed him to sacrifice eight animals (cows and bulls), on four altars, and to hang their carcasses in a leafy grove. When Aristaeus came back in nine day, he found a swarm of bees had made a hive of one of the carcasses.

Rhoecus (Gr.)--A dryad tried to communicate with him through her messenger, a bee. He brushed it aside, and the dryad avenged berself by making him blind.

BEFRIEND *See also* FRIENDSHIP

Alcinoüs (Gr.)-- *See same under* SHIP.

BEGGAR

Furies, The three (Gr.)--They visited earth often to punish unkindness to beggars.

Penelope (Gr.)--When her husband, Ulysses, returned from his years of wandering, he punished her suitors by disguising himself as a beggar, and seeking them out to kill one at a time.

BEGINNINGS

Janus (Ro.)--A god of doors, or material openings, but more truly of beginnings, especially of good beginnings which insure good endings. Hence, he is represented as facing both ways, for the Romans believed that beginnings and endings were of the same piece, and that an undertaking ill begun could not achieve success.

BEHEADING *See also* MURDER

Hercules (Ro.)--He overcame Lityerses, King of Phrygia, by cutting off his head and throwing his body into the Meander River.

Lityerses (Gr.)--King of Phrygia. He had a custom of holding a corn reaping contest with strangers. If he won, he beheaded them and concealed their bodies in the sheaves, singing a song all the while.

Medusa (Gr.)--The most terrible monster of the three Gorgon sisters, had her miserable existence come to an end when Perseus cut off her head as she slept.

Perseus (Gr.)--An older hero sent by King Polydectes of Seriphus, to conquer the Gorgon Medusa. After he cut off her head, he flew far and wide, turning all to stone who even glanced at it.

BETRAYAL

Nisus (Gr.)--He had a purple lock of hair, upon which depended his life and fortune. His daughter, Scylla, betrayed him by cutting off the tuft, and conveying it to his enemy, King Minos.

Tantalus (Gr.)--King of Phryia. He betrayed the secrets of the gods, for which he was condemned to Tartarus.

BIRDS *See also* CRANES; EAGLES; SWANS

Aëdon (Gr.)--Queen of Thebes, whom Zeus turned into a nightingale to relieve her grief over killing her own son, Itylus.

Aeneas (Gr.)--At the Island of the Harpies, he and his crew prepared a feast, but as soon as they began to eat, the disgusting birds (Harpies) zoomed in to seize the food with their talons and fly off with it.

Aloadae (Gr.)--These two monsters, Otus and Ephialtes, tried to dethrone the immortals, and for this they were struck by Jupiter's lightning and sent to Hades. There they were bound to a pillar with serpents, and tormented by the perpetual hooting of a screech owl.

Aphrodite (Gr.); Venus (Ro.)--The swan, sparrow, and dove were sacred to her.

Calaïs (Gr.)--A winged warrior on the Argonautic expedition, who served well in an encounter with those monstrous birds, the Harpies.

Coronis (Gr.)--She was killed by Apollo after a raven or crow, told him she had been unfaithful to him. In his anger, the god changed the color of the raven or crow from white to black.

Gryphons (Gr.)--Guardians of gold; they had the head and wings of an eagle, and the body of a lion.

Halcyone (Gr.)--When her husband, Ceyx, was drowned in a shipwreck, she in her grief, threw herself into the sea. Out of compassion, the gods changed her and her mate into kingfishers.

Harpies (Gr.)--They were disgustingly foul creatures, with heads and bosoms of maidens, and wings, tail, legs, and claws of cirds.

Hercules (Ro.)--For his fifth Labor, he had to destroy birds in the valley of Stymphalus, which had been harassing and devouring many inhab-itants. He did so by rousing the birds with cymbals, then shooting them with arrows dipped in Hydra's poison.

Hero (Gr.)--She lived on the Hellespont at Sestos, and there tended Aphrodite's swans and sparrows.

Icelus (Gr.)--A producer of dreams; he was also able to personate birds, beasts and serpents.

Io (Gr.)--To disguise his love for Io, Jupiter changed her into a heifer. His wife, Juno, then begged it from him as a gift, and had it watched by the 100-eyed Argus. When Mercury came along to slay the mon-ster and set Io free, Juno took the eyes and scattered them as orna-ments on the tail of her peacock. They remain on all peacocks to this day.

Jupiter (Ro.); Zeus (Gr.)-- *See same under* EAGLE.

Leucothea (Gr.)--This was Ino transformed into a goddess of the sea. It was she in the form of a cormorant who alighted on Ulysses' raft to give him a life-belt to buoy him up in the waves.

Mars (Ro.); Ares (Gr.)--Patron god of the Romans; his chosen bird was the vulture.

Memnon (Gr.)--King of the Ethiopians. At his funeral pile, Jupiter caused the cinders and sparks of the fire to turn into birds, which, dividing into two flocks, fought over the pile until they all fell into the flame.

Minerva (Ro.); Athena (Gr.)--The owl, the cock and the crow were sacred to her.

24

BIRDS (cont.)

Nisus (Gr.)--He took the form of a sea-eagle. *See same under* HAIR. *See also* Scylla, *under* BIRDS.

Orpheus (Gr.)--The Muses buried his body at Libethra, where the nightingale sings more sweetly over his grave than in any other part of Greece.

Perdix (Gr.)--His uncle Daedalus pushed him off a tower and killed him. Minerva felt pity for the boy, and changed him into a bird, the partridge, which bears his name.

Philomela (Gr.)--The gods transformed her into a nightingale, forever bemoaning her nephew, Itylus, whom she helped kill.

Pierides (Gr.)--THey were changed into magpies.

Pleiades (Gr.)--Because Orion pursued them, they begged the gods to change their form. Jupiter turned them into pigeons, and then made them a constellation.

Polyphonte (Gr.)-- *See same under* CHANGE IN FORM.

Procne (Gr.)--For her part in killing her son, Itylus, she was changed into a swallow.

Prometheus (Gr.)--Because he stole fire from heaven for the use of man, Jupiter ordered him chained to a rock on Mt. Caucasus, and exposed to the attack of a vulture, which preyed on his liver for ages, yet never succeeded in consuming it.

Scylla (Gr.)--She betrayed her father to his enemy, Mino II, and for this King Minos, himself tied her to the rudder of his ship and dragged her through the waves toward Crete. She was then transformed into a bird, continually the prey of a sea-eagle, whose form Nisus had assumed.

Stymphalus (Gr.)--This was a valley which harboured the man-eating Stymphalian birds. They had cruel beaks and talons. It was Hercules' fifth Labor to destroy them.

Tereus (Gr.)--The cruel husband of Procne. After his wife had killed their son, Itylus, and served him as food to his father, the gods transformed her into a swallow; her sister, Philomela into a nightingale, and Tereus into a hawk, endlessly pursuing the sisters.

Tityus (Gr.)--For insulting the goddess, Latona, this giant was required to lie stretched across nine acres while a vulture preyed upon his liver.

Venus (Ro.)-- *See* Aphrodite *above. Also see* Polyphonte *under* CHANGE IN FORM.

BIRTHS: UNUSUAL

Bacchus (Gr.)--He came to birth from his mother's ashes.

Chrysaor (Gr.)--Son of Poseidon, who sprang with Pegasus from the body of Medusa.

Eurystheus (Gr.)--Hera hastened his birth, in order to precede that of Hercules; for it was decreed that the first boy born that day should rule the race of Perseus.

Hercules (Ro.)--The delay of his birth subordinated him to his cousin, Eurystheus, who became the King of Mycea.

Minerva (Ro.)--Daughter of Jupiter, who sprang from his brain, full-grown and fully armed.

Pegasus (Gr.)--The winged horse that sprang from the body of Medusa.

Uranus (Gr.)--In the conflict between the Titans and the Cyclopes, Cornus wounded Uranus with his sickle. From his blood leaped into being the Furies, whose heads writhed with serpents; the Giants, a novel race of monsters, and the Melic nymphs, maidens of the ashen spear.

BIRTHDAY

Genius (Ro.)--A Roman guardian spirit, to whom men made offerings on their birthday.

BLACK

Phaëton (Gr.)--When he tried to drive his father's (Apollo's) chariot, the horses went out of control. Clouds began to smoke, and trees on the mountains burned until the heat became intolerable. The people of Aethiopia turned black because the blood was drawn to the surface so suddenly.

BLACKSMITH

Vulcan (Ro.); Hephaestus (Gr.)--The blacksmith of the gods. The fumes and flames from his smithy poured forth from the crater of Moutain Aetna.

BLESSED

Hylas (Gr.)--The Naids had pulled him down into the depths of a spring. They kept him captive there, and he became numbered among the blessed.

BLESSING

Biton (Gr.)--He and his brother, Cleobis pulled their mother's chariot to a temple of Juno, where the goddess gave them the blessing of death.

BLINDNESS

Bellerophon (Gr.)--When by his pride he drew the anger of the Olympians Jupiter sent a gadfly to sting Pegasus, and cause him to throw his rider. From then on, Bellerophon wandered lame, blind and lonely through the Aleian field and perished miserably.

Cedalion (Gr.)--One of Vulcan's men who served as a guide for the blinded Orion. He sat on his shoulders and pointed him east until they met the sun-god who restored sight by his beam.

Daphnis (Gr.)--A Naiad fell in love with this handsome shepherd and threatened to blind him if he did not vow fidelity to her. He forgot the vow, and she did strike him blind.

27

BLINDNESS (cont.)

Eros (Gr.); Cupid (Ro.)--He was often represented with eyes covered because of the blindness of his actions.

Jupiter (Ro.); Zeus (Gr.)--He overcame the Titans by blinding them, and consigning them to Tartarus.

Orion (Gr.)--Because he tried to take Merope by force, her father, Oenopion, deprived him of his sight. He used Cedalion as a guide until he reached the abode of the sun god, Apollo, who restored his sight with the sun-beam.

Phineus (Gr.)--A Thracian King who was so cruel that Jupiter punished him by taking away his sight and transporting him to the Island of the Harpies.

Piplea (Gr.)--A Naiad, unrequited, struck him blind.

Plutus (Gr.)--The god of wealth; blinded by Zeus that he might bestow his gifts without discrimination of merit.

Polyphemus (Gr.)--To permit the escape of his men from the cave of this giant, Ulysses blinded his one eye with the end of a burning stake. *For more on this escape, see* Polyphemous *under* HAIR.

Rhoecus (Gr.)--He was blinded by a Dryad when he brushed aside her messenger, a bee.

Thamyris (Gr.)--A Thracian bard, who presumed to challenge the Muses. Conquered in the contest, he was deprived of his sight.

Tiresias (Gr.)--After he had by chance seen Minerva bathing he lost his sight.

BLOOD, TRANSFORMED

Acis (Gr.)--A rock thrown by a Cyclops destroyed him. Blood spurting from under the stone became a stream which still bears his name.

Adonis (Gr.)--After he was killed by a wild boar, Aphrodite caused the anemone to grow from the drops of his blood.

BLOOD, TRANSFORMED (cont.)

Alcyoneus (Gr.)--He was one of the Giants formed from the blood that fell from the wounded Uranus.

Alecto (Gr.)--One of the three Furies, who leaped from the spilled blood of Uranus.

Attis (Gr.)--A Phrygian god of vegetation, who mutilated himself and died from loss of blood. Violets sprang up from the drops. His death and resurrection were annually celebrated at a spring festival.

Dejanira (Gr.)--She soaked the robe of Hercules in the blood of the Centaur, Nessus, and its poison killed him.

Diomede (Gr.)--When Venus tried to rescue her son, Aeneas, during the Trojan War, Diomede grazed her palm with his spear, which caused her to lose ichor, the life-stream of the gods, and forced her to return to Olympus.

Erysichthon (Gr.)--He violated an oak grove sacred to Ceres. When he struck one tree with his ax, it shuddered and groaned and blood flowed from the wound. For this, Ceres dispatched Famine to give him a raging hunger. *See same under* HUNGER.

Furies, The three (Gr.)--Goddesses of vengeance who leaped from the spilled blood of Uranus.

Giants, The (Gr.)--When Cronus wounded Uranus with his sickle, these creatures akin to men, sprang into being from his blood.

Hercules (Ro.)-- *See* Dejanira.

Hyacinthus (Gr.)--A discus thrown by Apollo wounded him accidentally, and his blood which stained the ground, became a purple flower, now bearing his name.

Marsyas (Gr.)--After he challenged Apollo to a music contest and lost, Apollo punished him by flaying him alive. The River Marsyas was formed from his blood.

Melic Nymphs (Gr.)--These maidens of the ashen spear also sprang from the spilled blood of Uranus.

Nessus (Gr.)--A Centaur. *See* Dejanira.

Polydorus (2); (Gr.)--A young prince of Troy, murdered by many arrows. A bush grew from his blood.

Pyramus (Gr.)--He threw himself on his own sword, and his blood spurted onto a nearby white mulberry tree, tinging its berries a reddish purple. From that time on, the mulberry tree has produced nothing but purple berries.

Talus (Gr.)--Had only one vein in his body, and that plugged on the top of his head with a nail. Medea drew out the stopper.

Tisiphone (Gr.)--The avenging goddess of the three Furies, who sprang from the blood of Uranus.

Uranus (Gr.)--In the struggle between the Titan and the Cyclopes, Cronus wounded Uranus with his iron sickle. From his blood leaped into being the Furies, whose heads writhe with serpents; the Giants, a novel race of monsters; and the Melic nymphs.

BOAR

Admetus (Gr.)-- *See same under* ANIMAL.

Adonis (Gr.)--He was killed by a wild boar.

Ancaeus (Gr.)-- *See same under* HERO.

Arcadia (Gr.)--A mountainous, picturesque district of Greece, where Hercules performed his third Labor of capturing the boar that haunted Mount Erymanthus.

Atalanta (Gr.)--The wife of Mars, and a famed huntress. She took part in the Calydonian boar hunt.

Attis (Gr.)--In one version of his part in myths, he was slain by a boar.

Calydonian Boar Hunt (Gr.)--This was the pursuit of a boar which had been sent by the goddess, Artemis, to ravage the fields of Calydon. She did this because King Oeneus of Calydon, had neglected to pay due honor to her in offering his sacrifices. His son, Meleager, head of the renowned Hunt, finally killed the boar.

Hercules (Ro.)-- See Arcadia.

Idas (Gr.)--With his inseparable brother, Lynceus, he took part in the Calydonian Boar Hunt.

Jason (Gr.)--He was scarcely more than a boy when he went on the Calydonian Boar Hunt.

Lynceus (Gr.)-- *See* Idas.

Meleager (Gr.)--Being in love with Atalanta, he gave her the trophies of the Calydonian chase. It was he who killed the boar.

Neptune (Ro.); Poseidon (Gr.)--In his honor, black and white bulls, white boars, and rams were sacrificed.

Oeneus (Gr.)-- *See* Calydonian Boar Hunt.

Orthia (Gr.); Diana (Ro.)--This was the same as Diana, or Artemis, who sent the wild boar to Calydon.

Pentheus (Gr.)--He was torn to pieces by his mother and sisters, and other Bacchanalians, who mistook him for a wild boar.

Plexippus (Gr.)--He and Toxeus were brothers of Queen Althaea; braggarts and envious of her son, Meleager. During a boar hunt, the two were killed by Meleager.

Toxeus (Gr.)--He joined the Calydonian Boar Hunt with his brother Plexippus, *which see.*

BOAST *See also* BRAGGART

Cassiopeia (Gr.)--*See same under* BEAUTY.

Niobe (Gr.)--Pride in her numerous children led her to boast of her superiority over the goddess Latona, who only had two. For this, Apollo and Artemis killed all the children, except one, and Zeus changed Niobe, herself, into stone.

BOATMAN

Charon (Gr.)--The grim boatman who ferried the souls of the dead across the River Styx in Hades, if their bodies had been duly buried in the world above.

Phaon (Gr.)--He ferried a boat between Lesbos and Chios.

BODY *See also* GIANTS; MONSTERS

Centaurs (Gr.)--Creatures who were half-horse, half-men, often very intelligent.

Chimaera (Gr.)--A fire-breathing monster; the fore part of his body was half lion, half goat, and the hind part was dragon.

Chrysaor (Gr.)--Son of Poseidon, who sprang with Pegasus from the body of Medusa.

Cyclopes (Gr.)--Men of gigantic size, more like monsters, who had one enormous eye set in the middle of their foreheads.

Glaucus (Gr.)--He became immortal by tasting magic herbs, which changed him to a strange half-man, half-fish, similar to the sea-gods.

Harpies (Gr.)-- *See same under* BIRDS.

Hermaphroditus (Gr.)--Son of Hermes and Aphrodite, who became united with the nymph, Salmacis, in a single body.

Itylus (Gr.)--In revenge, the sisters, Procne and Philomela, killed him and served his body up as food to his father, King Tereus of Thrace.

Minotaur (Gr.)--He was a bull-headed, man-bodied monster, a terror to Crete.

Pan (Gr.); Faunus (Gr.)--He had the horns, ears and legs of a goat.

Satyrs (Gr.)--They appeared in early myth as bearded creatures with snub noses, goat's ears and horse's tails. Later, they resembled youths, with sprouting horns.

BOUNDARY

Dido (Gr.)--She escaped from Tyre; set the boundaries of a new site

BOUNDARY (cont.)

Dido (cont.)--with strips of a bull's hide. It became the city of Carthage, and she its queen.

Mercury (Ro.); Hermes (Gr.)--He was the guardian of boundaries and of roads.

Silvanus (Ro.)--A rural deity; genius of the woods and fields; guardian of rural boundaries.

BOX

Acamas (Gr.)--Phyllis gave him a box and warned him not to open it unless he had no intention of returning it to her. Eventually he opened it anyway, and its contents so terrified him that he galloped away wildly on his horse until he was thrown and died by falling on his own sword.

Acrisius (Gr.)--Because he was told that he would meet death at the hands of a son of Danaë, he enclosed her and her new infant, Perseus, in a big chest and set it adrift on the sea.

Althaea (Gr.)--Because the Fates had told her her son, Meleager, would die when the brand burning in the hearth was consumed, she withdrew it and stored it carefully in a box.

Herse (Gr.)--Athena gave her a box which was to remain closed. Herse yielded to curiosity, opened it. But she lifted the lid and let escape a multitude of plagues for hapless man. One thing that remained inside the box was hope.

Perseus (Gr.)-- See Acrisius *above.*

Psyche (Gr.)--She was told not to open a box given to her in Hades. But when she lifted the lid, Sleep escaped and made her unconscious.

BOY

Ganymede (Gr.)--A beautiful Trojan boy, who succeeded Hebe as cupbearer to the gods.

BRAGGART

Minos II (Gr.)--When aiming for the crown of Crete, he boasted he could

BRAGGART (cont.)

Minos II (cont.)--get anything he wanted by prayer.

Plexippus (Gr.)--Brother of Queen Althaea; a braggart, and envious of her son, Meleager.

Toxeus (Gr.)--Brother of Plexippus. In a family quarrel, his nephew, Meleager, killed both him and Plexippus.

BRAIN *See also* HEAD

Minerva (Ro.)--Sprang full-grown from the brain of Jupiter.

BRAND, BURNING *See* BURNING

BRASS

Minos II (Gr.)--King of Crete, whose domain was protected by the huge man of brass, Talus.

Pollux (Gr.)--With his brother, Castor, they captured the man of brass, Talus.

Salmoneus (Gr.)--Built a bridge of brass over which he could drive his chariot, to make sounds like thunder.

Talus (Gr.)--A giant of living brass made by Vulcan. Had only one vein in his body. On the top of his head it was plugged by a nail. Medea drew out the stopper.

BRAVERY *See also* HEROES

Antilochus (Gr.)--The brave son of Nestor.

Memnon (Gr.)--Fought bravely. Slew Antilochus.

BREAST--PLATE *See also* SHIELD

Aegis (Gr.)--A sacred breast-plate.

Athena (Gr.); Minerva (Ro.)-- *See same under* SYMBOLS.

BREAST—PLATE (cont.)

Jupiter (Ro.)--Wore a breast-plate of storm-cloud.

BREEZES See also WIND

Aura (Gr.)--Goddess of the mild and gentle breezes.

Eos (Gr.)--Mother of the morning and evening breezes.

BRIBERY

Alcmaeon (Gr.)--For his mother, Eriphyle's had accepted a bribe of Har-monia's necklace from Polynices to continue the war against Thebes, and for her having sent her husband, Amphiaraüs to his death, Alc-maeon returned and killed her.

Hippodamia (Gr.)--Bribed a charioteer to remove a bolt from her father Oenomaus's chariot, to allow her favorite, Pelops to win a race.

Myrtilus (gr.)--Was the charioteer bribed by Hippodamia.

BRIDGE

Salmoneus (Gr.)--Built a bridge of brass, over which he drove his chariot, to make sounds like thunder.

BRIDLE

Minerva (Ro.)--Fashioned a golden bridle, with which Pegasus could speed through the air.

Bellerophon (Gr.)--Secured the magic bridle from Minerva, to perform miracles with Pegasus.

BROOKS *See also* STREAM; WATERS

Artemis (Gr.)--Favored woodland brooks and streams in which she could bathe.

Fontus (Ro.)--God of brooks and springs.

BROOKS (cont.)

Juturna (Ro.)--A water-nymph; goddess of brooks and springs, whose pool in the Forum was sacred.

BROTHER *See also* TWINS

Idas (Gr.)--Was the brother of Lynceus.

BULL *See also* MINOTAUR

Acheloüs (Gr.)--Changed into a bull while trying to wrestle Hercules.

Androgeüs (Gr.)--Was sent by Aegeus, King of Athens, to fight the Marathonian bull, she was saved by her two sons.

Cadmus (Gr.)--Searched for his sister, Europa, who had been carried away by Jupiter, in the guise of a bull.

Cretan Bull (Gr.)--Neptune sent this bull to King Minos II, for sacrifice, but because it had great beauty, Minos refused to give it up. Neptune, infuriated, drove the bull wild and sent Minos' wife, Pasiphaë, into a frenzy of love for it. It was overcome by Hercules and killed by Theseus. His offspring, the Minotaur, remained long a terror to Crete.

Dido (Gr.)--On a new site, she asked of the natives only so much land as could be enclosed with a bull's hide. This granted, she cut the hide into strips and enclosed an area large enough to contain a citadel. *See more under* INVENTION.

Dirce (Gr.)--In reprisal, she was tied by the hair to the tail of a bull and dragged to her death.

Europa (Gr.)--Was carried off by Jupiter, who in the form of a white bull, swam with her to Crete, where she became the mother of Minos.

Hercules (Ro.)--Conquered the Cretan bull.

Jason (Gr.)--Had to perform certain tasks for his uncle Pelias, such as harnessing two fire-breathing, brazen-hoofed bulls to a plow.

Marathonian Bull *(Gr.)-- Same as* the Cretan bull. His offspring was the Minotaur.

BULL (cont.)

Minos II (Gr.)--Asked Neptune to send him a bull for sacrifice, but he kept it.

Minotaur, The (Gr.)--This bull-headed, man-bodied monster was a terror to Crete, until Daedalus, the artificer, built a labyrinth in which to contain it.

Neptune (Ro.)--In his honor, black and white bulls were sacrificed.

Pasiphae (Gr.)--Neptune drove her into a passion for the Cretan bull. She gave birth to the Minotaur.

Poseidon (Gr.); Neptune (Ro.)--Drove the Cretan bull wild.

Proteus (Gr.)--To allay the vengeance of some nymphs, he told Aristaeus to select four bulls and four cows, of perfect form and beauty, for sacrifice on four altars.

Zethus (Gr.)--Son of Antiope, and brother of Amphion, who tied Dirce's hair to a bull.

BURIED

Antigone (Gr.)--*See same under* FUNERAL.

Creon (Gr.)--Antigone's uncle, the usurping king of Thebes, who ordered her buried.

Manes (Ro.)--They were shades that hovered over places of burial.

Pyramus (Gr.)--He and his loved one, Thisbe, were buried in the same sepulchre.

BURNING

Aeneas (Gr.)--Carried his aged father, Anchises, on his shoulders from the burning city of Troy.

Althaea (Gr.)--Quenched a burning brand and stored it in a box, because the Fates had told her her son would live no longer than the brand.

Anchises (Gr.)-- *See* Aeneas.

Cyclops (Gr.)– *See* Polyphemus.

Meleager (Gr.)-- *See* Althaea *above.* Enraged after Meleager killed two uncles, Althaea threw the fatal brand in the fire, causing Meleager's death.

Polyphemus (Gr.)--The Cyclops whose eye Ulysses plunged out with a burning pole.

Vulcan (Ro.)–His Greek name, Hephaestus, meant "burning."

C

CADUCEUS *See also* STAFF; WAND

Caduceus (Gr.)–The magic wand of health, happiness and dreams, given to Mercury by Apollo.

Hermes (Gr.)--Wore winged shoes fastened to his ankles, a winged cap, and carried a caduceus.

Mercury (Ro.)--Bore a caduceus of wood or gold, twined with snakes and surmounted by wings.

CALYDONIAN *See* HUNT

CANNIBALISM

Atreus (Gr.)–After killing three sons of his faithless brother, Thyestes, he caused him to eat the flesh of his own children at a banquet.

Cronus (Gr.)--To assure his not losing the throne to an heir, he swallowed his first five children as soon as they were born.

CANNIBALISM (cont.)

Diomedes (Gr.)--Owned two fearful horses which fed on human flesh. Hercules killed him, after which he threw the king into the stalls to be devoured by his own steads.

Glaucus of Corinth (Gr.)--Fed his mares on human flesh. One day they turned on him and tore him to pieces.

Itylus (Gr.)–He was killed and served up as food to his father, Tereus.

Laestrygones (Gr.)--A race of cannibal giants who killed many of Ulysses' comrades.

Minotaur, The (Gr.)--A monster who lived on human victims.

Pelops (Gr.)--Was a victim, whose father served his roasted flesh at a banquet.

Procne (Gr.)–Helped to kill Itylus, and served him as food.

Tantalus (Gr.)--Wanting to ridicule the reputed omniscience of the gods, he tried to deceive them into eating the roasted flesh of his own son, Pelops.

Tereus (Gr.)–Ate the roasted flesh of his own son, Itylus, at table.

Thyestes (Gr.)--Brother of Atreus, who brought vengeance on him by causing him to eat the flesh of his own children.

CAPTIVE

Andromeda (Gr.)--Had been chained to a rock.

Briseïs (Gr.)--A captive handmaiden of Achilles, who gave him up to Agamemnon in a division of spoils in the Trojan War.

Cassandra (Gr.)-- *See same under* CARRIED OFF.

Hecuba (Gr.)–Wife of King Priam, taken captive to Greece.

Hercules (Ro.)--A captive of Queen Omphale for three years.

Omphale (Gr.)--Condemned Hercules to spin wool with her handmaidens for three years.

Perseus (Gr.)--Released the captive Andromeda and claimed her for his wife.

Pirithoüs (Gr.)--Chained to a rock by Pluto in Hades. Left there.

Prometheus (Gr.)--Jove ordered him chained to a rock on Mount Caucasus, where he was exposed to the attack of a vulture.

Proteus (Gr.)--Even in chains, he could assume many forms, to fire, to a flood, to a horrible wild beast, etc., in rapid succession.

Theseus (Gr.)--With Pirithoüs, he was chained to a rock in Hades, but released by Hercules.

Ulysses (Gr.)--Remained with the sea-nymph, Calypso, seven years.

CARE

Lyaeus (Gr.)–The loosener of care.

Nyx (Night) (Gr.)--The mother of care.

CARRIED OFF *See also* ABDUCTION

Andromache (Gr.)--After the death of her husband, Hector, she was carried off to be the wife of Neoptolemus, and to bear him three sons.

Boreas (Gr.)--Carried off by the nymph, Orithyia.

Cassandra (Gr.)–During the Trojan War, she and her mother, Hecuba, were carried off to Greece.

Castor (Gr.)-- *See* Hilaira.

Chryseïs (Gr.)--Carried off by the Greeks for Agamemnon.

Dejanira (Gr.)--Carried across a river by Nessus, who then tried to kidnap her from her husband, Hercules.

CARRIED OFF (cont.)

Europa (Gr.)--Jupiter, in the form of a white bull, carried her off, and swam with her to Crete.

Hades (Gr.); (Pluto)--Carried off Persephone from the upper world and made her his Queen.

Harpies (Gr.)--Foul creatures who carried off the souls of the dead.

Hecuba (Gr.)--She and her daughter, Cassandra, were carried off by the enemy to Greece, after the fall of Troy.

Hilaira (Gr.)--She and her sister, Phoebe, were carried off by Castor and Pollux.

Idas (Gr.)--Carried off Marpessa, after she had declined the love of Apollo.

Iphigenia (Gr.)--Was snatched by the goddess, Artemis, and carried off to Tauris, where she was made a priestess.

Marpessa (Gr.)--Called "the fair-ankled", she was carried off by the strong man, Idas, assisted by Poseidon, who gave him a winged chariot.

Neoptolemus (Gr.)-- See Andromache

Paris (Gr.)--Carried off Helen from her husband, Menelaüs, thus bringing about the Trojan War, and the fall of Troy.

Persephone (Gr.); Proserpina (Ro.)-- See Hades.

Piplea (Gr.)--Carried off by robbers.

Proserpina (Ro.)--Whom Pluto (Hades) carried off to the Under World.

Theseus (Gr.)--In a campaign against the Amazons, he carried off their queen, Antiope, and married her.
It was Theseus who carried off Helen and returned her at short notice.

CARTHAGE

Dido (Gr.)--Queen of Carthage. She selected the site for Carthage. *See more on* Dido *under the heading* BULL.

CARTHAGE (cont.)

Dis (Gr.)--At the time of the struggle with Carthage, the worship of this underworld god was introduced into Rome.

CATTLE *See also* BULLS; COWS; HERDS

Cacus (Gr.)--A giant who stole some of Hercules' cattle. *See same under* STEALING.

Lampetia (Gr.)--With her sister, Phaëthusa, she tended her father's herds on the Island of Thrinacia. When Ulysses' ship landed at Thrinacia, the father, Helios, a sun-god, commanded the crew not to violate these herds. After a month famine pressed the men and in the absence of Ulysses they slew some of them.

Pales--The goddess presiding over cattle and pastures.

CAVE

Aristaeus (Gr.)--Found the old, prophetic sea-god, Proteus, in his cave, to learn why his bees had died.

Aeolus (Gr.); Hippotades (Gr.)--King of the winds, who confined them in a cavern and released them as he saw fit.

Cacus (Gr.)--A giant who hid Ulysses' cattle in his cave.

Cumaean Sibyl, (Gr.)--A young prophetess who lived in a deep cave at Cumae, Italy.

Echo (Gr.)--Because the satyr, Narcissus, did not return her love, she faded away until there was nothing left but her disembodied voice, which still may be heard in caves, and among rocky hills and mountains.

Endymion (Gr.)--A youth of great beauty, who was given a choice by Jupiter, of death in any manner he chose, or perpetual youth united with perpetual sleep. He chose the latter and still sleeps in the Carian cave.

Furies The (Gr.)--Spread their couches in the Cave of Avernus of the Infernal Region.

CAVE (cont.)

Medusa (Gr.)--Lived in a cavern surrounded by the stony figures of men and animals that became petrified at the sight of her.

Nereus (Gr.)--A genial old man of the sea who lived with his family below the waters in a great shining cave.

Oracles of the dead (Gr.)--Greeks communicated with the ghosts of Hades, through certain Oracles of the dead, situated in cavernous spots, deep and melancholy streams and baleful marshes.

Oreads (Gr.)--Were nymphs of grottoes, hills and mountains.

Orpheus (Gr.)--Was permitted to take his wife, Eurydice, away from the Lower World, on condition that he not turn around to look at her. In his excitement he turned around, and his wife disappeared like vapor. For seven months he sang his sorrow in a desert cave.

Pan (Gr.)--Dwelt in caves.

Polyphemus (Gr.)--One of the Cyclopes, a huge, shapeless monster with a beard and only one eye, who lived in a cave on the Cyclopes island.

Scylla (Gr.)--Lived in a cave high on a cliff of the Aeaean Isle. As Ulysses sailed through the channel, she reached out with her long necks and seized a sailor in the mouths of each of her six heads.

Ulysses (Gr.)--Discovered the cave of the Cyclops Polyphemous, who had been seizing and devouring two of Ulysses's men each day. *See more on* Ulysses *under the heading* BLINDNESS and RAMS.

CENTAUR

Centaurs (Gr.)--Were intelligent creatures, half-horse, half-men.

Chiron (Gr.)--A centaur renowned for his skill in healing, riding, hunting and music. Teacher of Achilles and Jason.

Dejanira (Gr.)--She and her husband, Hercules, came to a river across which the centaur Nessus, carried travelers for a fee. He tried to kidnap her, and for this Hercules shot the centaur in the heart with an arrow.

Eurytion (Gr.)--One of the Centaurs, who got drunk at a marriage feast, and caused a fight. *See also* Lapithae.

CENTAUR (cont.)

Jason (Gr.)–Son of Aeson, who sent him to be brought up by the Centaur, Chiron.

Lapithae (Gr.)--When Eurytion started a fight at the marriage feast of Pirithous and Hippodamia, he involved all the centaurs and the people of Thessaly, the Lapithae.

Nessus (Gr.)--As he died, the centaur told Dejanira to take a portion of his blood to be used as a charm to preserve the love of her husband.

Pholus (Gr.)--A centaur with whom Hercules formed a friendship during his third Labor of capturing the Arcadian boar.

CHAINS *See* CAPTIVE

CHALLENGE *See also* CONTESTS; RACES

Atalanta (Gr.)--A swift runner, she challenged her suitors to a race; her hand the prize; death for defeat.

CHAMBER

Danaë (Gr.)--Because her father, Acrisius' oracle had told him a son of Danaë would cause his death, he shut her in an underground chamber where no man could ever see her.

CHANCE *See also* GAMBLERS

Mercury (Ro.)--A god of chance.

CHANGE IN FORM *See also* BIRDS; BLOOD; STONE; SWAN; TREES

Acetes (Gr.)--A fisherman who deceived Bacchus by promising to take him to Naxos and heading for Egypt instead. Bacchus changed 20 of the crew into dolphins and kept Acetes to pilot the ship to Naxos.

CHANGE IN FORM (cont.)

Acheloüs (Gr.)--A river-god, who could change form. *See same under* WRESTLER.

Actaeon (Gr.)-- *See same under* HUNTER.

Aëdon (Gr.)--After she killed her son, Itylus, by mistake, Zeus relieved her grief by turning her into a nightingale.

Althaea (Gr.)--After she extinguished the life of her son, Meleager, she committed suicide, and the weeping women around her were changed into birds.

Arachne (Gr.)--A Lydian princess who challenged Minerva to a weaving contest and lost. This so humiliated her that she hanged herself and Minerva transformed her into a spider, forever spinning the thread on which she was suspended.

Arethusa (Gr.)--A woodland nymph. See *more under* BATHING.

Arsinoë (Coronis) (Gr.)--A raven told her husband, Apollo, she had been unfaithful. He changed the color of the raven from white to black. Changed Arsinoë into a stone.

Atlas (Gr.)-- *See same under* MOUNTAIN.

Cadmus (Gr.)--He killed a dragon. By order of Minerva, he took the dragon's teeth and sowed them in the earth. They sprouted into armed men, who fought one another until only five were left. These became the ancestors of the Thebans.

Calchas (Gr.)--Neptune assumed the form of this soothsayer to raise the ardor of the Greek warriors, to force the Trojans to give way.

Callisto (Gr.)-- *See same under* BEAR.

Cepheus (Gr.)--Was changed into a constellation.

Cercopes (Gr.)--Were thievish gnomes, captured by Hercules. Some of them, having deceived Jupiter, were changed into apes.

Ceres (Ro.)--Attempted to make Triptolemus immortal.

CHANGE IN FORM (cont.)

Circe (Gr.)-- *See same under* ANIMAL.

Coronis (Gr.)-- *See* Arsinoë.

Cyncnus (Gr.)--Was changed by kindly gods into a swan. *See more on* Cyncnus *under the heading* SWAN.

Electra (Gr.)-- *See same under* HEAVEN.

Galatea (Gr.)--An ivory statue, created by the king and sculptor, Pygmalion, who fell in love with it. He appealed to Aphrodite to make it come to life. She did so, and blessed their nuptials.

Glaucus (Gr.)--Became immortal by tasting magic herbs which changed him to a strange half-man, half-fish, similar to the sea-gods.

Halcyone (Gr.)--After being changed into a kingfisher, she brooded over her nest seven days before and seven days after the winter solstice, during which time Jove forbade the winds to blow, and the way was safe for seafarers.

Heliades (Gr.)--The daughters of Helios, who were changed into poplar trees.

Hippomenes (Gr.)-- *See same under* HAPPINESS.

Io (Gr.)-- *See same under* ANIMAL.

Latona (Gr.)--She wanted to drink from a pond of clear water but rustics there waded into the pond to stir up the mud. Latona had them changed into frogs.

Leucothea (Gr.)-- *See same under* BIRDS.

Medusa (Gr.)--Had been a maiden whose hair was her chief glory, but when she dared to vie in beauty with Minerva, the goddess changed her ringlets into hissing serpents.

Minerva (Gr.)-- *See* Arachne; Medusa.

Morpheus (Gr.)--Was expert in changing himself into the counterfeit forms of men.

CHANGE IN FORM (cont.)

Narcissus (Gr.)--After his death his body could not be found. In its place had sprung a flower, purple within, surrounded by white leaves.

Nisus (Gr.)--Assumed the form of the sea eagle, continually attacking the bird into which Scylla had been transformed.

Pan (Gr.)--Fell in love with the nymph, Syrinx. She ran away, but at a river bank he overtook her. When she called for help, her friends, the water-nymphs, changed her into a tuft of reeds. Finding he was embracing only these, Pan breathed a sigh, and the air through the reeds produced a plaintive melody.

Pleiades (Gr.)--Jupiter turned them into pigeons and made them a constellation.

Polyphonte (Gr.)--A victim of the vengeance of Venus, which turned him into an owl.

Proteus (Gr.)--His craft enabled him to assume many forms: a fire, a flood, or a wild beast, in rapid succession.

Scylla (Gr.)--Instead of aiding Glaucus to win Scylla, she used her sorcery to transform her rival into a hideous monster with twelve arms, twelve feet, six heads with rows of sharp teeth, and the yelp of a dog.

Tithonus (Gr.)-- *See same under* AGE, OLD.

Vertumnus (Ro.)-- *See same under* GUISE.

CHAOS

Erebus (Gr.)--The son of Chaos; brother of Nox. He dwelt in Hades.

Gaea (Gr.); Tellus (Ro.)--Mother Earth, in the older order of gods; the oldest offspring of Chaos.

CHARIOT

Achilles (Gr.)--Implacable to his foes, he killed Hector in revenge and dragged his body behind a chariot before the city of Troy.

CHARIOT (cont.)

Admetus (Gr.)-- *See same under* ANIMAL.

Apollo (Gr.)--Had a chariot of gold, the gift of Vulcan, with wheels of gold, and spokes of silver and diamond settings, and drawn by mighty steeds fed with ambrosia.

Ares (Gr.)-- *See same under* HORSE.

Biton (Gr.)--With the help of his brother, Cleobis, he pulled his mother's chariot to the temple of Juno, where the goddess gave them the blessing of death.

Cebriones (Gr.)--The charioteer of Hector.

Ceres (Gr.)--Drove a chariot drawn by winged dragons.

Cleobis (Gr.)-- *See* Biton.

Cybele (Gr.)--Her chariot was drawn by lions.

Cygnus (Gr.)--Stole his father's chariot and rode wildly across the heavens.

Cydippe (Gr.)--A priestess, whose sons, Biton and Cleobis, yoked themselves to her chariot to pull it many weary leagues to a temple.

Erechtheus (Gr.)--Inventor of the four-wheeled chariot.

Gemini (Castor and Pollus) (Gr.)--Patrons of chariot races.

Hector (Gr.)-- *See* Achilles.

Helios (Gr.)--The ancient sun-god, who drove a four-horse chariot through the heavens.

Hippodamia (Gr.)--Her father, Oenomaüs, offered her to the suitor who could defeat his horses in a chariot race.

Hippolytus (Gr.)--Driving along the shore, his horses were frightened by a sea monster, and ran away, dashing the chariot to pieces, and killing him.

Iolaüs (Gr.)--Sometimes he was the charioteer of Hercules.

CHARIOT (cont.)

Laiüs (Gr.)--In a narrow road, his chariot met that of Oedipus. When Oedipus refused to give way, Laiüs's attendant killed one of his horses. Enraged, Oedipus killed both attendant and Laiüs.

Machaon (Gr.)--After he had been wounded by an arrow from the bow of Paris in the Trojan War, he was taken from the field by Nestor in his chariot.

Marpessa (Gr.)--She was carried off by Idas, in the winged chariot given him by Poseidon.

Myrtilus--The charioteer of Oenomaüs, who was bribed by Hippodamia to remove a bolt from a wheel of her fathers chariot, to allow Pelops to win the race and her hand.

Neptune (Ro.)--Brazen-hoofed and gold-maned horses drew his chariot over the sea.

Nestor (Gr.)-- *See* Machaon.

Oedipus (Gr.)--When his chariot was blocked by the chariot of Laiüs in a narrow road, an argument resulted in Oedipus's killing Laiüs, who turned out to be his real father.

Oenomaus (Gr.)--King of Elis, who demanded that a suitor win his daughter, Hippodamia, only by worsting him in a chariot race.

Pelias (Gr.)--Usurping king of Iolcus, who promised the hand of his daughter, Alcestis, to the suitor who came for her in a chariot drawn by lions and boars.

Pelops (Gr.)--Obtained winged horses from Neptune to help him win the chariot race with Oenomaüs, and the hand of Hippodamia.

Phaëton (Gr.)--Asked his father, Apollo's permission to drive his gold chariot of the sun. The horses dashed the chariot around like a ship without ballast. After clouds began to smoke and mountains burned, Jupiter hurled a lightning bolt which struck him from existence. He fell headlong like a shooting star.

Priam (Gr.)--Father of Hector, who had been killed by Achilles, and his body dragged in disgrace behind Achilles chariot.

Proserpina (Ro.)--Met Pluto while he was making an inspection trip in the Mount Aetna region in his chariot drawn by black horses.

49

CHARIOT (cont.)

Salmoneus (Gr.)--A Titan, who built a bridge of brass over which he drove his chariot to make sounds like thunder.

Selene (Gr.)--Drove her chariot across the heavens.

Triptolemus (Gr.)--Was taken in Ceres' chariot drawn by winged dragons, through earth, to impart to mankind a knowledge of agriculture.

CHARITES

Charites (Gr.)--These were the three Graces; daughters of Eurynome and Jupiter: Euphrosyne, Aglaia and Thalia, who presided over the banquet, the dance and all social pleasures.

CHASE *See also* HUNTERS

Arethusa (Gr.)--A woodland nymph, who delighted in the joys of the chase.

Diana (Ro.)--A huntress. When weary of the chase, she turned to music.

Echo (Gr.)--A talkative nymph; a favorite of Diana, whom she attended in the chase.

Pan (Gr.)--He amused himself with the chase.

CHASTISE

Linus (Gr.)--The teacher of Hercules; when he chastised his pupil, he was killed by him with a lute.

CHIEFTAIN *See also* WARRIOR

Idomeneus (Gr.)--One of the great chieftains of Crete.

CHILDBIRTH

Artemis (Gr.); Eileithyia (Gr.)--Goddess of childbirth. *See also* Eileithyia.

CHILDBIRTH (cont.)

Auge (Gr.)--An Arcadian princess, who may have been originally a name for Artemis, worhipped as a goddess of childbirth.

Carmenta (Ro.)--A water goddess; guardian of women in childbirth.

Eileithyia (Gr.)--The goddess of childbirth; sometimes used as an epithet to describe Artemis (Diana), of Hera (Juno).

Lucina (Ro.)--The goddess who brings light, hence, goddess of childbirth; a title often applied to both Juno and Diana.

CHILDREN *See also* DAUGHTERS; INFANT; OFFSPRING

Aegyptus (Gr.)--Father of fifty sons, who married the fifty daughters of Danaüs.

Alcmene (Gr.)--Although married to the mortal, Alcaeus, she bore a son, Hercules, to Jupiter in Thebes.

Atreus (Gr.)--Killed three sons of his faithless brother, Thestes, and caused him to eat the flesh of his own children at a banquet.

Coroebus (Gr.)--A noble youth, who slew the monster that for a season was destroying the children.

Cronus (Gr.); Saturn (Ro.)–A Titan; married to Rhea he became the father of six gods. To assure his not losing the throne to an heir, he swallowed the first five as soon as they were born.

Danaïdes (Gr.)--The fifty daughters of Danaüs, who married the fifty sons of Aegyptus.

Doris (Gr.)--Wife of the genial old man of the sea, Nereus, by whom she had fifty fair daughters, the Nereïds.

Medea (Gr.)--After her husband, Jason, tired of her, the sorceress killed her own children, set fire to the palace and fled to Athens.

Nephele (Gr.)--To protect her children from her husband, Athamas's second wife, Ino, Nephele sent them on the back of the ram with the

CHILDREN (cont.)

Nephele (cont.)--golden fleece, to Colchis.

Nereus (Gr.)--Father of fifty daughters, he and his family lived below the waters in a great shining cave.

Niobe (Gr.)--Wife of Amphion, by whom she had seven sons and seven daughters. She boasted her superiority over the goddess, Latona, who had but two children, Apollo and Artemis. These two punished Niobe by slaying all her children, except one, who was abroad.

CHOICE

Endymion (Gr.)--Jupiter gave him a choice between death in any manner he chose, or perpetual youth with perpetual sleep. He chose the latter.

CHRIST

Pan (Gr.)--When the birth of Christ was announced, a deep groan heard through the isles of Greece told that Pan was dead, and the dynasty of Olympus dethroned.

CITADEL

Dido (Gr.)--Escaping from Tyre, she and some followers selected a site and asked the natives for only as much land as could be enclosed with a bull's hide. She cut the hide in strips, and stretched it large enough to contain a citadel. She called it Byrsa (hide). Around it the city of Carthage rose.

Sischaeus (Gr.)--His treasures were placed in the citadel built by his fugitive wife.

CITIES *See also* KINGS; PLACES

Alcmaeon (Gr.)--Became a leader of the Epigoni against Thebes.

Amphilochus (Gr.)--Brother of Alcmaeon, impelled by their mother, Eriphyle, to renew the war against Thebes.

CITIES (cont.)

Anchises (Gr.)--He was carried by his son, Aeneas, from the burning city of Troy.

Ascanius (Gr.)--Founded the city of Alba Longa, the cradle of Rome.

Athena (Gr.)--The protectress of cities, especially worshipped in her own Athens.

Cadmus (Gr.)-- *See same under* THEBES.

Cybele (Gr.)--Was the protectress of cities, and the bringer of civilization.

Dido (Gr.)--Asked for as much land as could be enclosed in a bull's hide. Around this the city of Carthage rose.

Enyo (Gr.)--One of three hoary witches; she, the ruiner of cities.

Minerva (Ro.)--Won over Neptune in a peaceful contest for the possession of Athens.

Paphos (Gr.)--Offspring of Cupid and Psyche, after whom the city of Paphos is named.

Perseus (Gr.)--Devoted himself to the founding of cities and the introduction of civilization.

Phoebus (Apollo) (Gr.)--A founder of cities, and promoter of colonization.

Phoroneus (Gr.)--Founded the city of Argos.

Rhea (Gr.)-- *See* Cybele.

Troy (Gr.)--The battle for this city lasted nine years, and was finally won by the Greeks, after the wooden horse was carried into Troy.

CIVILIZATION

Bacchus (Gr.)--Was a promoter of civilization, a lawgiver and lover of peace.

Consivius (Gr.)--God of civilization, sometimes known as the Sower.

CIVILIZATION (cont.)

Cybele (Ro.)--The bringer of civilization.

Janus (Ro.)-- *Same as* Consivius.

Perseus (Gr.)--Devoted to the service of mankind and the introduction of civilization.

CIVIC LIFE

Athena (Gr.)--Goddess of civic life.

CIVIL LIFE

Demeter--Guardian of civil life.

CIVIL RIGHTS

Orthia (Gr.); Diana (Ro.)--Guardian of civil rights.

CLOTHES *See* DRESS

CLOUD

Aeneas (Gr.)--In combat with Achilles he was spared by Neptune's spreading a cloud between them.

Horae (Gr.)--The three goddesses of the seasons, hours and orderliness, who took charge of the gate of clouds at Olympus, which they opened to permit the passage of Celestials to and from earth.

Phoebus Apollo (Gr.)--Wrapped Aeneas in a cloud, and bore him to that god's temple, where he was healed.

CLUB

Heracles (Gr.); Hercules (Ro.)--Is represented with a club in his hand and a lion-skin over his shoulder.

Periphetes (Gr.)--A ferocious savage, always armed with a club of iron.

COLONIZATION

Dido (Gr.)-- *See same under* LAND.

Evander (Gr.)--Led a colony from Arcadia to Latinum.

Phoebus Apollo (Gr.)--Was a promoter of colonization.

COLOR

Adrastus (Gr.)-- *See same under* PALENESS

Coronis (Gr.)--When a raven told Apollo this princess of Thessaly was unfaithful to him the god killed her and in his anger changed the color of the raven from white to black.

Elysian Fields (Gr.)--Residents here were the happy who had rendered service to mankind. They breathed freer air, and saw all objects in a purple light.

Eos (Gr.)--Robed in saffron, she rose from the streams of Ocean, to bring the light to gods and men.

Narcissus (Gr.)--Where his body had lain after his death, there sprung a flower, purple within, surrounded by white leaves.

Phaëton (Gr.)--When he tried to drive the chariot of the sun, the horses went out of control; clouds began to smoke and trees on the mountains burned with intense heat. The people of Aethiopia turned black because their blood was drawn to the surface so suddenly.

COLOSSUS

Colossus of Rhodes (Gr.)--Was a statue of Helios, the ancient sun-gods, later indentified as Apollo.

COMBAT *See also* SLAIN; WAR

Aeneas (Gr.)--In one combat with Achilles, he was saved by Neptune, who spread a cloud between them.

Ajax (Gr.)--In a duel, he wounded Hector.

Castor (Gr.)-- *See* Idas.

Diomede (Gr.)--In combat, with the help of Minerva, he wounded Mars.

Eteocles (Gr.)--In a quarrel with his brother, Polynices, they decided to settle it by a single combat. They fought and felled each other.

Hector (Gr.)--Pierced Patroclus with his spear and mortally wounded him. He, in turn, was killed by Achilles.

Hercules (Ro.)--Strangled two serpents while he was still in his cradle. Juno had sent them to destroy him. In combat with a lion in the valley of Nemea, he strangled it, also, as a part of his twelve labors. In a fit of madness, he killed his friend, Iphitus.

Idas (Gr.)--His brother, Lynceus, and he were in combat with their cousins, Castor and Pollux. Idas killed Castor; his brother slew Pollux, and Idas was slain by Zeus.

Lynceus (Gr.)-- See Idas.

Pollux (Gr.)-- See Idas.

Polynices (Gr.)-- See Eteocles.

COMEDY

Comus (Gr. and Ro.)-- See same under MIRTH.

Thalia (Gr.)--She was the daughter of Jupiter and Mnemosyne. She was the Muse of comedy. Another Thalia was the daughter of Jupiter and Eurynome. She was one of the three Graces.

COMET

Electra (Gr.)--Not wishing to witness the ruin of Troy, she left her place among the Pleiades, and became a comet, ranging the expanse of heaven, with her hair floating wildly behind her.

COMPANION See also FRIENDSHIP

Aeacus (Gr.)--Son of Zeus and Aegina. As a young man he lived alone on an uninhabited island. Praying to his father for companions, he saw the ants on the island transformed into men and women, and named

56

COMPANION (cont.)

Aeacus (cont.)--them Myrmidons.

Castor (Gr.)--Companion and half-brother of Pollux. Jupiter rewarded their attachment by placing them among the stars as Gemini, the Twins.

Hyacinthus (Gr.)--Was loved by Apollo, who made him a constant companion.

Hylas (Gr.)–Was Hercules' companion during the Argonautic expedition.

Idaeus (Gr.)--A companion and herald of King Priam.

Idas (Gr.)--The inseparable companion of his brother, Lynceus.

Iolaüs (Gr.)--Companion and sometimes charioteer of Hercules.

CONCEITED

Narcissus (Gr.)--In love with his own reflection.

Tantalus (Gr.)--Was so conceited he ridiculed the omniscience of the gods, and betrayed their secrets.

CONSTELLATION *See also* STARS

Callisto (Gr.)--To appease the jealously of Juno, Jupiter placed her and her son, Arcas, in the heavens as the Great and Little Bears.

Cassiopeia (Gr.)-- *See same under* HEAVEN.

Cepheus (Gr.)--One of the Argonauts, who was changed into a constellation at his death.

Merope (Gr.)--The invisible one of the Pleiades, who concealed herself out of shame for having loved a mortal (Sisyphus).

Orion (Gr.)--He was blinded by Merope's father for trying to take possession of her by force. Vulcan gave him a guide, Cedalion, who sat on his shoulders and pointed him east until they met the sun-god, Apollo, who restored his sight.

57

Pleiades (Gr.)--These seven nymphs of Diana's train, still fly before Orion in the heavens. Jupiter had changed them into a constellation.

CONTEMPLATION

Minerva (Ro.)--Was the goddess of contemplation, wisdom and skill.

CONTENTION

Paris (Gr.)--His mother had dreamed she was to give birth to a child who would stir up contention. He kidnapped Helen from her husband, Menelaüs, and this brought about the Trojan War.

CONTEST *See also* RACES; WRESTLERS

Antaeus (Gr.)--A giant wrestler. *See more under* LABORS.

Arachne (Gr.)--Challenged Minerva to a weaving contest. She lost and hanged herself.

Daphnis (Gr.)--Won in a reaping contest with Lityerses, and took the prize, the girl, Piplea.

Eurytus (Gr.)-- *See* Iole.

Iole (Gr.)--Her hand was offered to the winner in an archery contest, but when Hercules won, her father, Eurytus, refused to fill his agreement, fearing Hercules might become insane a second time.

Marsyas (Gr.)--Challenged Apollo to a music contest on a flute. The god won, and punished Marsyas by flaying him alive.

Midas (Gr.)--Was a judge, with Tmolus, a mountain-god, in the contest of musical skill between Pan and Apollo. Tmolus chose Apollo, but Midas dissented, after which the god changed his ears into those of an ass.

Minerva (Ro.)--In a peaceful contest with Neptune for possession of the city of Athens, she won.

Pan (Gr.)-- *See* Midas.

58

CONTEST (cont.)

Thamyris (Gr.)--Challenged the Muses to a trial of skill. Conquered in the contest, he was deprived of his sight.

CORN

Ceres (Ro.)--Golden sheaves of corn and poppies were sacred to her.

Demeter (Gr.)-- *See same under* SYMBOLS.

Proserpina (Ro.); Persephon (Gr.)--Golden sheaves of corn, and soporific poppies were sacred to her.

CORNUCOPIA

Acheloüs (Gr.)--While he was in the form of a bull, Hercules dragged him to the ground and rent one horn away. The Naiads consecrated it and filled it with flowers for the goddess of Plenty.

Naiads (Gr.)--These nymphs made a cornucopia ot of a bull's horn.

Plenty--This goddess adopted the cornucopia as her symbol.

Pluto (Class.)--Carried the cornucopia as a symbol of inexhaustible riches.

Proserpina (Ro.)--Bore a cornucopia overflowing with flowers.

COUNCIL

Idomeneus (Gr.)–A great Greek chieftain, among those in a council of the Greeks called by Agamemnon.

Jupiter (Ro.); Zeus (Gr.)--At the council of the gods, he was chosen Sovereign of the World.

Thersites (Gr.)--Among those at the council called by Agamemnon, he clamored for a Greek retreat.

COUNSELOR

Nestor (Gr.)--Became King of Pylos; noted for being a wise and trusted counselor, especially to Agamemnon.

Polyidus (Gr.)--A soothsayer who counseled Bellerophon to procure Pegasus.

COUNTRY

Nymphs, The Sleepless (Gr.)--These were the dread goddesses of the country people.

COURAGE

Otus (Gr.)--He and his brother, Ephialtes, were monsters, renowned for their courage, strength and stature.

COVETOUS

Pygmalion (Gr.)--Because he was covetous of Sicaeus's treasures, Pygmalion caused him to be put to death.

Scylla (Gr.)--Since Circe was covetous of the sea-green god, Glaucus, for herself, she transformed her rival, Scylla, into a hideous monster.

COW See also CATTLE; CHANGE IN FORM

Cadmus (Gr.)--The oracle, Apollo, told him to find a cow, and to follow her. See same under ADVENTURES.

Dione (Gr.)--Was a nymph, to whom the cow was sacred.

COWHERD

Geryon (Gr.)--The three-headed cowherd son of Callirrhoë and Chrysoar.

CRANES

Ibycus (Gr.)--Attacked by robbers, he had a witness in a flock of cranes that flew overhead.

Semnae (The Three Furies) (Gr.)--Worked with the cranes to detect the

CRANES (cont.)

Semnae (cont.)--murderers of Ibycus.

CREATOR

Prometheus (Gr.)--Became a creator, modelling man out of earth.

CRETE

Europa (Gr.)--Jupiter, in the form of a white bull, swam off with her to Crete.

Idomeneus (Gr.)--King of Crete; leader of the Cretans against Troy.

CRIME *See* MURDER

CRIPPLER

Gyges (Gr.)--Called "The crippler", or "The Vaulter"; had 100 hands.

CRITICISM

Momus (Gr.)--The god of adverse criticism, ridicule, blame and mockery.

CROSS ROADS

Hecate (Gr.)--A goddess of the cross-roads.

Hercules (Ro.)--One day at a cross-road he met two women—Pleasure and Duty. Asked to make a choice, he chose Duty and followed her through life.

CROWN

Adradne (Gr.)-- *See same under* STARS.

Cybele (Ro.)--Known as Mater Turrita.

CROWN (cont.)

Jason (Gr.)--Surrendered his crown to his half-brother, Pelias, on condition that he retrieve it on reaching his majority.

CRUELTY *See also* CHILDREN; TORMENT

Antiope (Gr.)--Was treated with extreme cruelty by her uncle Lycus, the usurping King of Thebes, and his wife, Dirce.

Apollo (Gr.)--He could punish with severity.

Lycus (Gr.)-- *See* Antiope.

Mezentius (Gr.)--A monster of cruelty, inventing unheard of torments to gratify his vengeance.

Persephone (Gr.)--Queen of Hades; wife of Pluto, and like her husband, cruel and unyielding.

Phineus (Gr.)--A Thracian king, so cruel that Jupiter punished him by making him blind.

Pluto (Class.)--Was hard and inexorable.

Proserpina (Ro.); Persephone (Gr.)--When she was the goddess of death, she was cruel and gave harsh orders to the Furies.

CUNNING *See also* TRICKERY

Cronus (Gr.)--In art, his head is veiled to conceal his cunning and reserve.

Mercury (Ro.)--His cunning made him a dangerous foe, for he could play the trickster and thief.

Prometheus (Gr.)--Was bold and cunning of heart. He stole fire from heaven for the use of man.

Vulcan (Ro.)--Could be cunning, even vengeful, and he was more feared than courted.

CUPBEARER

Ganymede (Gr.)--A beautiful Trojan boy who succeeded Hebe as cup-

CUPBEARER (cont.)

Ganymede (cont.)--bearer to the gods.

Hebe (Gr.)--Poured the nectar for the gods in Olympus.

CURE

Triptolemus (Gr.)--He was cured of a fever by Ceres, who rid him of it with poppy juice, milk and a kiss.

CURETES

Curetes (Gr.)-- Earth-born demons who raised Jupiter in Crete.

CURIOSITY *See* BOX

CURSE

Cadmus (Gr.)--Killed a dragon sacred to Mars, and had to serve penance to the god for eight years. This curse followed nearly every scion of his house.

Eriphyle (Gr.)--She was bribed by Polynices with the necklace of Harmonia, which was still fraught with the curse of Cadmus.

Eteocles (Gr.)--He and his brother, Polynices, felled each other, fulfilling the curse of Oedipus.

Harmonia (Gr.)--Married Cadmus, and Vulcan gave her a necklace of unsurpassed brilliance, which he had forged himself. This brought a curse on the family, which did not pass until their great-great-grandson, Oedipus, had by fraternal strife put an end to the family.

Melicertes (Gr.)--Being a grandson of Cadmus, the curse of the house followed him, too.

CYCLOPES

Cyclopes (Gr.)--A race of men of gigantic size, with one enormous eye set in the middle of their foreheads.

Gaea (Gr.)--One of the older order of gods; wife of Uranus; from their

Gaea (cont.)--union came the Cyclopes, Titans, and the 100-handed monsters.

Hades--The Cyclopes gave him the helmet of darkness, with which he could move anywhere unseen.

Nausithoüs (Gr.)--King of the Phaeacians, who had been oppressed by that savage race, the Cyclopes.

Polyphemus (Gr.)--A huge, shapeless monster, one of the Cyclopes, who had a beard, coarse looks, and only one eye.

D

DACTYLS

Dactyls--Attendants of Cybele near Mt. Ida in Crete. *See also* IRON WORKING; RHYTHM.

DIAMONES

Diamones --A large class of supernatural beings, or spirits, that may or may not be personified. Among the many divinities described as daimones were nymphs, satyrs, river-gods, benates and genii. They generally resided in a particular object, place, or natural phenomenon.

DANAÏDES

Amymone (Gr.)--One of the Danaïdes.

Danaïdes (Gr.)--These were the fifty daughters of Danaüs, who married the fifty sons of Aegyptus, all but one of whom murdered their husbands on their wedding night. Hypermestra is the one who abstained.

DANCE

Charites (Gr.)--The Three Graces. They presided over the dance and all

DANCE (cont.)

Charites (cont.)--social pleasures.

Diana (Ro.)--She turned to music and dance.

Graces, The Three (Gr.)--Agalaia, (brilliance); Euphorsyne, (joy), and Thalia (bloom), who presided over the dance and polite accomplishments.

Maenades (Gr.)--Were women attendants of Bacchus, who, as they danced and sang, waved a staff. *See same under* STAFF.

Pan (Gr.)--Played upon the syrinx (Pan's pipes), and led the dances of the wood-nymphs.

Terpsichore (Gr.)–The Muse of choral dance and song.

Thalia (Gr.)--Presided over the dance.

DARKNESS *See also* NIGHT

Death (Thanatos) (Gr.)--Dwells in subterranean darkness.

Erebus (Gr.)--A place of nether darkness, through which souls passed to Hades.

Hades (Gr.)--With his helmet of darkness, he could move anywhere unseen.

Hecate (Gr.)--Represented darkness and terrors.

Latona (Ro.)--Goddess of darkness.

Light (Gr.)--Night and darkness were the prime elements of Nature, and from them sprang Light.

Sleep (Gr.)--He and Death were the sons of Night, who lived in subterranean darkness.

Somnus (Gr.)-- *Same as* SLEEP.

Thanatos (Gr.)-- *Same as* DEATH.

DAUGHTER

Danaüs (Gr.)-- *See heading* DANAÏDES.

Erysichthon (Gr.)--His punishment, a raging hunger. He sold his daughter for edibles.

Leucippus (Gr.)--His daughters were the cause of a rift between Castor and Pollus, and their cousins, Idas and Lynceus.

Nereids (Gr.)--Were the fifty mermaid daughters of Nereus and Doris.

Nereus (Gr.)--Father of fifty daughters, all of whom lived with him below the waters in a large, shining cave.

Pierides (Gr.)--Were the nine daughters of Pierus, later changed into magpies.

Thetis (Gr.)--One of the most famous of the daughters of Nereus.

DAY

Diana (Ro.)--Goddess of the bright day.

DEATH *See also* MURDER; SLAIN; VENGEANCE

Apollos (Gr.)--Was the giver of sudden death.

Ares (Gr.); Mars (Ro.)--Freed death from Sisyphus.

Biton (Gr.)–Juno gave him and his brother, Cleobis, the blessing of death.

Ceres (Ro.)--Was associated with the alternate death and life in nature, which simulated the resurrection and immortality of man.

Charon (Gr.)--Ferried the dead across the River Styx.

Cleobis (Gr.)– *See* Biton.

Death (Gr.)--Closes forever the eyes of men.

Endymion (Gr.)--Jupiter gave him a choice of death in any manner he chose, or perpetual youth united with perpetual sleep. He chose the latter.

DEATH (cont.)

Harpies (Gr.)--Snatched up and carried off the souls of the dead.

Mors (Ro.)--The god of death.

Naiads (Gr.)--Were nymphs, responsible for the death of the shepherd, Daphnis, as well as that of the young lad, Hylas.

Nyx (Gr.)--Mother of Death.

Oracles (Gr.)--Sometimes the Greeks communicated with the ghosts of Hades, through certain oracles of the dead.

Orcus (Ro.); (Pluto), (Dis)--This Roman god is Death, or ruler of the Underworld.

Persephone (Gr.)--Goddess of death.

Protesilaüs (Gr.)--Mercury led him back to the upper world; when he died a second time, his wife, Laodamia, died with him.

DECEPTION *See also* TRICKERY

Cercopes (Gr.)--Thievish gnomes, some of whom once deceived Jupiter, and were changed into apes.

DEDICATE

Jason (Gr.)--After delivering the Golden Fleece to the usurping King Pelias, of Thessaly, Jason dedicated their ship, the *Argo*, to Neptune.

DEER

Hercules (Ro.)--Pursued the Cerynean doe for one year, completing his fourth Labor.

DEFORMITY

Vulcan (Ro.)--Was born lame, and his mother, Juno, chagrined by his deformity, cast him from Heaven, out of sight of the gods.

DEITIES *See also* DIVINITIES; GODS; GODDESSES

Janus (Ro.) (Consivius)--Ancient, and most important of the Roman deities.

Juno (Ro.) (Hera)--Sister and wife of Jupiter. Deity of the light and the sky. Mother of Hebe, Mars, and Vulcan.

Jupiter (Ro.) (Jove), (Zeus)--After the Titan War, in a council of the gods, he was chosen Sovereign of the World.

Satyrs (Gr.)--Deities of the woods and fields.

Vesta (Ro.)--A divinity of the home, settled rather than nomadic in habit.

Zephyrus (Gr.)--Mildest and gentlest of all sylvan deities.

DELUGE *See also* FLOOD

Neptune (Ro.)--He and his brother, Jupiter, swept away the race of man with a deluge.

DEMOGOGUE

Thersites (Gr.)--An insolent brawler and a demogogue, killed by Achilles for ridiculing his grief.

DEMONS

Ares (Gr.); Mars (Ro.)--Was attended by a retinue of blood-thirsty demons.

Curetes (Gr.)--Were earth-born demons, who raised Jupiter in Crete.

DESERT

Phaëton (Gr.)--Drove the chariot of his father, Apollo, out of control until mountains caught fire, and the Libyan desert dried up, and the Nile hid his head in it.

DESERTED

Adriadne (Gr.)--When Theseus deserted her, she was comforted by Bacchus and married him.

DESIRE

Eros (Gr.); Cupis (Ro.)--He shot darts of desire into the bosoms of men.

DESPISER

Erysichthon (Gr.)--He was a despiser of the gods.

DESTINY

Aeneas (Gr.)--During his adventures, he came to Carthage, where Queen Dido fell in love with him and kept him there until he was reminded of his destiny, and sailed again for the shores of Italy.

Fates, The (Gr.)--Three goddesses who were supposed to determine the course of human life; called The Destinies.

DEW

Aglauros (Gr.)--Daughter of Cecrops, and with her sisters, Herse and Pandrosos, personifications of the dew.

Clytie (Gr.)--Since her love for Apollo was unrequited, she pined for him and sat on the ground for nine days, with only the chilly dew as sustenance.

Herse (Gr.)-- *See* Aglauros.

Memnon (Gr.)--After his death, his mother, Aurora, remained inconsolable. The dewdrops are her tears.

Palinurus (Gr.)--Somnus made him sleepy by waving over him a branch moistened by Lethaean dew.

Pandrosos (Gr.)-- *See* Aglauros.

DICE

Rhoecus (Gr.)--Joining some comrades over a game of dice, he forgot to be constant to a loving dryad.

DISAPPEARED

Orpheus (Gr.)--He was allowed to lead his wife, Eurydice, out of the Lower World, provided he did not turn to look at her. In his excitement he looked back, and she disappeared like a vapor in the air.

DISAPPOINTMENT

Echo (Gr.)--Pining from disappointment that Narcissus did not return her love, she faded away until there was nothing left but her disembodied voice.

DISCUS

Acrisius (Gr.)--Was killed accidentally by his son, Perseus, when a discus bounded the wrong way.

Zephyrus (Gr.)--The west wind; he blew a discus thrown by Apollo, off its course to kill Hyacinthus.

DISCORD

Eris (Gr.)--Goddess of discord or strife. She threw the golden apple into an assembly of the gods, to cause contention.

DISCOVERY

Dactyls (Gr.)--Were credited with the discovery of iron-working.

DISEASES

Phoebus (Gr.)--Warded off the dangers and diseases of summer and autumn.

DISGUISE

Battus (Gr.)--A peasant who promised secrecy to Mercury, then told the whole story to Mercury in disguise.

Ganymede (Gr.)--He was seized by Jupiter, disguised as an eagle, and borne to Heaven.

Palladium, The (Gr.)--This celebrated statue of Minerva was stolen by Ulysses and Diomede, who had entered the city of Troy in disguise.

Penelope (Gr.)--Ulysses' wife, who remained faithful during his 20-year absence, in spite of being importuned by many suitors. Upon his return, Ulysses, disguised as a beggar, sought them out one at a time, to punish them.

Vertumnus (Gr.)--In disguise he wooed Pomona.

DISOBEDIENCE

Furies, The (Gr.)--Often they visited earth to punish filial disobedience.

DIOSCURI

Dioscuri--These were Castor and Pollux, brothers, whose attachment Jupiter rewarded by placing them among the stars as Gemini, the Twins.

DIVERS

Glaucus (Gr.)--Guardian of divers, sailors, and fish.

DIVINE

Dioscuri (Gr.)--Received divine honors under this name (sons of Jove.)

DIVINITY

Jove (Ro.)--Chief divinity of the ancient Romans.

Zephyrus (Gr.)--With the other winds, he was among the lesser divinities of Heaven.

DIVINITY

Zeus (Gr.)--Supreme ruler of the Universe, he was the wisest of the divinities.

DOE *See* DEER

DOCTORS *See* HEALING; MEDICINE; SURGEON

DOG

Argus (3), (Gr.)--Ulysses' old dog, who recognized him after his return from ten years of adventures.

Cereberus (Gr.)--Was a three-headed dog with a serpent tail, which guarded the gate to the Underworld.

Eurytion (Gr.)--One of the giants, who, with his two-headed dog, guarded the oxen of Geryon.

Hecate (Gr.)--The hound was sacred to her.

Linus (Gr.)--In his youth, he was torn to pieces by dogs.

Mars (Ro.)--His chosen animals were haunters of the battlefields—the dog and the vulture.

Syclla (Gr.)--A fair virgin, who was transformed by Circe, into a hideous monster with the yelp of a dog.

Sirius (Gr.)--The dog of Orion, transformed into a star.

DOORS

Janus (Ro.)--An ancient Roman deity, the god of doors, or material openings, but more truly of beginnings.

DRAGON

Aeëtes (Gr.)--Keeper of the Golden Fleece, who placed it in a consecrated grove under the watchful care of a sleepless dragon.

Atlas (Gr.)--*See same under* APPLES, GOLDEN.

72

DRAGON (cont.)

Cadmus (Gr.)--During his adventures, he killed a dragon sacred to Mars, and had to serve penance for eight years. *See same under* ADVENTURES.

Ceres (Ro.)--Drove a chariot drawn by winged dragons.

Chimaera (Gr.)--A monster whose fore part was half lion, half goat, and the hind part, a dragon.

Typhon (Gr.)--A hundred dragon heads spread from his neck.

DRAMA

Dionysus (Gr.)--Patron of the drama.

DREAD

Deimos (Gr.)--The personification of dread or terror.

Pan (Gr.)-- *See same under* PANIC.

DREAMS

Hypnos (Gr.)--Brought to mortals solace and fair dreams.

Icelus (Gr.)--Brother of Phantasus, and Morpheus, he was a producer of dreams.

Nyx (Gr.)--Mother of the Fates; Death; Sleep; Dreams; and Care.

DRESS

Athena (Gr.)--Wore a tasseled breast-plate of goatskin.

Erato (Gr.)--Wore a thin garment and held a lyre.

Giants, The (Gr.)--Monsters who clothed themselves in skins of beasts.

Hercules (Ro.)--Wore the dress of a woman and spun wool during his three years as a slave of Queen Omphale.

DRINKING *See also* INTOXICATED

Agave (Gr.)--Killed her son, Pentheus, during a Bacchanalian revel.

Bacchantes (Gr.)--These were women worshippers of Bacchus, who indulged in wild orgies.

DROWNED

Ceyx (Gr.)--Was drowned in a shipwreck.

Halcyone (Gr.)--After her husband, Ceyx, was drowned, she threw herself into the sea.

Hero (Gr.)--Cast herself into the sea, after her lover, Leander, was drowned.

Hylas (Gr.)--The Naiads pulled him by the hand down into the depths of a spring.

Ino (Gr.)--To escape her mad husband, Learchus, she held her child, Melicertes, in her arms, and jumped from a cliff into the sea.

Jupiter (Ro.)--After ruling the world for several eons, he grew tired of the fraud, violence, and wars of the earth, and proceeded to drown all its inhabitants.

Leander (Gr.)--Swam the Hellespont each night to visit his loved one, Hero. One night the sea was so rough that his strength failed and he was drowned.

DRUNKENNESS

Comus (Gr. and Ro.)--Was the god of drunkenness, festive joy and mirth.

Silenus (Gr.)--Oldest of the Satyrs, jovial, tutor of Bacchus, and generally tipsy.

DRYADS

Dryads (Gr.)--Were wood-nymphs. Each nymph's life began and ended with a particular tree.

Erysichthon (Gr.)--The Dryads invoked punishment on him when he cut down an oak in a grove sacred to Ceres.

Hamadryads (Gr.)--Wood-nymphs; inferior divinites of nature.

Nymphs (Gr.)--Two of the six classes of these beautiful maidens were wood-nymphs.

Pan (Gr.)--Was the son of Mercury and a Dryad.

Rhocecus (Gr.)--When he saved a tree from falling he was rewarded by being given the love of the dryad of that tree.

DUTY

Hercules (Ro.)--Met two women at a cross-roads. *See same under* CROSS-ROADS.

E

EAGLE

Ganymede (Gr.)--Was carried to Heaven by Jupiter disguised as an eagle.

Gryphons (Gr.)--Were creatures with heads and wings of an eagle.

Jupiter (Ro.)--His special messenger was the eagle.

Nisus (Gr.)--Assumed the form of the sea eagle, continually preying upon Scylla transformed into a bird.

EARS

Midas (Gr.)--When, as a judge, he chose Pan over Apollo in a music contest, the god changed his ears into those of an ass.

Pan (Gr.)--Had the ears, horns and legs of a goat.

Ulysses (Gr.)--In order to pass safely by the coast of the Sirens, by being deaf to their seductive music, Ulysses stopped the ears of his men with wax.

EARTH

Consus (Ro.)--Was an early Roman god of the earth.

Dionysus (Gr.)--A deity of earth.

Endymion (Gr.)--Originally an earth divinity.

Gaea (Gr.)--In the older order of gods, she was Mother Earth.

Hecate (Gr.)--She combined the characters of moon, earth, and Underworld goddess.

Naiads (Gr.)--Although they were immortal, being the daughters of Jupiter, they maintained an intimate association with the deities of earth.

Tellus (Ro.); Gaea (Gr.)--Goddess of the earth.

Terra (Gr.); Gaea (Gr.)--The earth goddess.

ECHO

Echo (Gr.)--Because she was too talkative, she was condemned to the loss of her voice, except for the purpose of replying.

Juno (Ro.)--Was displeased with Echo, and caused her to lose her voice.

Narcissus (Gr.)--Echo's unrequited love for him caused her fade away.

EDIBLES *See* FOOD

EFFEMINATE

Hercules (Ro.)--A slave to Queen Omphale for three years, he lived effeminately, wore dresses and spun wool.

Salmacis (Gr.)--Was a nymph of a fountain in ancient Caria, the waters of which rendered effeminate all who drank them.

ELOPEMENT *See also* MURDER

Medea (Gr.)--She eloped with Jason.

ELOQUENCE

Hermes (Gr.); Mercury (Ro.)--He was sweet-voiced and had the power of persuasion by eloquence.

Mercury (Ro.)--Was described as the god of eloquence.

Phoenix (Gr.)--Educated Achilles in eloquence and the arts of war.

ELYSIAN FIELDS

Anchises (Gr.)--Was visited by his son, Aeneas, in the Elysian Fields.

Elysian Fields--Were groves where the happy, including those who had rendered service to mankind, resided.

ENEMIES *See* FEUD

ENRAGED *See* MADNESS

ENVIOUS

Aëdon (Gr.)--Queen of Thebes, envious of her sister-in-law, Niobe, for having borne 14 children.

Daedalus (Gr.)--Was envious of the ingenuity of his nephew, Perdix; pushed him off a tower and killed him.

Plexippus (Gr.)--He and Toxeus were brothers of Queen Althaea, braggarts and envious of her son, Meleager.

EPITHET *See also* NAME; PATRONYM

Enyalius (Gr.)--A god of war; an epithet of Mars.

Nomius (Gr.)--One of the epithets applied to Apollo.

Scamandrius (Gr.)--A nickname used by Hector for his son, Astyanax.

Thalassios (Gr.)--An epithet for Hymen, who returned a shipload of kidnaped Athenian maidens to their home.

EPONYM *See* PATRONYM

ESCAPE *See* PURSUIT

Polyphemus *under* RAM

ETERNITY

Danaïdes (Gr.)--*See same under* TARTARUS.

EVENING *See* NIGHT

EXILE

Oedipus (Gr.)--Was cast into exile by his sons, Eteocles and Polynices.

EXPEDITION

Adrastus (Gr.)--King of Argos, he was a leader of the expedition of the Seven against Thebes, and its sole survivor.

Amphiaraüs (Gr.)--Being a soothsayer, he opposed the Seven against Thebes expedition, knowing that none of the leaders but Adrastus would like to return.

Argonautic expedition--Was the search for the Golden Fleece.

Calydonian Hunt (Gr.)--This was the pursuit of a boar sent by the goddess Artemis to ravage Calydon.

Eteocles (Gr.)--His refusal to share the kingdom of Thebes with his brother, Polynices, led to the expedition, Seven against Thebes.

Hylas (Gr.)--Was a lad who attended Hercules during the Argonautic expedition.

Jason (Gr.)--Took part in the Calydonian Boar Hunt when scarcely more than a boy. Later, he assembled fifty famous heroes to cross the seas to the kingdom of Colchis, in search of the Golden Fleece, an enterprise known as the Argonautic Expedition.

EXPIATION

Hercules (Ro.)-- In expiation for slaying his children during a period of insanity, he was made subject to his cousin, Eurystheus, who enjoined upon him a succession of desperate undertakings, called the Twelve Labors of Hercules. *See same under* LABORS.

EYES

Argus (2), (Gr.)-- *See same under* ORNAMENTS.

Arimasps (Gr. and Ro.)--A race of one-eyed men. *See same under* GRYPHONS.

Cyclopes (Gr.)--A race of giants with one enormous eye set in the middle of their foreheads.

Death (Gr.)--Closes forever the eyes of men.

Graeae, The (Gr.)--Were three hoary witches: Deino (the Terrifier); Enyo (the Shaker), and Pephrede (the Horrifier), who had only one eye among them, which they handed from one to the other, and only one tooth.

Mercury (Ro.)--Was sent by Jupiter to overcome the 100-eyed Argus guarding Io. After he killed the monster, Juno took the eyes and scattered them as ornaments on the tail of her peacock, where they remain to this day.

Nycheia (Gr')--The nymph with the "April eyes."

Oedipus (Gr.)--Discovering that he had married his own mother, he punished himself by tearing out his eyes.

Orion (Gr.)--Was deprived of his sight by Oenopion; Apollo restored it with a sun-beam.

Polyphemus (Gr.)--One of the Cyclopes, he was a shapeless monster with only one eye.

Ulysses (Gr.)--Plunged out the eye of Polyphemus, to escape from his cave.

FACING *See also* BEGINNINGS

Janus (Ro.)--Was an ancient Roman deity, represented as facing both ways, for the Romans believed that beginnings and endings were of the same piece.

FAITHLESS

Eteocles (Gr.)--The faithless son of Oedipus and Jocasta, who refused to give up the throne in Thebes to his brother, Polynices, as promised.

FAMILY

Lares (Ro.)--Were deified spirits of ancestors who protected their descendants. They were divinities who presided over the household and family.

Penates (Ro.)--Gods of the welfare and prosperity of the family.

Zeus (Gr.)--It was his to repay violation of duty in the family, in social relations and the State.

FAMINE *See* HUNGER

FALSE CHARGES

Phaedra (Gr.)--In despair over being repulsed by Hippolytus, she hanged herself after leaving a scroll containing false charges against him.

FATES, THE

Ademtus (Gr.)--When he fell ill, Apollo prevailed on the Fates to spare his life, but they agreed only on condition that someone else consented to die in his place.

Adrasta (Gr.)--Goddess of inevitable fate, who with her sister nymph, Ida, fed the rescued Jupiter on goat's milk until he reached maturity.

FATES, THE (cont.)

Althaea (Gr.)-- *See same under* BOX.

Atropus (Gr.)--The one of the three Fates who severed the thread of life with shears.

Clotho (Gr.)–Youngest of the three Fates who wound wool around the spindle.

Destinies, The (Gr.)--Were the same as the Three Fates.

Lachesis (Gr.)--The one of the three Fates known as the Disposer of Lots, and who determined the length of life.

Moerae (Gr.)--*Greek*, name of the Fates.

Moeragetes (Gr.)--A name applied to Zeus, as leader of the Fates.

Night (Gr.); Nox (Ro.)--A prime element of Nature; mother of the Fates, and others.

Nyx (Gr.)– *See* Night.

Parcae (Ro.)--The three Fates, corresponding to the three Moerae of the Greeks.

FATHER *See* OFFSPRING

FAUNS

Faunus (Ro.)--A rural, Roman deity. To the Greeks, his pastoral character is identical to that of Pan.

Pan (Gr.)--Led the dances of the wood-nymphs. He had the ears, legs and horns of a goat.

Satyrs (Gr.)--Bearded creatures with snub noses, goats' ears and horses' tails. The goat-legged satyr is found in Roman poetry.

FEAR

Phobos (Gr.)--A son and attendant of Mars, named Fear. Another Phobos was a goddess who personified panic fear which overtook armies and put them to flight.

FEAR (cont.)

Vulcan (Ro.)–A good-natured god, but cunning and even vengeful, and more to be feared than courted.

FEAST

Aeneas (Gr.)--On the island of the Harpies, he and his companions prepared a feast, but as soon as they began to eat, the disgusting Harpies (birds with heads of maidens), flew in to seize the food with their talons and carry it off.

Hymen (Gr.)--A divine youth; personification of the wedding feast.

FEET

Achilles (Gr.)-- *See same under* HEEL.

Acrisius (Gr.)--Was hit in the foot by a discus thrown by his grandson, Perseus. This caused his death, and fulfilled a prophecy.

Atalanta (Gr.)--Fleet of foot. She offered herself as a prize to him who could defeat her in a race. Hippomenes won by strewing golden apples in her path.

Oedipus (Gr.)--As a baby his feet had been pierced by a herdsman, to cause his death, as instructed. He was adopted by King Polybus, and dubbed "Oedipus," or "Swollen–Foot."

Sciron (Gr.)--Was a giant who kept watch over a cliff. He forced travelers to look at the feet, and when they knelt down he kicked them into waters below.

Vulcan (Ro.)--He was lame because Cronus had picked him up by the foot and hurled him from Heaven.

FERRYMAN

Charon (Gr.)--The grim boatman who ferried the dead across the River Styx.

Nessus (Gr.)--A centaur who carried travelers across a river for a stated fee.

FERRYMAN (cont.)

Phaon (Gr.)--Ferried a boat between Lesbos and Chios.

FERTILITY

Bacchus (Gr.)--Represented the power of fertility and of joyful life.

Earth Goddess (Gaea) (Gr.)--A goddess concerned with fertility and vegetation.

Iasion (Gr.)--A mortal, possibly a hero or deity of agriculture; his myth, from a ritual symbolizing fertilization of the fields.

FESTIVAL

Ceres (Ro.)--Goddess of harvest festivals.

Erechtheus (Gr.)--King of Athens, founder of the ancient festival in honor of Athena.

Ibycus (Gr.)--A poet who was killed by two robbers on his way to a music festival at Corinth.

Munychia (Gr.)--An ancient festival of Artemis.

FEUD *See also* AVENGE

Aegisthus (Gr.)--He and Agamemnon revived a treacherous feud which had existed between their fathers.

Atreus (Gr.)--In a family feud, he and his brother, Thyestes, killed their brother, Chrysippus.

FEVER

Triptolemus (Gr.)--His fever was cured by Ceres, with poppy juice and a kiss.

FIDELITY

Daphnis (Gr.)–A handsome shepherd; A Naiad, in love with him, threat-

Daphnis (cont.)--ened to blind him if he did not vow fidelity to her.

Penelope (Gr.)--Wife of Ulysses, whose fidelity to him over many years was the marvel of the *Odyssey*.

FIELDS

Faunus (Gr.)--A rural deity, worshiped as a god of the fields, fruitfulness and animal life.

Pan (Ro.)--Was a god of woods and fields.

FIGHTING *See* COMBAT; FEUD; SLAIN; STRIFE; WAR

FIRE

Chimaera (Gr.)--A fire-breathing monster, which created great havoc.

Demeter (Gr.)-- *See same under* NURSE.

Demophoon (Gr.)-- *See same under* NURSE.

Dioscuri (Gr.)--These were Castor and Pollux, patrons of sailors, to whom they appeared as balls of fire (St. Elmo's fire), on the masts.

Hephaestus (Gr.); Vulcan (Ro.)--God of fire, volcanic eruption, incendiary flame, and of arts dependent on fire, such as metalworking.

Herostratus (Gr.)-- *See same under* TEMPLE.

Jason (Gr.)--After he tired of Medea, she set fire to his palace and fled to Athens.

Man (Gr.)--Began with Prometheus, who brought him fire with which he could develop commerce, science, and the arts.

Medea (Gr.)-- *See* Jason.

Paris (Gr.)--Before he was born, his mother, Hecuba, dreamed she would give birth to a child who would stir up contention (a "firebrand").

FIRE (cont.)

Porphyrion (Gr.)--The fire-king, leader of the more mighty Giants.

Priam (Gr.)--King of Troy. Although he was old when the siege of Troy began, he lived to see the wooden horse smuggled into the city, and to see Troy burned to the ground.

Prometheus (Gr.)--Stole fire from heaven for the use of man.

Vesta (Gr.)--Goddess of the hearth and its fire. From her altars other gods obtained their fires.

Vulcan (Ro.)--Was the blacksmith of the gods. Mount Aetna poured forth the fumes and flames of his smithy.

FISH

Dagon (Gr.)--The fish-god who swam nightly in the subterranean waters.

Glaucus (Gr.)--One of the lesser powers of the Ocean. Once a fisherman, he became immortal by tasting magic herbs which changed him to a strange half-man, half-fish similar to the sea-gods.

Perdix (Gr.)--Learned the mechanical arts. Imitating the spine of a fish in iron, he invented the saw.

Portumnus (Gr.)--Was invoked by sailors. Represented as riding on a dolphin.

Priapus (Gr.)--Protector of herds, bees, and fish.

FISHERMAN

Acetes (Gr.)--A fisherman of Maeonia, who acquired the art of steering by the stars.

Dictys (Gr.)--A fisherman of Seriphus, who rescued Danaë and Perseus from the waves.

FLATTERER

Damocles (Gr.)--A flatterer in the court of Dionysius I. *See same under* BANQUET.

FLEECE *See* GOLDEN FLEECE

FLOCKS *See also* HERDS; SHEPHERDS

Pan (Gr.)--Was a god of flocks and shepherds.

Phaëthusa (Gr.)--With her sister, Lampetia, she guarded their father Helios's flocks on the island of Thrinacia.

FLOOD *See also* DELUGE

Baucis (Gr.)--Because she and her husband, Philemon, had been hospitable to Jupiter and Mercury, the two gods saved their home when they sank the rest of the village in a lake.

Deucalion (Gr.)--They (he and his wife, Pyrrha), were the only two survivors, finding refuge on Mt. Parnassus, after Jupiter and Neptune brought on a great flood.

Hesione (Gr.)--She was offered by her father, Laomedon, to a hungry sea monster which came with floods sent by Neptune.

Philemon (Gr.)-- *See* Baucis.

FLOWERS

Aphrodite (Gr.)--The rose, myrtle and apple were sacred to her.

Attis (Gr.)--Following his self-mutilation, violets sprang up from the drops of his blood.

Chloris (Gr.)--Goddess of flowers.

Clytie (Gr.)--In love with Apollo, unrequited, she sat on the ground until her limbs took root in the ground, and her face became a sun-flower, turning on its stem to follow the sun-god across the sky.

Dryope (Gr.)--Plucked the purple blossoms of a lotus plant, and discovered it to be none other than the transformed nymph, Lotis. *See same under* NYMPHS.

Flora (Gr.)--An ancient goddess of flowers or of blooming vegetation.

Hyacinthus (Gr.)--Killed by a quoit flung by Apollo, his blood stained

FLOWERS (cont.)

Hyacinthus (cont.)--the ground and became a purple flower. Apollo marked the petals with his sorrow, inscribing "Ai! Ai!" upon them, and named the flower Hyacinthus.

Linus (Gr.)--Died young. His fate like that of others who succumbed in the springtime of life, typifies the sudden withering of herbs, flowers, animal life, under the fierce shafts of summer.

Lotus-Eaters, The (Gr.)--Gave Ulysses' men the lotus plant to eat, which made them lose all thought of home and wish to remain there.

Midas (Gr.)--His hair-dresser whispered the secret of his having ass's ears, to a hole in the ground. A thick bed of reeds growing nearby began to whisper the story, and continue to do so everytime a breeze passes.

Naiads, The (Gr.)--They put flowers in the bull's horn which Hercules brought, and presented it to the goddess of Plenty. She named it Cornucopia.

Narcissus (Gr.)--After his death, his body was nowhere to be found. In its place there sprung a flower, purple within, surrounded by white leaves, which preserves his name and memory.

Venus (Ro.)--Was the goddess of gardens and flowers.

FLUTE See MUSIC

FLYING

Daedalus (Gr.)--A famous artificer, who, while imprisoned, constructed wings made of feathers, fastened on with wax. With these, he and his son, Icarus, flew out of prison.

FOES See COMBAT; WAR

FOOD

Aeneas (Gr.)-- *See same under* FEAST.

Ceres (Ro.)--Goddess of agriculture in general. *See also* Proserpina.

FOOD (cont.)

Erysichthon (Gr.)-- *See same under* HUNGER.

Furies, The (Gr.)--One of them stood by a table loaded with dainties, and snatched food away as fast as the victims prepared to taste them.

Harpies, The (Gr.)--Seized or defiled the food of their victims.

Phineus (Gr.)--Jupiter transported him to the island of the Harpies, where he was punished by having them snatch or befoul his food.

Proserpina (Ro.)--She was tempted to eat a pomegranate which delayed her release from the Lower World, which her mother, Ceres, had tried for many years to effect.

Vesta (Ro.); Hestia (Gr.)--Being the goddess of the hearth and its fire, she was also goddess of the preparation of food.

FOOL

Vulcan (Ro.); Hephaestus (Gr.)--One of the great gods; a blacksmith. He was good-natured, and seems to have been the cause of "inextinguishable laughter" to the other gods, yet he was by no means a fool.

FORCE *See also* CARRIED OFF

Orion (Gr.)--Was a giant who tried to gain possession of Merope by force. For this, he was blinded.

FOREST

Atlas (Gr.)-- *See same under* MOUNTAIN.

Cybele (Ro.); Rhea (Gr.)--Mother of the gods. She haunted mountain and forest fastnesses.

Dryads (Gr.)--Were wood-nymphs who lived in forests.

Pan (Gr.)--A god of the forest, he was dreaded by those who had to pass through the woods at night.

FORGERS *See also* IRON WORKING

Cyclopes (Gr.)--Were giants who forged the thunderbolts for **Zeus**.

Vulcan (Ro.)--The god of fire, and the glow of the forge.

FORGETFULNESS

Lethe (Gr.)--A river of oblivion in Hades, a drink of which brought forgetfulness of the past.

FORT

Dido (Gr.)--She erected a fort, around which the city of Carthage rose.

FORTUNE

Fortuna (Ro.)--Goddess of fortune. Being the first-born daughter of Jupiter, she was called *Fortuna Primigenia*.

Tyche (Gr.)-- *Same as* Fortuna.

FOUNDER

Aeolus (Gr.)--Ancestor of the Aeolians.

Därdansu (Gr.)--Son of Electra and Zeus; the true founder of the Trojan race.

Dorus (Gr.)--Son of Hellen; became an ancestor of the Dorians.

Hellen (Gr.)--Was the founder of the Hellenic race.

Ninus (Gr.)--Husband of Semiramis; founder of the city of Ninevah.

Quirinus (Ro.)--An ancient god of war, whose chief shrine was on the Quirnal. Said to be no other than Romulus, founder of Rome.

Romulus (Ro.)--First king of Rome. He slew his twin brother, Remus, for leaping scornfully over the wall of his new city, Rome. He was deified by the Romans.

FOUNTAIN

Arethusa (Gr.)--Diana cleft the ground for her protection when Alpheüs frightened her. A cold sweat came over her, changing her into a fountain.

Camenae, The (Ro.)--Were nymphs of fountains and springs in ancient Rome; later, the Greek Muses.

Carmenta (Ro.)--A water or spring goddess; leader of the fountain nymphs.

Egeria (Ro.)--Associated with Carmenta.

Helicon (Ro.)--A mountain in Greece, which contained the fountains of Aganippe and Hippocrene.

Hippocrene (Gr.)--A mountain on Mt. Helicon, fabled to have burst forth when the ground was struck by the hoof of Pegasus.

Salmacis (Gr.)--A nymph of a fountain in ancient Caria, the waters of which rendered effeminate all who drank of them.

FREEDMEN

Feronia (Gr.)--Goddess of groves and freedmen.

FRENZY See MADNESS

FRIENDSHIP

Achates (Gr.)--A friend of Aeneas, and his loyal companion throughout the Aeneïd.

Pirithoüs (Gr.)--A famous friendship between him and Theseus originated in the midst of arms.

Pylades (Gr.)--Grew up with Orestes and formed a lasting friendship with him.

FRIGHT

Adrastus (Gr.)--King of Argos. Witnessing the deaths of his sons—in—law

FRIGHT (cont.)

Adrastus (cont.)–caused him such fright, he turned pale and remained so.

Erechtheus (Gr.)–In the form of a serpent, in a basket, he gave such fright to the three daughters of Cecrops, they jumped off the Acropolis.

Pan (Gr.)– *See same under* PANIC.

FROGS

Latona (Ro.)–Because some rustics had stirred up a pond of clear water with their feet to make it undrinkable, Latona had them changed into frogs.

FRUCTIFICATION

Liber (Ro.)–An ancient Roman god of fructification; later identified with Bacchus of the grape.

FRUITFULNESS

Aphrodite (Gr.)– *See same under* GODDESSES.

Demeter (Gr.); Ceres (Ro.)–Goddess of the fruitfulness of mankind.

Faunus (Ro.)–A rural deity, worshiped as a god of animal life, fields, fruitfulness.

FRUITS

Aristaeus (Gr.)–Was the protector of vine and olive.

Atlas (Gr.)–Was the possessor of an orchard bearing apples of gold.

Pomona (Gr.)–Was a Hamadryad; guardian of fruit groves, especially apple orchards.

Pyramus (Gr.)–Believing his loved Thisbe to be dead, he threw himself on his own sword, and his blood spurted onto the white mulberries. Thenceforth the mulberry produced nothing but purple berries.

91

FUNERAL

Anaxerete (Gr.)– *See same under* STONE.

Antigone (Gr.)--Her uncle, Creon, usurping king of Thebes, had her buried alive because she performed funeral rites over the body of her traitor brother, Polynices.

Dido (Gr.)--After Aeneas left her she mounted a funeral pyre, and stabbed herself for the flames to consume her.

Evadne (Gr.)--During the obsequies of her husband, Capaneus, she cast herself on his funeral pyre.

Philoctetes (Gr.)--After Hercules built his own funeral pile, he asked Philoctetes to apply the torch.

Poeas (Gr.)--Helped his son, Philoctetes to apply the torch to Hercules' funeral pile.

Proteus (Gr.)--Paid funeral honors to Orpheus and Eurydice.

FURIES

Alcmaeon (Gr.)-- *See same under* MADNESS.

Alecto (Gr.)--One of the three Furies who leaped from the spilled blood of Uranus.

Amata (Gr.)--Queen of the Trojans, who, being possessed by a Fury, opposed the alliance of the Trojans with the Latins.

Ares (Gr.); Mars (Ro.)--Offspring of the North Wind and a Fury.

Discord (Gr.)--In the chamber of the Furies, she was mad.

Eumenides (Gr.); Erinnyes--A euphemistic name of the Furies, meaning the well-intentioned, intended to soothe them.

Furies, The (Gr.)--The three goddesses of vengeance.

Megaera (Gr.)--One of the three Furies, sister of Alecto and Tisiphone.

Orestes (Gr.)--After he killed his mother, Clytemnestra, in retribution, he was pursued from land to land by the Furies.

FURIES (cont.)

Persephone (Gr.)--Queen of Hades; goddess of death, she directed the Furies.

Poenae (Gr.)--A title used sometimes for the Furies.

Semnae (Gr.)--The three Furies, Alecto, Megaera and Tisiphone; attendants of Persephone.

Tisiphone (Gr.)--One of the three Furies; the avenging goddess.

FURY

Polyphemus (Gr.)--In love with Galatea, he became so furious when he saw her with Acis that he struck the young man with a rock, and killed him. Later, in his cave, he discovered Ulysses and his men awaiting him. In a fury he seized two of them and dashed out their brains against the side of the cave.

FUTURE

Tiresias (Gr.)--A soothsayer, who obtained from Minerva knowledge of future events.

G

GADFLY

Bellerophon (Gr.)--When he, by his pride, drew the anger of the Olympians, the king of gods sent a gadfly to sting his horse, Pegasus, causing him to throw his rider.

Io (Gr.)--Through jealousy, Juno sent a gadfly to sting her.

GAMBLERS

Mercury (Ro.)--Was the patron of gamblers and a god of chance.

GAMES

Acrisius (Gr.)--During an athletic contest, the discus of his grandson, Per-

GAMES (cont.)

Acrisius (cont.)--eus, bounded the wrong way and killed him, fulfilling a prophecy.

Gemini (Gr.)--Castor and Pollux, the twins, were horsemen and patrons of games.

Hyacinthus (Gr.)--Killed by a discus hurled too high and far by Apollo during a game of quoits.

Python (Gr.)--Apollo commemorated his conquest of this enormous serpent by organizing the Pythian games, in which the victors in feats of strength, or speed, were crowned with wreaths of beech leaves.

GARDENS

Priapus (Gr.)--A god; protector of the life of vineyards and gardens.

Venus (Ro.)--Goddess of gardens and flowers.

Vertumnus (Gr.)--The deity of gardens and changing seasons.

GATE *See also* GHOSTS

Cerberus (Gr.)--A three-headed dog with a serpent-tail and his necks bristling with snakes, which guarded the gate to the Underworld.

Horae (Gr.)--The three goddesses of the seasons and hours, who guarded the gate of clouds at Olympus. *See same under* CLOUD.

Iphis (Gr.)--Spurned by Anaxarete, he hung himself to her gatepost.

Olympus (Gr.)--The heaven of the Greek gods, protected by a gate of clouds.

GENERATIVE

Priapus (Ro.)–The male generative power, personified as a god.

GHOSTS

Lemures (Ro.)--Spirits to whom the Romans directed their prayers; they correspond to our ghosts.

Oracles (Gr.)--Sometimes the Greeks communicated with the ghosts of Hades, through certain oracles of the dead.

Psychopompus (Gr.)--This was Mercury when he conducted the outworn ghosts of mortals past the gates of the sun to the dark realm of Hades.

GIANT *See also* MONSTER

Alcyoneus (Gr.)--Was an earth-born giant, of the winter storms and ice-bergs.

Aloadae (Gr.)-- *See same under* MONSTER.

Antaeus (Gr.)--A giant wrestler, son of Gaea, whose strength was invincible as long as he remained in contact with his mother, Earth. He was strangled in mid-air by Hercules.

Atlas (Gr.)--A giant who stood in the far west, bearing the heavens on his head and hands, as a penalty for warring against Zeus.

Cacus (Gr.)--A giant who lived in a cave on Mt. Aventine and hid some of Hercules' cattle here. For this, Hercules killed him.

Clytias (Gr.)--A well–known Greek giant.

Cyclopes (Gr.)--A race of giants, who had one eye set in the middle of their foreheads.

Enceladus (Gr.)--One of the many 100-armed giants, who warred against the gods, and was overthrown by Athena.

Ephialtes (Gr.)--One of the two giant sons of Neptune, who tried to attack the Olympians.

Eurytion (Gr.)--A giant who, with his two-headed dog, guarded the oxen of Geryon.

Giants, The (Gr.)–Were a novel race of monsters, more akin to men than to the Titans. Their bodies and lower limbs were of snakes.

Iphimedia (Gr.)--Mother of the two giants, Otus and Ephialtes.

Juno (Ro.)--With Minerva and Hercules, she defeated the Giants.

GIANTS (cont.)

Laestrygones (Gr.)--A race of cannibal giants who killed many comrades of Odysseus (Ulysses).

Mimas (Gr.)--A famous Greek giant.

Orion (Gr.)--A giant and mighty hunter whose prowess gained for him the rare good will of Diana.

Otus (Gr.)--The giant brother of Ephialtes.

Pallas (Gr.)--One of the more mightly of the giants.

Phoebus (Gr.); Apollo (Gr.)--Subdued the giant Titylus, and overthrew Otus and Ephialtes.

Polybotes (Gr.)--Was among the most famous of the giants.

Porphyrion (Gr.)--One of the more mighty giants, the fire-king, leader of the crew.

Poseidon (Gr.); Neptune (Ro.)--Father of the two giants, the Aloadae.

Procrustes (Gr.)--"The Stretcher." He tied travelers to his iron bedstead; if they were too short, he stretched them to fit; if too long, he lopped off their limbs.

Proserpina (Ro.)--Met Pluto in the Mount Aetna region, where the giants had been imprisoned by Jupiter.

Rhoetus (Gr.)--A well-known giant.

Talus (Gr.)--A giant of living brass, fashioned by Vulcan.

Theseus (Gr.)--Slaughtered the giant, Procrustes.

Tityus (Gr.)--A giant so immense that lying down, he stretched across nine acres.

GIFT *See also* BLESSING

Cumaean Sibyl (Gr.)--Apollo promised her any gift. She chose to live as many years as there were grains of sand on the shore, but forgot to ask for eternal youth with it.

GIFT (cont.)

Scylla (Gr.)--Cut off the purple lock of hair of her father, Nisus, and gave it to his enemy, Minos II, of Crete. But Minos recoiled from this treacherous gift.

GIRDLE

Admeta (Gr.)--Daughter of Eurystheus, who asked for the girdle of Hippolyta. Hercules obtained it for her.

Amazons (Gr.)--A nation of war—like women, whose queen, Hippolyta (Antiope), possessed a magic girdle.

Cestes (Gr.)--Was the girdle of Venus, which enhanced the charm of the wearer.

Cyane (Gr.)--A Sicilian nymph who found Proserpina's girdle floating on the Anapus River.

Hercules (Ro.)--As his Ninth Labor, he killed Hippolyta, and carried her girdle to Eurystheus for his daughter, Admeta.

Hippolyta (Gr.); Antiope (Gr.)--Queen of the Amazons, had been given the prized girdle, by Ares.

Ulysses (Gr.)--During a storm at sea a passionate sea-nymph, Leucothea, in the form of a cormorant, lit on his raft to give him a girdle (life-belt), to buoy him up.

Venus (Ro.)--Her girdle enhanced the charm of the wearer.

GLANCE *See also* LOOK BACK

Gorgons (Gr.)--The three monster sisters, Euryale, Medusa and Stheno. No living thing could glance at them without turning to stone.

Medusa (Gr.)--One of the three Gorgons. Around the cave where she lived were the stony figures of men and animals who had chanced to glance at her, and had been petrified.

GNOMES

Cercopes (Gr.)--Thievish gnomes. *See same under* THIEVES.

GOAT

Amalthea (Gr.)--Was a goat on the Island of Crete, whose milk nourished the rescued infant, Jupiter.

Chimaera (Gr.)--A fire--breathing monster. The front of his body was part lion, part goat; the hind part, a dragon. He was destroyed by Bellerophon.

Jupiter (Ro.); Zeus (Gr.)--As an infant, he was concealed on the island of Crete, nurtured by nymphs and fed on the milk of the goat Amalthea.

Pan (Gr.)--A god of the woods and fields. He made love to the nymphs, but frequently to no avail, for he was not prepossessing, having the horns, ears and legs of a goat.

Satyrs (Gr.)--Deities of the woods and fields, they appeared as bearded creatures, with snub noses, goat's ears and horse's tails.

GODS *See also* CUPBEARER; EARTH

Aesculapias (Ro.)--The god of medicine.

Apollo (Gr.)--God of the sun, of poetry and music; the source of inspiration for oracles.

Ares (Gr.); Mars (Ro.)--The war-god.

Asclepius (Gr.); Aesculapius (Ro.)--The god of medicine.

Asopus (Gr.)--A river-god.

Bacchus (Gr.); Dionysus (Gr.); Iacchus (Gr.); Liber (Ro.)--God of wine; a deity of earth.

Bellerophon (Gr.)--Seeing that this hero was beloved of the gods, King Iobates of Lycia, gave him his daughter, Antea, and made him successor to his throne.

Cephissus (Gr.)--A river-god.

Chronos (Gr.)--The god of Time; a power which destroys whatever it has brought into existence.

Comus (Gr. and Ro.)--The god of festive joy, mirth and drunkenness.

GODS (cont.)

Consivius (Gr.); Janus (Ro.)--The god of civilization, sometimes known as the Sower.

Consus (Ro.)--An early Italian god of the earth; keeper of the stores; god of the stored-up harvest.

Cronus (Gr.)-- *See* Rhea.

Cupid (Ro.); Eros (Gr.)--The god of love; son of Venus.

Cybele (Ro.)--Mother of the gods.

Dagon (Gr.)--The fish-god who swam nightly through subterranean waters.

Dionysus (Gr.)-- *See* Bacchus.

Dis (Ro); Pluto (Gr.)--An underworld god whose worship was introduced into Rome with that of Proserpina at the time of the struggle at Carthage.

Enceladus (Gr.)--One of the mighty 100-armed giants who warred against the gods.

Enyalius (Gr.)--A god of war; an epithet of Mars.

Eros (Gr.); Cupid (Ro.)--First of the gods; the small, powerful god of love.

Erysichthon (Gr.)--A despiser of the gods.

Eurus (Gr.)--God of the southeast wind.

Faunus (Ro.); Pan (Gr.)--A rural deity, worshipped as a god of animal life, fields, fruitfulness, shepherds and prophecy.

Fontus (Ro.)--God of flowing waters, springs, brooks and healing.

Gaea (Gr.); Tellus (Ro.)--Mother Earth. She belonged to the older order of gods.

Hades (Gr.); Pluto (Class.); Orcus (Ro.); Dis (Ro.)--The grim god of the Lower World.

Helios (Gr.)--The ancient sun-god who drove a four-hrose chariot across

GODS (cont.)

Helios (cont.)--the heavens. Later identified as Apollo.

Hephaestus (Gr.); Vulcan (Ro.)--God of fire, especially of volcanic eruption, incendiary flame, and of arts dependent on fire, such as metalworking.

Hermes (Gr.); Mercury (Ro.)--The herald and messenger of the gods.

Hymen (Gr.)--The god of marriage.

Hypnos (Gr.); Somnus (Ro.)--The winged god of sleep.

Iacchus (Gr.); Bacchus (Gr.); Liber (Ro.)--The god of wine; especially the god of animal life and vegetation.

Inachus (Gr.)--A river-god.

Iobates (Gr.)-- *See* Bellerophon.

Janus (Ro.); Consivius (Gr.)--An ancient and important Roman deity; the god of doors, of beginnings.

Jove (Ro.); Jupiter (Ro.)--God of the sky; the chief divinity of the ancient Romans.

Jupiter (Ro.); Zeus (Gr.); Jove (Ro.)-- *See* Jove; Zeus.

Juventus (Ro.)--The god of youth, worshipped by the Romans.

Kronos (Gr.); Saturn (Ro.)--A god of the harvests.

Liber (Ro.); Bacchus (Gr.)--An ancient Italian god of fructification; later identified with Bacchus of the grape.

Lyaeus (Gr.)--A god called the loosener of care; identified with Bacchus.

Lycius (Gr.)--Another name for Apollo; the wolf-god or the golden-god of light.

Mars (Ro.); Ares (Gr.)--One of the great gods of Heaven; the patron god of the Romans.

Melicertes (Gr.)--After he drowned he was made the sea-god Palaemon.

GODS (cont.)

Mercury (Ro.); Hermes (Gr.)--The god of commerce and gain, whose cult was derived from that of the Greek Hermes.

Momus (Gr.)--The god of ridicule and adverse criticism.

Mors (Ro.); Thanatos (Gr.)--The god of death.

Mulciber (Ro.); Hephaestus (Gr.); Vulcan (Ro.)--A descriptive name for Vulcan; from *mulceo,* meaning to soften.

Neptune (Ro.); Poseidon (Gr.)--God of the sea and of all waters.

Oceanus (Gr.)--Oldest of the Titans, he was the Neptune of the older dynasty of gods.

Orcus (Ro.)--Known among the Romans also as Dis or Tartarus, he was Pluto or Hades to the Greeks, the god Death, ruler of the Underworld.

Paean (Gr.)--The family physician of the gods.

Pan (Gr.)--God of woods and fields, and of flocks and shepherds.

Pandora (Gr.)--Every god contributed something to her pefection, then named her Pandora, "the gift of the gods."

Penates (Ro.)--The gods of the household, the welfare and prosperity of the family.

Peneus (Gr.)--A river-god.

Perseus (Gr.)--One of the older heroes endowed with godlike qualities.

Phaëton (Gr.)--Asked his father, Apollo, to let him drive the chariot of the sun.

Philemon (Gr.)--He and his wife, Baucis, were the only ones in their village to give the two gods, Jupiter and Mercury a hospitable reception.

Phoebus (Apollo) (Gr.)--A god of life and peace; a pure and just god.

Pluto (Class.)-- *See* Hades.

Plutus (Gr.)--The god of wealth.

GODS (cont.)

Pontus (Gr.)--God of the deep sea or the waterways.

Poseidon (Gr.); Neptune (Ro.)--God of the kingdom of the sea.

Priapus (Gr.)--The male generative power personified as a god.

Proteus (Gr.)--A prophetic sea-god in the service of Neptune.

Psychopompus (Gr.)--This was Mercury when he was serving his gravest function of conducting ghosts of mortals to Hades.

Quirinus (Ro.)--An ancient Roman god of war.

Rhea (Gr.)--Wife of Cronus, she gave birth to six gods: Demeter, Hades, Hera, Hestia, Poseidon, and Zeus; hence called "Mother of the Gods."

Saturn (Ro.); Cronus (Gr.)--An ancient deity of seeds and sowing.

Satyrs (Gr.)--Deities of the woods and fields.

Scamander (Gr.)--A river-god.

Selene (Gr.)--An ancient goddess of the moon, descended from gods on both sides.

Silvanus (Ro.)--A rural deity.

Terminus (Ro.)--The god of landmarks.

Vulcan (Ro.)--One of the great gods; son of Jupiter and Juno; the god of fire; blacksmith of the gods.

Zeus (Gr.); Jupiter (Ro.)--At the council of the gods, he was chosen Sovereign of the World.

GODDESSES

Aphrodite (Gr.)--The smiling goddess of love, beauty and fruitfulness.

Artemis (Gr.); Diana (Ro.)--A virgin goddess; ideal of modesty, grace and maidenly vigor. Identified with the chaste brilliance of the moon.

Astraea (Gr.)--Goddess of innocence and purity.

GODDESSES (cont.)

Ate (Gr.)--Goddess of infatuation.

Athena (Gr.)--The virgin goddess; goddess of the thundercloud.

Aura (Gr.)--Goddess of the mild and gentle breezes.

Aurora (Ro.)--The rosy-fingered goddess of the Morn.

Bellona (Gr.)--A goddess personifying war.

Carmenta (Ro.)--A water or spring goddess.

Ceres (Ro.); Demeter (Gr.)--The goddess of sowing, reaping, of harvest festivals, and of agriculture in general.

Chloris (Gr.); Flora (Ro.)--Goddess of flowers.

Cybele (Ro.); Rhea (Gr.)--Mother of the gods. *See* Rhea *under* GODS. She was the protectress of cities and fortified places, and she wore a turreted crown which resembled the wall of a city.

Cynthia (Gr.); Diana (Ro.)--Goddess of the moon; also known as Luna.

Demeter (Gr.)-- *See* Ceres. Goddess of the fruitfulness of mankind.

Diana (Ro.); Artemis (Gr.)--Goddess of the moon.

Dictynna (Gr.)--A Cretan goddess, protectress of hunters and seafarers.

Earth Goddess (Gaea) (Gr.)--A goddess of fertility and vegetation.

Eileithyia (Gr.)--Goddess of childbirth.

Enyo (Gr.)--Daughter of Mars; ruiner of cities; goddess of war.

Eos (Gr.); Aurora (Ro.)--Goddess of the Morn.

Epona (Ro.)--Goddess of horses, mules and asses.

Eurynome (Gr.)--A sea-goddess.

Fauna (Ro.)--Known as the good goddess.

Feronia (Gr.)--Goddess of groves and freedman.

GODDESSES (cont.)

Flora (Ro.); Chloris (Gr.)--Goddess of flowers, and blooming vegetation.

Fortuna (Gr.)--Goddess of fortune. The first-born daughter of Jupiter.

Gaea (Terra) (Gr.)--Mother Earth, in the older order of goddesses.

Graces (Gr.)--Graceful and beautiful goddesses.

Hecate (Gr.)--A three-headed goddess, with six arms; goddess of the crossroads.

Hera (Gr.); Juno (Ro.)--An Olympian queen of Heaven.

Hestia (Gr.); Vesta (Ro.)--Goddess of the hearth, of the home or city.

Horae (Gr.)--Three goddesses of the hours, seasons, and of orderliness.

Hygeia (Gr.)--Recognized as a goddess, she was the personification of health.

Ino (Gr.)--The gods made her a goddess under the name of Leucothea.

Iris (Gr.)--Goddess of the rainbow.

Juno (Ro.); Hera (Gr.)--A deity of light and the sky.

Juturna (Ro.)--Goddess of springs and brooks.

Latona (Ro.)--Goddess of darkness.

Leto (Gr.)--Another name for Latona.

Leucothea (Gr.)--A sea-goddess; once Ino.

Libera (Ro.); Proserpina (Ro.)--A goddess associated with Liber.

Lucina (Ro.)--The goddess who brings to light; goddess of childbirth.

Luna (Ro.)--The moon, worshipped by the Romans.

Magna Mater (Ro.); Rhea (Gr.); Cybele (Ro.)--The great mother of the gods.

Maia (Majesta) (Ro.)--An ancient goddess in Roman religion.

104

GODDESSES (cont.)

Minerva (Ro.)--A virgin goddess, gentle, fair and thoughtful; goddess of storms and of the thunderbolt; goddess of wisdom, of skill, contemplation, spinning and weaving, of horticulture and agriculture.

Nemesis (Gr.)--An ancient Greek goddess, daught of Night.

Nike (Gr.); Victoria (Ro.)--The goddess of Victory.

Nymphs, Sleepless (Gr.)--The dread goddesses of the country people.

Ops (Ro.)--An ancient Italian goddess of sowing and the harvest.

Pales (Ro.)--The Roman goddess presiding over cattle and pastures.

Pandemos (Aphrodite) (Venus) (Gr.)--Goddess of vulgar love.

Persephone (Gr.)--Queen of Hades; goddess of death.

Phobos (Gr.)--A goddess who personified panic fear.

Plenty (Gr.)--The cornucopia was the symbol of the goddess of Plenty.

Poena (Gr.)--The goddess of punishment.

Proserpina (Ro.)--She was the goddess of spring, bearing a cornucopia.

Tellus (Ro.); Gaea (Gr.)--Goddess of the earth.

Terra (Gr.); Gaea (Gr.)--The earth goddess.

Themis (Gr.)--Goddess of Justice.

Trivia (Ro.)--She was one of the heads of the three-headed goddess, Hecate.

Tyche (Gr.)--The goddess of Fortune.

Venus (Ro.); APhrodite (Gr.)--The goddess of gardens, and flowers; of love and beauty.

Vesta (Ro.); Hestia (Gr.)--Goddess of the hearth and its fire, and the preparation of food.

Victoria (Ro.); Nike (Gr.)--Goddess of victory.

GOLD

Arimasps (Gr. and Ro.)--A race of one-eyed men. *See same under* GRYPHONS.

Bacchus (Gr.); Liber (Ro.)--Gave the power of changing everything into gold to Midas.

Danaë (Gr.)--Jupiter appeared before her distilled into a shower of gold.

Gryphons (Gr.)--Guardians of gold.

Hesperides (Gr.); Atlantides (Gr.)--These were four nymphs who guarded the orchard of the golden apples.

Midas (Gr.)--After finding that even his food turned to gold when he touched it, he went to the river Pactolus, and washed away his gold-creating power into the water.

Pegasus (Gr.)--The winged horse that wore a golden bridle.

Phoebus (Gr.); Apollo (Gr.)--The golden god of light.

GOLDEN AGE

Saturn (Ro.); Cronus (Gr.)--He came to the site of the future Rome, formed a society and gave it laws. Such peace and plenty ensued that men called his reign "The Golden Age."

GOLDEN APPLES *See* APPLES, GOLDEN

GOLDEN FLEECE

Aeëtes (Gr.)--King of Colchis, who received the Golden Fleece from Phrixus, and placed it in a consecrated grove under the watchful care of a sleepless dragon.

Argonauts (Gr.)--These were the companions of Jason, who sailed to the kingdom of Colchis in search of the Golden Fleece.

Gemini (Gr.)--The twins, Castor and Pollux, who rendered noteworthy service to the Argonauts returning from Colchis with Medea and the Golden Fleece.

Golden Fleece (Gr.)--This belonged to a valuable ram which could speak and vault through the air. It carried Phrixus to Colchis.

Helle (Gr.)--Sister of Phrixus who tried to ride with him on the ram, but fell into the strait between Europe and Asia. This was later named the Hellespont, now the Dardanelles.

Jason (Gr.)--Assembled fifty famous heroes to join him in the glorious quest of the Golden Fleece. This was called the Argonautic Expedition.

Medea (Gr.)--She was a sorceress at Colchis, who enabled Jason to find the Golden Fleece.

Nephele (Gr.)--Mother who sent her children, Phrixus and Helle, on back of the ram with the Golden Fleece.

Pelias (Gr.)--The ursurping King of Iolcus, who sent his nephew, Jason, after the Golden Fleece, to keep him from the throne.

Phrixus (Gr.)--After arriving in Colchis, he sacrificed the ram with the Golden Fleece to Jupiter, and delivered the fleece to King Aeëtes;

Pollux (Gr.)--*See* Gemini.

Theseus (Gr.)--He joined Jason in the Argonautic search for the Golden Fleece.

GOOD

Fauna (Ro.); Maia (Ro.)--Known as the good goddess; not to be confused with the Greek Maia.

GORGONS

Athena (Gr.); Minerva (Ro.)--*See same under* SYMBOLS.

Atlas (Gr.)--While he was guarding the golden apples, Perseus came along with the head of the Gorgon Medusa, the sight of which changed Atlas to stone.

Ceto (Gr.)--Mother of the three Gorgons.

Gorgons (Gr.)--The three monster sisters, Euryale, Medusa and Stheno, who had claws of bronze and serpents for hands, and snaky hair. No living thing could look at them without turning to stone.

Graeae, The (Gr.)--Hoary witches who served as sentinels for the Gorgons.

Medusa (Gr.)--The most terrible Gorgon, had once been a maiden whose hair was her chief glory, but she dared to vie in beauty with Minerva. The goddess then changed her ringlets into hissing serpents.

Perseus (Gr.)--Hero of Argos, he approached Medusa by looking at her reflection in his bright shield. When close enough he cut off her head. With this Gorgon head, he turned Atlas, Phineas and King Polydectes to stone.

Phineus (Gr.)--A rival for the hand of Perseus's wife, Andromeda; changed into stone by looking at the Gorgon head.

Stheno (Gr.)-- *See* Gorgons.

GOVERNMENT

Priam (Gr.)--King of Troy, was a wise ruler, strengthening his state by good government at home and powerful alliances with his neighbors.

GRACE

Artemis (Gr.); Diana (Ro.)--A virgin goddess; the ideal of modesty and grace.

Charis (Gr.); Aglaia (Gr.)--The youngest of the three Graces; the personification of grace and beauty.

Daphne (Gr.)--A graceful nymph, daughter of the river-god Peneüs.

GRACES, THE

Aglaia (Gr.)--One of the three Graces; daughter of Jupiter and Eurynome. In the *Illiad*, she was the wife of Vulcan. Aglaia signifies brilliance.

GRACES, THE (cont.)

Charites (Gr.)--The three Graces; goddesses Euphrosyne, Aglaia and Thalia, who presided over the banquet, the dance and all social pleasures.

Euphrosyne (Gr.)--One of the three Graces, signifying mirth or joy.

Graces, The (Gr.)--The three sisters were graceful and beautiful goddesses, attendants of Venus, and inspirers of the qualities which gave charm to nature, love, social intercourse, etc. *See* Aglaia, Euphrosyne, and Thalia.

Thalia (Gr.)-- *See* Charites; Graces. She helped to preside over polite accomplishments.

GRAEAE, THE (PHORCYDES)

Graeae, The (Gr.)--They were three hoary witches, known as the Gray Women. They had only one eye among them, which they handed from one to the other, and only one tooth.

GRAPE *See also* VINE

Dionysus (Gr.); Bacchus (Gr.)--The god of wine. He discovered the culture of the vine.

Liber (Ro.); Bacchus (Gr.)--An ancient Italian god of fructification; later identified with Bacchus of the grape.

Pomona (Ro.)--Was a Hamadryad. Vertumnus tried to woo her in many guises. He spoke of the dependence of a grapevine, clinging to a nearby tree, and advised her to be likewise as dependent on him.

GRASSHOPPER

Tithonus (Gr.)--Aurora turned him into a grasshopper.

GRIEF *See also* MOURNING

Aëdon (Gr.)--A queen of Thebes. After she killed her own son by mistake, Zues relieved her grief by turning her into a nightingale.

Lyde (Gr.)--She was loved by the satyr Narcissus, who was loved by Echo. She in turn was loved by Pan; all of whom grieved because they were scorned.

Niobe (Gr.)--Because of her pride and superiority over Latona, she was changed by Zeus into stone, yet her tears continued to flow. She remains a mass of rock from which a trickling stream flows, a tribute to her never-ending grief over having lost all fourteen children.

GROVES

Elysian Fields (Gr.)--Groves where the happy resided, including those who had rendered service to mankind.

Feronia (Ro.)--The goddess of groves and freedmen.

GRYPHONS

Arimasp (Gr. and Ro.)--One of a race of one-eyed men of Scythia, who were in constant strife with the Gryphons for the gold they were guarding.

Gryphons (Gr.)--These were creatures with the head and wings of an eagle, and the body of a lion. They were guardians of gold.

GUARDIAN

Genius (Ro.)--A Roman guardian spirit. On their birthdays men made their offerings to their Genius; women to their Juno.

Iacchus (Gr.)--The god of wine, who when young, had as guardian and tutor, the jovial Silenus, oldest of the Satyrs.

GUARD

Aegle (Gr.)--One of the four daughters of Atlas, (the Hesperides), assigned to guard the trees of the Golden Apples.

Argus (2), (Gr.)-- *See same under* HEIFER.

Briareus (Gr.)--A monster with 100 hands, assigned to guard the descent to Hades.

GUARD (cont.)

Furies, The (Gr.); Erinnyes--The three goddesses of vengeance, Alecto, Megaera, and Tisiphone, who spread their couches in the Cave of Avernus in the Infernal Region. Tisiphone kept guard in an iron tower by the entrance.

Golden Apples (Gr.)--These had been given to Hera as a wedding present. They were guarded by the nymphs (Hesperides) with the aid of a dragon.

Gryphons (Gr.)--Guardians of gold.

Hades (Gr.)--The entrance to this Underworld was guarded by Cerebus, a three-headed dog with a serpent-tail, and his neck bristling with snakes.

Hesperides (Gr.); Atlantides--These were four nymphs: Aegle, Arethusa, Erytheia and Hestia, who, with their mother, Hesperis, and the aid of the dragon, Ladon, guarded the garden where grew the tree with the golden apples.

Ladon (Gr.); Peneus (Gr.)--He was the serpent that guarded the apples of the Hesperides.

Talus (Gr.)--The giant of living brass who guarded the domain of King Minos in Crete.

GUIDE

Ariadne (Gr.)-- *See same under* LABYRINTH.

Cedalion (Gr.)--One of Vulcan's men who served as a guide for the blinded Orion.

Cumaean Sibyl (Gr.)--A young prophetess who acted as a guide to Aeneas in his descent to Hades.

Mercury (Ro.); Hermes (Gr.)--Was a messenger of the gods, and conductor of souls to the Lower World.

Orion (Gr.)--Vulcan took pity on him, and gave him as a guide, Cedalion, who led him to the sun—god, Apollo, who restored his sight with a sun—beam.

GUIDE (cont.)

Psychopompus (Gr.); Mercury (Ro.)--He conducted the outworn ghosts of mortals past the gates of the sun to Hades.

GUILTLESS

Elysian Fields (Gr.)--The souls of the guiltless passed to the Elysian Fields, where each followed the chosen pursuit of his former life in a land of sunlight, happiness, and song.

GUISE *See also* DISGUISE

Vertumnus (Ro.) He wooed Pomona in the guises of reaper, fisherman, soldier, etc., but won her only when he stood before her as a comely youth.

GYMNASTICS

Hermes (Gr.); Mercury (Ro.)--He was the first of inventors, the god of science, of youth and gymnastic exercises.

H

HADES See *also* LOWER WORLD; STYX; UNDER WORLD

Aeacus (Gr.)--Famed for his justice on earth, he became after his death one of the three judges (with Minos and Rhadamanthus) in Hades, before whom souls were brought to trial.

Aeneas (Gr.)--He was one of few mortals who visited the Stygian Realm and returned from it.

Aesculapius (Ro.); Asclepius (Gr.)--The god of medicine, whose skill was so great that Pluto complained the population of his realm, Hades, was being reduced. Jupiter obliged his brother, Pluto, by killing Aesculapius with a thunderbolt, but received him into the circle of gods.

Alcestis (Gr.)--When the Fates decreed that the life of her husband, King Admetus, could be saved only if someone consented to die in his stead, she came forward, went to Hades, and was restored later to the Upper World by Hercules.

112

HADES (cont.)

Aloadae (Gr.)--The two monsters representing the unregulated forces of vegetation, tried to dethrone the immortals. Jupiter killed them with his lightning, and they atoned in Hades by being bound to a pillar with serpents, and having to listen to the perpetual hooting of a screech owl.

Castor (Gr.)--Was slain in combat. His inconsolable brother, Pollux, pleaded with Jupiter to let him give his own life as ransom. Jupiter consented to let them enjoy life alternately, each spending half his time in Hades, and the rest on earth.

Ceres (Ro.); Demeter (Gr.)--After her daughter, Proserpina, had been carried off by Pluto to become the queen of Hades, Ceres tried for many years to restore her to the Upper World, but became discouraged.

Cumaean Sibyl (Gr.)--She acted as a guide for Aeneas during his descent to Hades.

Demeter (Gr.); Ceres (Ro.)--Goddess of fruitfulness of mankind. After Pluto carried off her daughter, Persephone, to be Queen of Hades, Demeter in her anger and despair made the earth barren. Finally it was arranged for her to spend at least half of each year with Persephone.

Erebus (Gr.)--The son of Chaos, he dwelt in Hades.

Eurydice (Gr.)--A nymph loved by Orpheus. After she died he descended to Hades and so pleased Pluto with his music that the god allowed him to lead Eurydice back to earth provided he did not look back until they reached the Upper World. By mistake, he glanced behind him and Eurydice vanished to rejoin the shades in Hades.

Furies, The (Gr.); Dirae (Ro.); Erinnyes (Gr.)--The three goddesses of vengeance, Alecto, Magaera, and Tisiphone, were attendants to Persephone, Queen of Hades.

Hecatonchires (Gr.)--These three hundred-handed monsters were Briareus, "The Stong;" Cottus, "The Striker;" and Gyges, "The Crippler." Their father, Uranus, feared them and tried to destroy them by thrusting them into Hades.

Hermes (Gr.); Mercury (Ro.)--His most grave function was to conduct the outworn ghosts of mortals to Hades.

Ixion (Gr.)--King of the Lapithae, who, because he aspired to the love of a goddess, Hera, was sent to Hades, and bound to an endlessly revolving wheel.

Lethe (Gr.)--This was a river in Hades, a drink of which brought forgetfulness of the past.

Minos I (Gr.)--A famous lawgiver and king of Crete, who became a judge of the souls of the dead in Hades.

Orpheus (Gr.)-- *See also* Eurydice. After losing his wife, Eurydice in Hades, he sang his sorrow for seven months in a desert cave. Some Thracian maidens there, finding they could not captivate him, tore him limb from limb. The Muses buried his body at Liberthra, and his shade went for a second time to Hades were he rejoined Eurydice.

Persephone (Gr.); Proserpina (Ro.)--Queen of Hades. *See also* Ceres and Demeter.

Pluto (Class.); Hades (Gr.); Orcus (Ro.)--Jupiter assigned him the government of the Under World. He was hard and inexorable.

Pollux (Gr.)-- *See* Castor.

Proserpina (Ro.)-- *See* Persephone.

Psychopompus (Gr.); Mercury (Ro.); Hermes (Gr.)-- *See* Hermes.

Rhadamanthus (Gr.)--Brother of Minos I, and Sarpedon, who became with them, after their deaths, judges in the Lower World where the souls of the dead were brought to trial.

Sarpedon (Gr.)--Jupiter gave him the privilege of living three generations. *See also* Rhadamanthus.

Sisyphus (Gr.)--For his disclosure that he had witnessed the intrigue of Jupiter with Aegina, the vengeance of the gods fell on him, and he was condemned to Hades and eternal punishment.

HAIR *See also* THREAD

Discord (Gr.); Eris (Gr.)--In the chamber of the Furies she is mad, and her snaky locks are bound with bloody fillets.

Erinnyes (Gr.); Furies, The (Gr.)--They were snaky-haired women who pursued an offender and inflicted madness.

Gorgons (Gr.)--Three monster sisters with claws of bronze, serpents for hands, and snaky hair.

Medusa (Gr.)--As a maiden she had dared to vie in beauty with Minerva, but the goddess took away her charm, and changed her hair into hissing serpents.

Midas (Gr.)--After he chose Pan over Apollo in a music contest, the sun-god changed his ears into those as an ass. Midas tried to hide his misfortune, but his hairdresser whispered the secret into the ground. Reeds sprang up and began to whisper the story, and do so every time a breeze passes over them.

Nisus (Gr.)--King of Megara, had on his head a purple lock of hair, on which depended his fortune and his life. His daughter, Scylla, cut it off and treacherously gave it to his enemy, Minos.

HAMADRYADS

Hamadryads (Gr.)--These were dryads; wood-nymphs; female, and of the lesser gods of earth.

Pomona (Ro.)--Was a Hamadryad, guardian of fruit groves, especially apple orchards.

HAMMER

Hephaestus (Gr.); Vulcan (Ro.)--God of fire, usually represented as a vigorous man equipped with hammer and tongs.

Vulcan (Ro.); Hephaestus (Gr.)--He was the blacksmith of the gods.

HANDMAIDEN

Briseïs (Gr.)--The captive handmaiden of Achilles who was relinquished by him to Agamemnon in a division of spoils in the Trojan War.

Omphale (Gr.)--The queen of Lydia, for whom Hercules was condemned to spin wool with her handmaidens.

HANDS

Centimanus (Gr.); Gyges (Gr.)--One of the Hecatonchires, called "The Vaulter," or "The Crippler." His name means hundred-handed.

Hecatonchires (Gr.) Hundred handed monsters

HANDSOME *See* BEAUTY

HANGING

Arachne (Gr.)--Losing to Minerva in a weaving contest so humiliated her that she hanged herself. Minerva changed her into a spider, forever spinning the thread by which she was suspended.

Dejanira (Gr.)--Because she had unwittingly caused the death of Hercules by poisoning his robe, she hanged herself.

Iphis (Gr.)--The worthy lover of Anaxarete, who hung himself to her gatepost after she spurned him.

Oenone (Gr.)--Remorseful over not having tried to heal the wound of her former husband, Paris, she hanged herself.

HAPPINESS

Caduceus (Gr.)--This magic wand given to Mercury by Apollo gave wealth, dreams and happiness.

Elysian Fields (Gr.)--A land of spring, sunlight, song and happiness.

116

HAPPINESS (cont.)

Galatea (Gr.)--A sea-nymph who loved Acis, but found her happiness disturbed by the jealous attentions of the Cyclops, Polyphemous.

Hippomenes (Gr.); Milanion (Gr.)--Venus told him how to win the beautiful Atalanta in a race. When the couple, in their happiness, forgot to pay Venus due honor, she arranged deviously through Cybele to have them transformed into lions to haul her chariot.

HARPIES

Aëllo (Gr.)--A Harpy.

Aeneas (Gr.)--During his wanderings he landed at the Island of the Harpies. They prepared a feast, but as soon as he and his companions began to eat, the disgusting birds seized the food with their talons and flew away with it.

Calais (Gr.)-- *See* Iris.

Celaeno (Gr.)--A Harpy.

Harpies (Gr.)--Foul creatures with heads and bosoms of maidens, and wings, tail, legs, and claws of birds. Their faces were pale with hunger; they snatched up and carried off the souls of the dead.

Iris (Gr.)--Goddess of the rainbow; sister of the Harpies. When the winged warrior sons of Boreas (Calaïs and Zetes) had encounter with the Harpies, it was she who prevented their killing the monstrous birds.

Ocypete (Gr.)--A Harpy.

Thaumas (Gr.)--Father of the Harpies and of Iris.

Zetes (Gr.)-- *See* Iris.

HARVEST

Ceres (Ro.); Demeter (Gr.)--Goddess of sowing, reaping and harvest festivals.

HARVEST (cont.)

Consus (Ro.)--An early Italian god of the earth; god of the stored-up harvest.

Cronus (Gr.); Saturn (Ro.)--A Titan; the god of harvests.

Demeter (Gr.); Ceres (Ro.)--Goddess of the fruitfulness of mankind; goddess of marriage. She is worshipped by harvesters.

Kronos (Gr.)--A Titan. *See* Cronus.

Ops (Ro.)--An ancient Italian goddess of sowing and the harvest.

Phoebus (Gr.); Apollo (Gr.)--He brought not only the warm spring and summer, but the blessings of the harvest.

HATRED

Iapetus (Gr.)--One of the Titans, instigators of hatred and strife.

Styx (Gr.)--The river of hate in Hades.

Titans, The (Gr.)--They appeared to be the personification of mighty convulsions, such as volcanic eruptions and earthquakes. *See* Iapetus *above.*

HEAD

Athena (Gr.); Minerva (Ro.)--The virgin goddess, sprang from the brain of Jove, brandishing a spear.

Harpies, The (Gr.)--These bird-like creatures had the head and bosoms of maidens.

Hecate (Gr.)--A three-headed goddess with six arms.

Hydra (Gr.)--A water serpent that ravaged the country of Argos. It had nine heads, any one of which when cut off was succeeded by two others, unless the wound were cauterized. It was finally slain by Hercules.

Medusa (Gr.)--The most terrible of the Gorgons, whose head had been cut off by Perseus. One glance at the head turned every observer to stone.

Metis (Gr.)--The first love of Jupiter. She warned him that if she bore him a child, it would be greater than he. In fear, he swallowed her, and in time there sprang from his head the goddess Athena.

Scylla (Gr.)--She was transformed by her rival, Circe, into a hideous monster, with twelve arms, twelve feet, and six heads armed with sharp teeth and the yelp of a dog.

Talus (Gr.)--A giant of brass who had in his body only one vein which was plugged with a nail on the top of his head.

Vulcan (Ro.); Hepheastus (Gr.)--One of the great gods. He took part in the making of the human race, and assisted at the birth of Minerva by splitting open Jupiter's head with an ax to facilitate it.

HEALING

Aesculapius (Ro.); Asclepius (Gr.)--God of medicine, so skilled in healing that he was sometimes able to restore the dead to life.

Apollo (Gr.); Lycius (Gr.)--The god of the sun, was also a god of healing, and the stayer of plagues.

Carmenta (Ro.)--A water or spring goddess, and goddess of healing and prophecy.

Chiron (Gr.)--A centaur, skilled in riding, music and the art of healing.

Diana (Ro.); Artemis (Gr.)--A goddess of the moon, gentle and a healer of ills.

Diomede (Gr.)--In the Trojan War, he wounded Mars, felled Pandarus, and crushed Aeneas with a stone. Phoebus Apollo wrapped Aeneas in a cloud and bore him to his temple, where the warrior was healed.

HEALING (cont.)

Fontus (Ro.)--God of flowing waters and of healing.

Juturna (Ro.)--Goddess of springs and brooks; goddess of healing.

Latona (Ro.); Leto (Gr.)--When Aeneas was wounded and carried to the temple of Phoebus Apollo, Diana and Latona helped to heal him there.

Paean (Gr.)--The family physician of the gods. He healed one of the wounds of Mars.

Phoebus (Gr.); Apollo (Gr.)--He warded off diseases and healed the sick.

Vulcan (Ro.); Hephaestus (Gr.)--A good-natured god, honored as a god of healing and prophecy.

HEALTH

Caduceus (Gr.)--The wand of health and happiness.

Hygeia (Gr.)--The personification of health; associated as the daughter of Aesculapias.

HEART

Andromache (Gr.)--Daughter of the great-hearted Eëtion.

Cupid (Ro.); Eros (Gr.)--With his bow and arrows he pierced the hearts of both gods and mortals, using gold-tipped arrows to inspire love; lead-tipped to produce hate.

Daphne (Gr.)--Because Cupid had pierced her heart with a lead-tipped arrow, she repelled love, first rejecting Leucippus, then Apollo. When she could no longer run from him, she appealed to a woodland divinity who transformed her into a laurel tree.

Eëtion (Gr.)--Father of the "white-armed" Andromache. Called the great-hearted.

120

HEARTH

Hestia (Gr.); Vesta (Ro.)--Goddess of the hearth; of the home and city.

Penates (Ro.)--Gods of the household, they were worshipped in close connection with Vesta.

Vesta (Ro.); Hestia (Gr.)--Divinity of the home; goddess of the hearth, public and private.

Vulcan (Ro.); Hephaestus (Gr.)--God of fire, the glow of the forge or the hearth.

HEAVEN

Asteria (Gr.)--The starry heavens.

Atlas (Gr.)--A giant who bore the heavens on his head and hands, as a penalty for warring against Zeus.

Cassiopeia (Gr.)--Wife of one of the Argonauts, Cepheus, and mother of Andromeda. In the heavens she is a northern constellation, shining between the two.

Daphnis (Gr.)--Because he had been blinded, he called on his father, Mercury, for aid. Mercury transported him to heaven and caused a well to gush forth on the spot from which he was ascended.

Electra (Gr.)--One of the Pleides, daughters of Atlas, who still fly before Orion in the heavens. Though their number was seven, only six are visible, since Electra left her place that she might not witness the ruin of Troy. Instead, she became a comet, with her hair floating wildly behind her, ranging the heavens inconsolably.

Helios (Gr.)--The ancient sun-god, who drove a four-horse chariot through the heavens.

Hercules (Ro.); Heracles (Gr.)--His most difficult labor (11th) was the robbery of the golden apples of the Hesperides. Since Atlas was the father of the Hesperides, he sought him out and held up the heavens for him while he obtained some apples.

HEAVEN (cont.)

Hyades (Gr.)--Nymphs; daughters of Atlas, placed by Zeus in the heavens.

Juno (Ro.); Hera (Gr.)--With Minerva, she was also a divinty of the new dynasty of heaven.

Jupiter (Ro.); Zeus (Gr.)--In a council of gods following the Titan War, he was made Sovereign of the World. He doomed Atlas to bear the heavens on his shoulders; made Prometheus a creator by means of fire.

Ophion (Gr.)--One of the Titans. In legend they ruled over heaven before the age of Saturn.

Psyche (Gr.)--After many earthly misadventures, she was taken to the heavenly abodes by Cupid, where she was received by Jupiter, given ambrosia to drink and made an immortal.

Romulus (Ro.)--The first king of Rome; finally he was carried to heaven by his father Mars, and was deified by the Romans.

Uranus (Gr.)--The personified heaven; became the husband of Gaea, the Earth.

HECATONCHIRES

Briareus (Gr.)--One of the shadowy giants assigned to guard the descent to Hades. Called "The Strong."

Cottus (Gr.)--A 100-handed monster, called "The Striker."

Gyges (Gr.)--One of the Hecatonchires, known as "The Vaulter," or "The Crippler." Also called Centimanus.

Hecatonchires (Gr.)--The three hundred-handed monsters, sons of Uranus, who tried to destroy them by thrusting them into Hades.

HEEL

Achilles (Gr.)--His mother, Thetis, tried to make her infant invulnerable by holding him by the heels and plunging him into the river Styx. One day in the temple of Apollo, he was still young when Paris shot a poisoned arrow at him and fatally wounded him in the heel.

Thetis (Gr.)--One of the most famous of the fifty Nereids; the mother of Achilles, who tried to make him invulnerable by dipping him into the river Styx, forgetting his heels did not get wet.

HEIFER

Argus (Gr.)--The hundred-eyed creature assigned by Juno to guard the young woman, Io, who had been changed into a heifer by Jupiter.

Io (Gr.)--She was loved by Jupiter, who tried to disguise his love, and spare himself the jealousy of Juno, by changing Io into a heifer.

HEIRS *See also* USURPERS

Amulius (Gr.)--A Trojan whose ambition caused him to rob his brother, King Numitor, of his power. To avoid future trouble with heirs, he killed Numitor's son.

Cronus (Gr.); Saturn (Ro.)--A Titan; lord of Heaven and Earth; called "The Crafty." Married to Rhea, he became the father of six gods, and to assure his not losing his throne to an heir, he swallowed the first five as soon as they were born.

Pelias (Gr.)--The usurping King of Iolcus, who sent Jason after the Golden Fleece to keep him from his throne.

HELIADES

Heliades (Gr.)--These were Lampetia and Phaëthusa, daughters of Olymene and the ancient sun-god, Helios, who tended their father's flocks and herds on the island of Thrinacia. After Jupiter struck their brother, Phaëton, with a thunderbolt, they lamented his fate, turned into poplar trees and dropped tears of amber.

HELLESPONT

Helle (Gr.)--She fell from the back of the ram with the Golden Fleece into a strait between Europe and Asia, and it was later named for her.

Leander (Gr.)--Swam the Hellespont each night to meet his loved one, Hero. When he was caught in a tempest and drowned, she threw herself into the sea.

HELMET

Hades (Gr.); Pluto (Class.)--The grim god of the Lower World. By virtue of the helmet of darkness given him by the Cyclopes, he could move anywhere, unseen and hated by mortals.

Perseus (Gr.)--By borrowing the helmet of Hades, and Minerva's shield, he was able to conquer Medusa and cut off her head.

Pluto (Class.)-- *See* Hades.

HERALD

Hermes (Gr.); Mercury (Ro.)--Famed for his fleetness, he was herald and messenger of the gods.

Idaeus (Gr.)--Companion and herald of King Priam.

Mercury (Ro.); Hermes (Gr.)--The god of eloquence, he was also herald and messenger of the gods, and conductor of souls to the Lower World.

HERBS

Glaucus (Gr.)--One of the lesser powers of the Ocean, he became immortal by tasting magic herbs which changed him to a strange half-man, half-fish similar to the sea-gods.

124

HERDS; HERDSMEN *See also* FLOCKS; SHEPHERDS

Apollo (Gr.)--Spent many of his younger years as a herdsman for mortal masters in Arcadia, Laconis and Thessaly. He also herded a year for King Laomedon in Mount Ida, by order of Jupiter.

Aristaeus (Gr.)--An Arcadian deity, he was the guardian of herds and flocks.

Diana (Ro.); Artemis (Gr.)--Guardian of wild beasts. She had sacred herds, and was quick to resent injury to them.

Epimenides (Gr.)--A Cretan herdsman, who awoke from a fifty seven years sleep to find himself endowed with gifts of prophecy.

Faunus (Ro.); Pan (Gr.)--A rural deity; patron of husbandry, hunting and herding.

Hecate (Gr.)--A three-headed goddess with six arms; fosterer of herds and human children.

Hercules (Ro.)--For killing his music teacher, he was sent off to the mountains to live among the herdsmen and the cattle.

Laïus (Gr.)--Being warned by an oracle that he would be killed by his son, he sent the new-born boy off with a herdsman, supposedly to die.

Lampetia (Gr.)--One of the two daughters of Helios, who tended their father's herds and flocks on the island of Thrinacia.

Mercury (Ro.); Hermes (Gr.)--He was the guardian of boundaries, and the fiver of increase to herds.

Nomius (Gr.)--Apollo as a herdsman.

Priapus (Ro.)--Protector of vineyards, gardens, as well as of herds, bees and fish.

Silvanus (Ro.)--A rural deity; genius of woods, fields, and homes of herdmen.

HERDS; HERDSMEN (cont.)

Tyrrheus (Gr.)--The king's herdsman.

HERMAPHRODITE

Hermaphroditus (Gr.)--Son of Hermes and Aphrodite, who became united with the nymph Salmacis, in a single body.

HERO

Achilles (Gr.)--The ideal hero of the Greeks; most famous of the Trojan warriors.

Aeneas (Gr.)--A Trojan prince; hero in the battle to save Troy.

Agenor (Gr.)--One of the bravest of the Trojan heroes.

Ajax, The Great (Gr.)--First cousin of Achilles; one of the most valiant of the Greek heroes at Troy.

Alcmene (Gr.)--A hero laid low with a mortal wound inflicted by the Calydonian boar.

Antilochus (Gr.)--Brave son of Nestor; friend of Achilles.

Bellerophon (Gr.)--Hero who was sent by King Iobates to destroy the Chimaera.

Diomede (Gr.)--Second only to Achilles in having the qualities of a hero.

Dioscuri (Gr.)--The twins Castor and Pollus, who received heroic honors as the *Tyndaridae*.

Elysian Fields (Gr.)--Groves where the happy resided, including priests, poets, and great-hearted heroes.

Gemini (Gr.)--Brothers Castor and Pollux, heroes conceived at Rome as patrons of knightly caste.

Hector (Gr.)--The handsome hero of the seige of Troy.

126

HERO (cont.)

Heracles (Gr.)--An earthly son of Jupiter; the greatest of the heroes.

Hercules (Ro.)--Son of Jupiter and Alcmene; celebrated for his strength. The national hero of Greece.

Idas (Gr.)--In legend, a hero; had great strength. He was slain by Zeus.

Iolaüs (Gr.)--A Boeotian hero; devoted friend and sometimes charioteer of Hercules.

Jason (Gr.)--He assembled fifty famous heroes to go on the Argonautic Expedition.

Meleager (Gr.)--A hero of importance. He took part in the Calydonian Boar Hunt.

Memnon (Gr.)--Brave son of Nestor. In the Trojan War he held the Greeks at bay until Achilles appeared and killed him.

Nestor (Gr.)--Bore arms with Achilles and Ajax in the Trojan War, and performed the brave feat of carrying Machaon from the battle field in his chariot.

Odysseus (Gr.); Ulysses (Gr.)--Hero of the Odyssey.

Orpheus (Gr.)--Was counted among the older heroes, contributing his part, especially with the Argonautic Expedition.

Palamedes (Gr.)--A hero of the Trojan War who tried to persuade Ulysses to embark with him to take part in it.

Peleus (Gr.)--One of the older Greek heroes, who accompanied Hercules during his Labors.

Perseus (Gr.)--One of the Older Heroes. Hero of Argus; endowed with god-like qualities.

Protesilaüs (Gr.)--One of the most admirable of the Greek heroes. Tried to land along the coast of Troy.

127

HERO (cont.)

Seven Against Thebes (Gr.)--This was the expedition of seven heroes against the city. They were Adrastus, Amphiaraüs, Capaneus, Hippomedon, Polynices, Parthenopaeus and Tydeus. The Expedition ended in defeat, and the deaths of all the heroes except Adrastus.

HEROINE

Atalanta (Gr.)--A beautiful heroine, widely famed for her swift running.

Athena (Gr.); Minerva (Ro.)--The goddess of war, who sprang from the brain of Jove, agleam with the panoply of war.

HIDE

Dido (Gr.)-- *See same under* CITADEL.

HILLS

Echo (Gr.)--A talkative nymph, fond of woods and hills.

Oreads (Gr.)--Nymphs of mountains, hills and grottoes.

Sisyphus (Gr.)--The vengeance of the gods condemned him to Hades, where he had to roll a huge stone uphill endlessly.

HISTORY

Clio (Gr.)--The Muse of History.

HOLES

Danaïdes (Gr.)--For slaying their husbands, forty-nine of these daughters of Danaüs were condemned to spend eternity in Tartarus, trying to fill with water a vessel full of holes.

HOME

Baucis (Gr.)-- *See same under* HOSPITABLE.

Hestia (Gr.); Vesta (Ro.)--Goddess of the hearth, of the home and the city.

Vesta (Ro.); Hestia (Gr.)--Divinity of the home, settled rather than nomadic.

HONORS

Dioscuri (Gr.)--Twin brothers, they received heroic honors as the *Tyndaridae,* and divine honors under the name of *Dioscuri.*

Memnon (Gr.)--He was received by King Priam with honor.

Tyndaridae (Gr.)-- *See* Dioscuri.

HOPE

Pandora (Gr.)--Jupiter had given her a box and told her never to open it. She lifted the lid and all the plagues for hapless man escaped. The one thing that remained in the box was hope.

Persephone (Gr.); Proserpina (Ro.)--Queen of Hades, she was cruel, and hostile to youth, life and hope.

HORAE

Horae (Gr.)--Three goddesses of the hours and seasons, who took charge of the gate of clouds at Olympus.

HORN

Acheloüs (Gr.)--A river-god who could change form. After wrestling with Hercules as a serpent, he lost and changed into a bull. Hercules dragged his head to the ground and rent one horn away for his fourth labor.

129

HORN (cont.)

Naiads (Gr.) and (Ro.)--These nymphs consecrated the horn of Acheloüs, filled it with flowers and presented it to the goddess of Plenty, who named it Cornucopia.

HORRIBLE

Enyalius (Gr.)--A god of war; called "The Horrible." His name was an epithet for Mars.

HORRIFIER

Pephredo (Gr.)--Was one of three hoary witches, known as the Gray Women. They had only one eye among them, which they handed from one to the other, and only one tooth. Pephredo was called "The Horrifier." Enyo was called "The Shaker," and Deino, "The Terrifier."

HORSE See also WOODEN HORSE

Abderus (Gr.)--A son of Hermes. Heracles left him to guard the man-eating mares of Diomedes, and returned to find the youth had been eaten.

Ares (Gr.); Mars (Ro.)--The god of war. He usually fought on foot, but sometimes from a chariot drawn by four horses.

Arion (Gr.)--The first and fleetest of horses; a horse-god.

Bellerophon (Gr.)--A hero to whom Minerva gave the winged horse, Pegasus, with the magic gold bridle, with which he sped through the air, and gained an easy victory over the Chimaera.

Castor (Gr.)--Famous as a trainer of horses.

Centaurs (Gr.)--Intelligent creatures, half-horse, half-men.

Chiron (Gr.)--One of the centaurs, skilled in riding, music, and the art of

HORSE (cont.)

Chiron (cont.)--healing; teacher of Achilles.

Colchas (Gr.)--A prophet who told the Greeks the Trojans would win if they took possession of the wooden horse.

Diana (Ro.); Artemis (Gr.)--Guardian of wild beasts, of horses and other domestic animals.

Diomedes (Gr.)--King of Thrace, who possessed two swift and fearful horses which fed on human flesh.

Epona (Ro.)--Goddess of horses, mules, and asses.

Erichthonius (Gr.)--He owned 3000 horses.

Gemini (Gr.)--Castor and Pollus, two horse-men and patrons of eqestraian exercises.

Glaucus of Corinth (Gr.)--Noted for his love of horse racing, and his fashion of feeding his mares on human flesh. They turned on him finally, and tore him to pieces.

Hercules (Ro.); Alcides (Gr.)-- His 8th Labor was to remove the man-eating horses of Diomedes. In order to do so, he had to kill their owner and feed him to the horses.

Hippocrene (Gr.)--A fountain on Mt. Helicon, which burst forth when Pegasus struck the ground with his hoof.

Laomedon (Gr.)--King of Troy, who reneged on his promise to reward Hercules with the horses of Neptune.

Medusa (Gr.)--From her body sprang the winged horse, Pegasus.

Minerva (Ro.); Athena (Gr.)--Goddess of war, protestress of war horses and warships.

Neleus (Gr.)--An offspring of Neptune; keeper of horses, and animals dear to Neptune.

131

HORSE (cont.)

Neptune (Ro.); Poseidon (Gr.)--He created the horse, and was the patron of horse-races. His own horses were brazen-hoofed and gold-maned, and as they drew his chariot over the sea, it became smooth before them.

Pegasus (Gr.)--A winged horse which had been caught and tamed by Minerva, and presented by her to the Muses.

Pelias (Gr.)--A keeper of horses.

Pelops (Gr.)--Was trained by Neptune to drive horses. With winged steeds, he won a race against Oenomaüs, which entitled him to the hand of Hippodamia.

Pollux (Gr.)-- *See* Gemini.

Polyidus (Gr.)--A soothsayer, who counseled Bellerophon to procure the horse Pegasus.

Tyro (Gr.)--A princess; mother of Neleus, and Pelias, *which see above.*

HOSPITABLE

Baucis (Gr.)--After she and her husband, Philemon, were hospitable to Jupiter and Mercury, the gods saved their home, and changed it into a temple.

Polydectes (Gr.)--His name, meaning the hospitable was also used by Hades.

HOSTILE

Hera (Gr.); Juno (Ro.)--Always hostile to the offspring of her husband, Jupiter, she declared war against Hercules from his birth.

Juno (Ro.); Hera (Gr.)--All the mistresses of Jupiter had to endure in one way or another, the fury and vengeance of Juno.

HOURS

Horae (Gr.)--Three goddesses of the hours, seasons and of orderliness, who took charge of the gate of clouds at Olympus.

Themis (Gr.)--Mother of the Horae by Jupiter; among the prominent Titans, she sat as goddess of justice.

HOUSE *See* HOME

HOUSEHOLD

Lares (Ro.)--The deified spirits of ancestors, who presided over the household or family.

Penates (Ro.)--Gods of the household, the welfare and prosperity of the family.

HUNGER

Erysichthon (Gr.)--For cutting down an oak tree, the Dryads commanded famine to enfold him in her wings. His hunger raged. The more he ate, the more he craved, and when he ran out of money he sold his daughter for edibles. Finally, he was compelled to devour his own limbs, and in due time finished himself off.

Harpies (Gr.)-- *See same under* PALENESS.

HUNT

Orthia (Gr.); Diana (Ro.)--When Oeneus neglected to pay her due honors, she became indignant and sent an enormous boar to ravage the fields of Calydon; thus originating the Calydonian Hunt.

HUNTER *See also* CHASE

Actaeon (Gr.)--A young hunter who happened upon Diana bathing in a forest pool. Taken by surprise, she dashed water into his face,

133

Actaeon (cont.)--which transformed him into a stag. His own dogs then pursued him and tore him to pieces.

Arcas (Gr.)--A hunter, whose mother, Callisto, had been changed into a bear. One day while hunting he spied a bear and was about to spear her when Jupiter snatched them both and placed them in the heavens as the Great and Little Bears.

Castor (Gr.)--He and his brother, Pollux, joined the Calydonian Hunt.

Centaurs (Gr.)--These creatures, half-horse, half-men, were intelligent, and renowned for various skills, including riding and hunting.

Cephalus (Gr.)--A young hunter married to Procris. He had been lured away by Aurora, and although he returned, his wife did not trust his loyalty. One day she spied on him from behind some bushes, and he, thinking she was a wild beast, threw a javelin which killed her.

Chiron (Gr.)--One of the centaurs, skilled in riding and hunting.

Dryads (Gr.)--Wood nymphs, who at times assumed the forms of peasant girls, shephredesses, or followers of the hunt.

Faunus (Ro.); Pan (Gr.)--A rural deity; patron of husbandry, herding and hunting.

Nestor (Gr.)--One of the numerous young men who joined Meleager and other heroes in the Calydonian Boar Hunt.

Oeneus (Gr.)--King of Calydon, who, because he did not pay Diana due honor, brought on the Calydonian boar ravage.

Orion (Gr.)--A giant and mighty hunter, whose prowess and manly favor gained for him the rare good will of Diana.

HUNTRESS

Artemis (Gr.)--The virgin goddess, sometimes known as Agroters--the huntress.

HUNTRESS (cont.)

Atalanta (Gr.)--In Arcadian legend, she is famous as a huntress.

Camilla (Gr.)--A huntress and warrior, who had been taught by her father Metabus, to use the bow and throw the javelin.

Diana (Ro.); Artemis (Gr.)--Goddess of the moon, and huntress.

Dictynna (Gr.)--A Cretan goddess, protectress of hunters and sea-farers; sometimes identified with Artemis.

Metabus (Gr.)--Father of Camilla, who saved her as an infant, by tying her to his lance with wrappers of bark and hurling the weapon across the Amasenus River.

HUSBAND

Danaides (Gr.)--The fifty daughters of Danaüs, of whom forty nine followed their father's command to slay their husbands on their wedding night.

HUSBANDRY

Faunus (Ro.); Pan (Gr.)--A rural deity; patron of husbandry, hunting, and herding.

HYADES

Hyades (Gr.)--Nymphs; daughters of Atlas.

I

ICEBERG

Alcyoneus (Gr.)--An earth-born giant, of the winter-storms and icebergs.

IDENTIFICATION

Cronus (Gr.); Saturn (Ro.)–A Titan, often erroneously identified with Chronos, god of Time.

ILLNESS *See* HEALING; MEDICINE

IMMORTALITY

Calypso (Gr.)--A sea-nymph who received Ulysses on her island, Oxygia. She tried to retain him by offering him immortality but he remained only seven years.

Ceres (Ro.); Demeter (Gr.)–Goddess of agriculture. She was associated with the alternate death and life in nature, which simulated the resurrection and immortality of man.

Dejanira (Gr.)–Daughter of King Oeneus of Calydon, she murdered her husband, Hercules, with a poisoned robe. He was admitted as a deity to the ranks of the immortals.

Demeter (Gr.)– *See same under* NURSE.

Glaucus (Gr.)--One of the lesser powers of the Ocean, who became immortal by tasting magic herbs which changed him to a strange half-man, half-fish, similar to the sea-gods.

Hercules (Ro.); Alcides (Gr.)– *See* Dejanira *above.*

Herostratus (Gr.)–A Greek who sought immortality by setting fire to one of the wonders of the world, the Temple of Ephesus.

Memnon (Gr.)--Fought bravely in the Trojan War, and was killed by Achilles. The Aethiopians raised a tomb in his honor, and Jupiter made him immortal.

Naiads (Gr. and Ro.)--Although they were immortal, being the daughters of Jupiter, they maintained an intimate association with the deities of earth.

Orpheus (Gr.)--He taught mysterious truths concerning the origin of

IMMORTALITY (cont.)

Orpheus (cont.)--things and the immortality of the soul.

Psyche (Gr.)--She and her husband, Cupid, finally ascended to the heavenly abodes, where Psyche was received by Jupiter, given a cup of ambrosia to drink and made an immortal.

Tithonus (Gr.)--He was a favorite love of Aurora, who asked Jupiter to grant him immortality. She forgot to have youth joined in the gift, and when he grew old and feeble she turned him into a grasshopper.

INCEST

Adrastus (Gr.)--By his niece, Amphithea, he had two sons and three daughters.

Canace (Gr.)--Daughter of Aeolus; sister of Macareus, with whom she committed incest.

Ceto (Gr.)-- *See* Phorcys.

Jocasta (Gr.)--Mother of Oedipus, who married him later, not knowing he was her son.

Juno (Ro.); Hera (Gr.)--She was jealous in disposition and always unhappy over the vagaries of her brother and spouse, Jupiter.

Macareus (Gr.)-- *See* Canace.

Oceanus (Gr.)--Oldest of the Titans, he married his sister, Tethys.

Oedipus (Gr.)--His father, King Laïus of Thebes, sent his newborn son, Oedipus, into the mountains. Years later, the young man returned a hero, and the grateful Thebans gave him their queen, Jocasta, in marriage. Neither knew the relationship of mother and son until many years afterward.

Phorcys (Gr.)--Married his sister, Ceto.

INDISCRETION

Sisyphus (Gr.)–A witness to the intrigue of Jupiter with Aegina, he was indiscreet enough to disclose it. The vengeance of gods and men fell upon him.

INDUSTRY

Mercury (Ro.); Hermes (Gr.)--Skilled in invention, the forerunner of mathematicians, he was also the furtherer of lawful industry.

INFANT *See also* CHILDREN; OFFSPRING

Achilles (Gr.)–When he was an infant, his mother, Thetis, tried to make him invlunerable by holding him by the ankles and dipping him in the river Styx.

Hercules (Ro.)–When Juno had two serpents put in his cradle to destroy him, the precocious infant strangled them with his hands.

Jupiter (Ro.); Zeus (Gr.)--His mother, Rhea, saved him from being swallowed by his father, Cronus, and concealed him on the island of Crete, where he was nurtured by nymphs.

Oedipus (Gr.)--As an infant, he was adopted by King Polybus, of Corinth.

Paris (Gr.)--Because she thought he would stir up contention, his mother, Hecuba, sent him shortly after his birth to be raised by shepherds on Mt. Ida.

Zethus (Gr.)–He and his brother, Amphion, were brought up by shepherds on Mount Cithaeron, not knowning their parentage.

INFATUATION

Ate (Gr.)–Goddess of infatuation.

INGENUITY

Perdix (Gr.)--He showed striking evidence of ingenuity. One day he observed the spine of a fish, imitated it in iron, and thus invented the saw.

INNOVATOR

Daphnis (Gr.)--The innovator of bucolic poetry.

INNOCENCE

Astraea (Gr.)–Goddess of innocence and purity. *See same under* STARS.

INSANITY *See also* MADNESS

Hercules (Ro.)-- *See same under* MADNESS.

Iole (Gr.)–Her father, King Eurytus, would not permit her to marry Hercules, fearing he might become insane a second time.

Leucothea (Gr.)--She became a goddess of the sea, after she had jumped off a cliff to escape the insane Athamas.

INSOLENT

Nemesis (Gr.)–Represented the righteous anger and vengeance of the gods toward the proud and the insolent.

Penelope (Gr.)--Wife of Ulysses. She had many suitors during his ten-year absence. The most insolent was Antinoüs, whom Ulysses shot with an arrow upon his return.

INSULT

Cassiopeia (Gr.)-- *See same under* BOASTING.

INTELLECT

Ajax, The Great (Gr.)--Although he was courageous, gigantic and handsome, he was dull of intellect.

INTENTIONED

Eumenides (Gr.)--A euphemistic name for the Furies, meaning the well-intentioned.

INTOXICATION *See also* DRINKING; DRUNKENNESS

Eurytion (Gr.)--One of the Centaurs, who became intoxicated at the marriage feast of Pirithoüs and Hippodamia, and threatened violence to the bride.

Silenus (Gr.)--A tutor; jovial and usually intoxicated. Once when he wandered away he was taken by some peasants to their king, Midas. When he offered the king a choice of a reward, Midas asked that whatever he touched be turned to gold.

INTRIGUE *See* INDISCRETION

INVASIONS

Hyllus (Gr.)--Son of Hercules, who headed the first and second invasions of the Peloponnesus, and was slain.

INVENTION *See also* INVENTOR

Cadmus (Gr.)--He was the inventor of many useful arts; introduced the alphabet from Phoenicia into Greece.

Dirce (Gr.)--The cruel wife of Lycus, who doomed Antiope to die by being dragged behind a bull. The victim's sons discovered her in time, tied Dirce's hair to the bull, and let her perish by her own invention.

140

INVENTION (cont.)

Pan (Gr.); Faunus (Ro.)--He played upon the syrinx, or "Pan's pipes," fabled to be his invention.

Perdix (Gr.)--Imitating the spine of a fish in iron, he invented the saw. He is sometimes credited for the invention of the compass and the potter's wheel.

INVENTOR *See also* INVENTION

Cadmus (Gr.)-- *See same under* INVENTION.

Erechtheus (Gr.)--Inventor of the four-wheeled chariot.

Hermes (Gr.); Mercury (Ro.)--He was the first of inventors fashioning a lyre from a tortoise shell.

Mercury (Ro.); Hermes (Gr.)--Having skill in invention, he was the forerunner of mathematicians and astronomers.

IRON WORKING

Dactyls (Gr.)--Attendants of Cybele, they were credited with the discovery of iron working.

Vulcan (Ro.); Hephaestur (Gr.)--Blacksmith of the gods, and the finest artificer in metal among them.

ITALY *See also* CITIES; ROME

Aeneas (Gr.)--A Trojan prince, who fought to save Troy, then embarked for Italy, where he was to found the Roman race.

Consus (Ro.)--An early Italian god of the earth. It is fabled that his altar was discovered underground by Romulus.

Cumaean Sibyl (Gr.)--A young prophetess who lived in a deep cavern at Cumae, Italy. It was the Sibyl who acted as a guide for Aeneas in his descent to Hades.

Cybele (Ro.)-- *See same under* CITIES.

Hippolytus (Gr.)--Killed in a chariot runaway, he was restored to life by Aesculapius, and placed in Italy under the protection of the nymph Egeria.

Latinus (Ro.)--Son of Faunus; King of Latium in Italy.

Lavinia (Ro.)--An ancient Italian god of fructification; later identified with Bacchus.

Ops (Ro.)--An ancient Italian goddess of sowing and the harvest; the wife of Saturn. Later confounded with Rhea.

Parthenope (Gr.)--A siren who was so discouraged at not being able to charm Ulysses that she threw herself into the sea. Her body was washed up on the Italian shore where now stands Naples, then called Parthenope.

Penates (Ro.)--Gods of the household, worhipped in close connection with Vesta, goddess of the hearth.

Rutuli (Ro.)--These were ancient Italian people, led by Turnus, their king. Their capital in 442 B.C. was Ardea.

Silvanus (Ro.)--A rural deity, guardian of rural boundaries, and country villas.

Tellus (Ro.); Gaea (Gr.)--Goddess of the earth.

Terminus (Ro.)--The god of landmarks. His statue was a crude stone or post set in the ground to mark boundaries.

JAVELIN

Aruns (Gr.)--An Etruscan warrior. *See same under* WARRIOR.

Cammilla (Gr.)--A huntress and warrior, who was taught by her father, Matabus, to use the bow and arrow, and to throw the javelin.

JAVELIN (cont.)

Cephalus (Gr.)--A young hunter. *See same under* HUNTER.

Metabus (Gr.)--Tied his infant daughter, Camilla, to a javelin, and hurled both across a flooded river.

Mezentius (Gr.)--In a battle between the Trojans and the Etruscans, he circled Aeneas three times, throwing one javelin after another, but when his horse was felled, Aeneas moved in and killed Mezentius.

Procris (Gr.)--She was given a javelin by Diana, which she turned over to her husband, Cephalus. By mistake, she was killed by this javelin while she was hiding in some bushes.

JEALOUS *See also* ENVIOUS

Callisto (Gr.)--To appease the jealous Juno, who had already changed her into a bear, Jupiter placed Callisto and her son, Arcas, in the heavens as the Great and Little Bears.

Hera (Gr.); Juno (Ro.)--An Olympian goddess; queen of heaven, she was jealous of Zeus (Jupiter) and all his loves.

Hippolytus (Gr.)--His father, Theseus, was jealous of his wife's (Phaedra's) interest in him, and imprecated the vengeance of Neptune upon him, causing his death.

Juno (Ro.)-- *See* Hera.

Polyphemus (Gr.)--A Cyclops who fell in love with Galatea. One day he came upon Galatea with her lover, Acis, in the woods, and the sight so infuriated him that he killed Acis with a tremendous rock.

Psyche (Gr.)--She was so beautiful that people strewed her way with chaplets and flowers. When Juno found her altar deserted, while men paid their vows to this virgin, she became jealous, and ordered Cupid to infuse in her a passion for some unworthy being. But Cupid fell in love with her himself.

Zephyrus (Gr.)--The west wind; lover of Flora. He was also fond of

JEALOUS (cont.)

Zephyrus (cont.)-Hyacinthus, and jealous of his preference for Apollo. He blew a disc out of its course to strike and kill Hyacinthus.

JOY

Bacchus (Gr.); Dionysus (Ro.)--He represented the joyful life.

Comus (Gr. and Ro.)--The god of festive joy and mirth.

Euphrosyne (Gr.)--One of the three Graces, signifying mirth or joy.

Graces, The Three (Gr.)--Inspirers of charm, grace and joy.

JUDGE

Aeacus (Gr.)-- *See same under* HADES.

Hades, The Realm of (Gr.)--This Underworld or region of darkness was inhabited by spirits of the dead and governed by Pluto (Hades), and Proserpina, his queen. After the souls were brought to trial before the three judges, they were assigned to two different regions: The condemned to a place where torment awaited them, and the guiltless to the Elysian Fields.

Midas (Gr.)--He was a judge, with Tmolus, to listen to a music contest between Pan and Apollo. When he chose Pan, the god changed his ears into those of an ass.

Minos I (Gr.)--King of Crete who became one of the judges of souls of the dead in Hades.

Rhadamanthus (Gr.)--He and his two brothers, Aeacus and Minos I, were sons of Jupiter and Europa. All three became judges of souls of the dead in Hades.

Sarpedon (Gr.)--Probably the same as Aeacus.

JUSTICE

Nereus (Gr.)--A genial old man of the sea, distinguished for his love of truth and justice.

Themis (Gr.)--She sat as goddess of justice beside Jupiter on his throne.

Zeus (Gr.); Jupiter (Ro.)--Justice was his; his to repay violation of duty in the family, social relationships and in the state.

K

KIDNAPPED *See also* CARRIED OFF

Dejanira (Gr.)--She was almost kidnapped by Nessus, while he was carrying her across a river, but her husband, Hercules, shot him in the heart with an arrow.

Paris (Gr.)-- See *same under* BEAUTY.

Thalassios (Gr.)--He brought a shipload of kidnapped Athenian maidens safely over the sea to their home.

KILLED *See* MURDER; SLAIN

KINGS AND THEIR LANDS *See also* REGENT

Abas (Gr.)--A king of Argos.

Acastus (Gr.)--King of Iolcus.

Acestes (Gr.)--The King of Sicily who gave Aeneas a hospitable reception.

Admetus (Gr.)--King of Thessaly.

Adrastus (Gr.)--King of Argos; later, King of Sicyon; leader of the expedition, the Seven against Thebes.

KINGS (cont.)

Aeacus (Gr.)--The righteous, first king of the island of Aegina.

Aeëtes (Gr.)--King of Colchis.

Aegus (Gr.)--King of Athens.

Aeolus (Gr.)--King of the winds with a palace on the isle of Aeolia.

Agamemnon (Gr.)--King of Argos or Mycenae; a Greek general in the war against Troy.

Agenor (Gr.)--A King of Argos.

Agenor (Gr.)--King of Tyre in Phoenicia.

Ajax, the Less (Gr.)--King of the Locrians.

Alcinoüs (Gr.)--A wise, just and beloved king of the Phaeacians in Scheria.

Amphion (Gr.)--King of Thebes.

Amphitryon (Gr.)--Warrior, and King of Thebes.

Aphareus (Gr.)--King of Messenia.

Atreus (Gr.)--King of Mycenae.

Augeas (Gr.)--King of Elis, who owned a herd of 3000 oxen.

Bacchus (Gr.); Dionysus (Gr.)--King of Phrygia; he gave the power of touching everything into gold to Midas.

Belus (Gr.)--King of Trye.

Busiris (Ro.)--A mythical Egyptian king who tried to sacrifice Hercules at the altar.

Cepheus (Gr.)--One of the Argonauts; King of Aethiopia.

Ceyx (Gr.)--King of Trachis in Thessaly.

KINGS (cont.)

Cocalis (Gr.)--King of Sicily.

Coronus (2), (Gr.)--King of Sicyon.

Cresphontes (Gr.)--King of Messenia.

Creusa (Gr.)--First wife of Aeneas.

Croesus (Gr.)--A king of Lydia, renowned for his vast wealth.

Cypselus (Gr.)--King of Arcadia.

Damocles (Gr.)--A flatterer in the court of Dionysius I of Syracuse, who constantly praised the happiness of kings. To rebuke him, Dionysius seated him at a royal banquet with a sword hung over his head by a single hair.

Deucalion (Gr.)--King of Thessaly.

Diomedes (Gr.)--King of Thrace, who owned man-eating horses, which finally devoured him.

Dionysius I (Gr.)-- *See* Damocles.

Epaphus (Gr.)--King of Egypt.

Epopeus (Gr.)--King of Sicyon.

Erechtheus (Gr.)--King of Athens; founder of the ancient festival in honor of Athena.

Erichthonius (Gr.)--King of Dardania.

Eteocles (Gr.)--He did not wish to share the throne in Thebes with his brother, Polynices. This led to the expedition, Seven against Thebes.

Eurystheus (Gr.)--King of Mycea, who imposed upon Hercules the Twelve Labors.

Eurytus (Gr.)--King of Oechalia.

Glaucus of Corinth (Gr.)--King of Corinth.

Gyges (Gr.)--The first king of Lydia, famous for his riches.

Helenus (Gr.)--Married Andromache; with her he ruled the realm of Epirus.

Idomeneus (Gr.)--King of Crete; one of the great Greek chieftains.

Iobates (Gr.)--King of Lycia, who sought a hero to destroy the fire-breathing monster that was devastating the land. He found Bellerophon, who rode Pegasus with the magic bridle, and killed the Chimaera.

Iphis (Gr.)--An Argive King.

Ixion (Gr.)--King of the Lapithae, who, because he aspired to the love of the goddess was sent to Hades, and bound to an endlessly revolving wheel.

Labdacus (Gr.)--King of Thebes; father of Laius.

Laertes (Gr.)--King of Ithaca; father of Ulysses.

Laius (Gr.)--King of Thebes; father of Oedipus, by his cousin Jocasta, whom he married in defiance of the gods.

Laomedon (Gr.)--Founder and King of Troy. Reneged on his promised to reward Hercules with the horses of Neptune.

Latinus (Ro.)--King of Latium in Italy.

Lityerses (Gr.)--King of Phrygia; son of Midas. He was overcome by Hercules.

Lycomedes (Gr.)--King of Scyros. Achilles was sent to his court to avoid taking part in the Trojan War.

Lycurgus (Gr.)--King of the Edones, who resisted the worship of Bacchus.

KINGS (cont.)

Lycus (Gr.)--King of Thebes, a usurper who took his niece, Antiope, from her protector, King Epopeus.

Memnon (Gr.)--King of the Aethiopians; served in the Trojan War.

Menelaüs (Gr.)--King of Sparta; ruled with dignity and splendor with Helen at his side.

Mezentius (Gr.)--King of the Etruscans; a cruel leader who invented unheard of torments to gratify his vengeance.

Midas (Gr.)--King of Phrygia; given the gift to turn all he touched to gold by Bacchus.

Minos I (Gr.)--A famous lawgiver and King of Crete.

Minos II (Gr.)--Grandson of MInos I; King of Crete, with his domain protected by the gigantic brass man, Talus.

Minyas (Gr.)--King of Orchomenus in Boetia.

Nausithoüs (Gr.)--King of the Phaeacians, who helped his people migrate to the isle of Scheria after they had been oppressed by the Cyclopes. Later he turned his throne over to his son, Alcinoüs.

Neptune (Ro.); Poseidon (Gr.)--His palace was in the depths of the sea, near the Greek coast, in Euboea.

Nestor (Gr.)--A hero among the Argonauts; later King of Pylos; noted for being a wise and trusted counselor.

Ninus (Gr.)--King of Babylonia.

Nisus (Gr.)--King of Megara; father of Scylla.

Numitor (Gr.)--King of Alba Longa.

Nycteus (Gr.)--King of THebes; father of Antiope.

Oedipus (Gr.)--Made ruler of Thebes; married his mother, Jocasta, unknowingly.

KINGS (cont.)

Oeneus (Gr.)--Ruler of Calydon in Aetolia; father of Dejanira.

Oenomaüs (Gr.)--King of Elis; father of Hippodamia.

Oenopion (Gr.)--King of Chios; father of Merope, who was wooed by Orion.

Oïleus (Gr.)--King of the Locrians; father of Ajax the Less.

Pelias (Gr.)--The usurping King of Iolcus; father of Alcestis.

Phineus (Gr.)--A Thracian king, a sage who instructed the Argonauts how to pass the Clashing Islands.

Pierus (Gr.)--King of Thessaly; his daughters were the Pierides.

Pirithous (Gr.)--King of the Lapithae.

Pluto (Class.); Hades (Gr.)--King of Hades; his queen was Persephone.

Polybus (Gr.)--King of Corinth, who with his queen, adopted Oedipus.

Polydectes (Gr.)--King of Seriphus, who took in Danaë and her son, Perseus, after they had been set adrift.

Polynices (Gr.)--He wanted to take his turn as King of Thebes, but his brother, Eteocles refused to surrender the throne to him.

Priam (Gr.)--King of Troy; a wise ruler; father of Paris.

Rhadamanthus (Gr.)--He became king as well as judge in Hades; tutor of Hercules.

Sarpedon (Gr.)--King of the Lycians.

Sisyphus (Gr.)--King of Corinth. He ended up in Hades rolling a stone perpetually uphill.

Strophius (Gr.)--King of Phocis.

Tantalus (Gr.)--King of Phrygia; conceited. He betrayed the secrets of the

KINGS (cont.)

Tantalus (cont.)--gods. Doomed to Tartarus he was offered food, only to have it snatched away from him.

Tereus (Gr.)--King of Thrace; cruel husband of Procne, who had her tongue plucked out to insure her silence.

Teucer (Gr.)--The best archer of the Greeks; became King of Cyprus, and founded Salamis.

Theseus (Gr.)--One of the older heroes; he became King of Athens.

Turnus (Gr.)--Chief of the Italian tribe, the Rutuli.

Tyndareus (Gr.)--King of Sparta.

KINGHT

Gemini (Gr.)--Conceived at Rome as patrons of knightly cast.

KNOWLEDGE

Nereus (Gr.)--Genial; distinguished for his knowledge and love of truth and justice.

L

LABORS

Antaeus (Gr.)--A giant wrestler, whose strength was invincible as long as he stayed in contact with mother Earth. He was finally vanquished by Hercules, who lifted him away from the earth and strangled him in the air. This was one of Hercule's labors not recorded among the other twelce.

Arcadia (Gr.)--It was here in a picturesque district of Greece that Hercules performed his third Labor al capturing the wild boar which Diana had sent in vengeance to haunt and ravage the fields around

151

LABORS (cont.)

Arcadia (cont.)--Mount Erymanthus.

Cacus (Gr.)--A giant who stole some of Hercules' cattle and hid them in his cave. Hercules killed Cacus, another exploit not recorded among his twelve Labors.

Eurystheus (Gr.)--King of Myces, and cousin of Hercules, who subordinated him and enjoined upon him a succession of desperate undertakings, called the Twelve Labors of Hercules.

Hercules (Ro.); Alcides (Gr.)--In expiation for killing his own children during a period of insanity, he was decreed by Juno, under the command of Eurystheus, to perform Twelve Labors:
1. To strangle the Nemean lion.
2. To destroy the nine-headed water-serpent, Hydra.
3. To capture the fierce wild boar in Arcadia.
4. To bring back the golden-horned doe from Cerynea.
5. To destroy the birds with the cruel beaks in the valley of Stymphalus.
6. To clean the stables where King Augeas of Elis kept 3000 Oxen.
7. To overcome the Cretan bull.
8. To remove the man-eating horses of Diomedes.
9. To obtain the girdle of Hippolyta, queen of the Amazons, for Admeta, daughter of Eurystheus.
10. To steal the red oxen of Geryon.
11. To rob the golden apples of the Hesperides.
12. To fetch the monster, Cerberus, from the Lower World.
Added to these, in another fit of madness, he killed his friend, Iphitus, and for this he was condemned to spend three years as the slave of Queen Omphale, spinning wool with the hand-maidens. After this he returned to Thebes and renounced his wife, Megara, fearing he might have a recurrence of his madness.

Megaera (Gr.)--A princess who was married to Hercules, and renounced by him.

LABYRINTH

Ariadne (Gr.)--She loved Theseus, and led him out of the labyrinth of

LABYRINTH (cont.)

Ariadne (cont.)--Daedalus by a thread.

Daedalus (Gr.)--A famous artificer who built the labyrinth to confine the monster, the Minotaur.

Minos II (Gr.)--King of Crete, who assigned Daedalus to construct the labyrinth. Later when the craftsman fell out of the king's favor, he made wings out of feathers and flew out of prison.

LAKE

Baucis (Gr.)--An old Phrygian peasant woman who, with her husband, Philemon, was so hospitable to Jupiter and Mercury in ther cottage that the gods saved their home from sinking into a lake with the rest of the village, and converted their abode into a temple.

LAME

Bellerophon (Gr.)--When he was thrown from the winged horse, Pegasus, he was made lame and blind.

Hephaestus (Gr.); Vulcan (Ro.)--God of fire, usually represented as a vigorous man with hammer and tongs, and having one short leg to show his lameness.

Vulcan (Ro.); Hephaestur (Gr.)--One of the great gods. His Greek name, meaning burning, shining, flaming, perhaps refers to the brilliance of the lightning. He was lame of gait, suggesting the flickering, unsteady nature of fire.

LANCE

Metabus (Gr.)--Father of Camilla; when she was an infant he tied her to a lance to throw her across a flooded river.

LAND

Dido (Gr.)--Selecting a site for a future home she asked for only so much land that she could enclose with a bull's hide. This granted, she cut the hide into strips and stretched it wide enough to contain a citadel. From this spot the city of Carthage rose.

LANDMARKS

Terminus (Ro.)--The god of landmarks.

LANGUAGE

Melampus (Gr.)--He had saved some young serpents, and one day when he was asleep under a tree, they licked his ears with their tongues, enabling him to understand the language of birds and creeping creatures.

LAPITHAE

Lapithae (Gr.)--Their leader, Coronis, in Thessaly. *See same under* CENTAUR.

LARES

Lares (Ro.)--These were the deified spirits of ancestors, who presided over the household or family. But there were also public lares; Lares of the precincts, of the fields, of the highways and of the sea.

LAUGHTER

Vulcan (Ro.); Hephaestus (Gr.)--He seemed to cause "inextinguishable laughter" among the gods, yet he was by no means a fool.

LAWS

Apollo (Gr.); Lycius (Gr.)--His life as a herdsman was spent in establish-

154

LAWS

Apollo (con't)--ing wise laws and customs.

Bacchus (Gr.); Liber (Ro.)--A promoter of civilization; lawgiver and lover of peace.

Minos I (Gr.)--King of Crete; a famous lawgiver, who became a judge of souls in Hades.

Nemesis (Gr.)--An ancient goddess; she personified retributive justice, and represented the vengeance of the gods toward the proud, the insolent and breakers of the law.

Phoebus (Gr.)--Better known as Apollo. He was a founder of cities, a promoter of colonization, a pure and just god, and giver of good laws.

LEG

Hephaestus (Gr.); Vulcan (Ro.)--He had one leg shorther than the other. According to one story, he was born halt and his mother, Juno, cast him from Heaven. In another, he was caught by the foot and hurled from the heavens by Cronus.

Vulcan (Ro.)-- *See* Hephaestus.

LEMURES

Lemures (Ro.)--These were spirits to whom the Romans addressed their prayers; corresponding to our prayers.

LIBERATOR

Liber (Ro.)--An ancient god, later identified with the Greek Bacchus, known as the Liberator.

LIFE

Atropus (Gr.); Morta (Ro.)--One of the three Fates; she who severed the

LIFE (cont.)

Atropus (cont.)--thread of life with shears.

Clotho (Gr.)--The youngest of the three Fates, who wound the wool around the spindle.

Fates, The Three (Gr.); Parcae (Ro.)--Daughters of Night: Clotho, Lachesis and Atropos, goddesses who determined the course of human life.

Lachesis (Gr.); Decuma (Ro.)--One of the three Fates, known as the Disposer of Lots, who determined the length of life.

Palinurus (Gr.)--When Venus asked Neptune to stop imperilling her son, Aeneas on the high seas, he demanded one life as ransom. Palinurus was the victim.

Pelops (Gr.)--Because his father, Tantalus, wanted to ridicule the omnicience of the gods, he served them the roasted flesh of his own son. The gods were not deceived, but restored Pelops to life.

Pygmalion (Gr.)--A sculptor who fashioned a statue of ivory so beautiful that he fell in love with it. He prayed to Aphrodite to make his creation come to life, and the goddess granted his plea.

Sarpedon (Gr.)--Jupiter gave him the privilege of living three generations.

LIFE-BELT

Leucothea (Gr.)--Formerly Ino, she was made a goddess of the sea under a new name. In the form of a cormorant, she lit on the raft of Ulysses to give him a life-belt.

LIGHT

Apollo (Gr.)--Sometimes called Lycius, the golden god of light.

Eos (Gr.); Aurora (Ro.)--Goddess of the Morn; she rises from the streams of Ocean to bring light to gods and men.

LIGHT (cont.)

Jove (Ro.); Jupiter (Ro.); Zeus (Gr.)--The supreme ruler, he was moderator of light and heat.

Juno (Ro.); Hera (Gr.)--A deity of light and the sky.

Light (Gr.)--In early myths, Night and Darkness were the prime elements of Nature, and from them sprang light.

Lycius (Gr.)-- *See* Apollo.

Zeus (Gr.)-- *See* Jove.

LIGHTNING

Aloadae (Gr.)--Two monster brothers, Otus and Ephialtes, who grew three cubits in height and one in breadth each year. When they tried to pile Mt. Ossa on Olympus and Mt. Pelion on top of that, Jupiter struck them dead with his lightning.

Hephaestus (Gr.); Vulcan (Ro.)--God of fire. His Greek name, meaning shining or flaming, perhaps referred originally to the brilliance of the lightning.

Jupiter (Ro.); Zeus (Gr.)--He was the moderator of the seasons; the thunderer, and wielder of the thunderbolt.

Minerva (Ro.); Athena (Gr.)--A virgin goddess, of the storms and the rushing thunderbolt.

Phaëton (Gr.)--After he drove Apollo's chariot wildly across the heavens, creating much damage to earth, Jupiter thundered and hurled a lightning bolt at him. He fell headlong like a shooting star.

LION

Admetus (Gr.)-- *See same under* ANIMAL.

Chimaera (Gr.)--A fire-breathing monster. The fore-part of his body was part lion, part goat, and the hind part a dragon.

157

Cybele (Ro.); Rhea (Gr.)--Wore a turreted crown like the wall of a city, and drove a chariot drawn by lions.

Echidna (Gr.)--A monster, half-serpent, half-woman. By Typhon she bore Cerebus, the three-headed dog; Hydra, the water-serpent in the Lerna swamp, and the fierce Newmean lion, which was finally killed by Hercules.

Gryphons (Gr.)--Guardians of gold. They had the head and wings of an eagle, and the body of a lion.

Heracles (Gr.); Hercules (Ro.)--An earthly son of Jupiter. He is represented with a club in his hand, and a lion-skin over his shoulder.

Hercules (Ro.)-- *See* Heracles. For his first Labor he was sent to slay the Nemean lion. After he was made a slave to Queen Omphale, he wore women's dresses and spun wool, while she wore his lion's skin.

Hippomenes (Gr.)--Because he and his new wife, Atalanta, did not pay due honor to Venus, the goddess caused them to offend Cybele, who transformed them into lions, yoked to haul her wherever she wanted to go.

Nemean Lion (Gr.)--An animal of great strength which was conquered and strangled by Hercules.

Pyramus (Gr.)--Thinking Thisbe, his beloved, had been killed by a lioness, he threw himself on his sword.

LIVER

Prometheus (Gr.)--Because of his devotion to humanity, he drew the anger of Jove, who ordered him to be chained to a rock on Mt. Caucasus, and attacked by a vulture, which forever preyed upon his liver, yet never consumed it.

Tityus (Gr.)--A giant who had ventured to insult the goddess, Latona. For this he had to lie eternally while a vulture preyed on his liver, which grew back as fast as it was consumed.

LOOK BACK

Eurydice (Gr.)--A nymph loved by Orpheus. He was allowed to lead her back from Hades, provided he did not look back. When he forgot and turned, she vanished immediately.

LOST

Creusa (Gr.)--Wife of Aenaes; mother of Ascanius; lost from them during their flight from the burning city of Troy.

Merope (Gr.)--The lost Pleiad, vested with mortality in consequence of her marriage to the mortal Sisyphus, King of Corinth.

LOTUS-EATERS, The

Lotophagi (Gr.)--They lived in a country discovered by Ulysses, and his crew. The men were kindly entertained and given the lotos plant to eat, with the effect that they lost all thought of home and wished to remain. Ulysses had to drag them away by main force, and tie them under the benches of his ship to take them home.

LOVE *See also* LOVE UNREQUITED; PASSION

Acis (Gr.)--Loved by Galatea, who was hindered by the jealousy of the Cyclops Polyphemous. The giant killed him.

Adonis (Gr.)--A young shepherd, with whom Aphrodite fell in love.

Aphrodite (Gr.); Venus (Ro.)–The sweetly smiling goddess of love.

Aphrodite Porne (Gr.)--Goddess of lust and venal love; the patroness of prostitutes.

Apollo (Gr.); Lycius (Gr.)--He made love to nymphs, as well as to mortal maidens. Although married, he had numberous love affairs.

Cupid (Ro.); Eros (Gr.)--The god of love; son of Venus, and one of her attendants. He was in love with Psyche, but visited her only at night.

Cybele (Ro.); Rhea (Gr.)--Mother of the gods, in love with the god of vegetation, Attis.

Daphne (Gr.)--A nymph, whose heart had been pierced with one of Cupid's lead-tipped arrows, causing her to repel love.

Daphnis (Gr.)--A Sicilian shepherd, in love with Piplea.

Diana (Ro.); Artemis (Gr.)--Despising the weakness of love, she imposed upon her nymphs vows of perpetual maidenhood.

Dido (Gr.)--Queen of Carthage. She conceived an ardent passion for Aeneas, and when he left her, she stabbed herself. See same under CITADEL.

Eros (Gr.); Cupid (Ro.)--The small, powerful god of love.

Eurydice (Gr.)--A nymph loved by Aristaeus; also the beloved of Orpheus, whom she married.

Galatea (Gr.)--An ivory statue created by the king and sculptor Pygmalion, who fell in love with it.

Haemon (Gr.)--Son of Creon; lover of Antigone.

Himeros (Gr.)--Brother of Eros; personification of the longing of love; also an attendant of Aphrodite.

Idas (Gr.)--After his loved Marpessa declined the love of Apollo, Idas carried her away in the winged chariot which Neptune had given him.

Iole (Gr.)--Hercules was in love with her, but her father refused their marriage, fearing that madness might strike him a second time.

Iphis (Gr.)--The worthy lover of Anaxarette, who, spurned, hung himself to her gatepost.

Ixion (Gr.)--King of the Lapithae, who was sent to Hades because he aspired to the love of a goddess, Hera.

Jason (Gr.)--He won the love of King Aeëtes' daughter, Medea.

Juno (Ro.); Hera (Gr.)--She was always jealous of her husband, (Jupi-

LOVE (cont.)

Juno (cont.)--ter's) love affairs.

Leander (Gr.)--The lover of Hero who swam the Hellespont each night to
meet her.

Lyde (Gr.)--She was loved by the satyr Narcissus, who was loved by
Echo, who in turn was loved by Pan; all of whom grieved because
they were scorned.

Marpessa (Gr.)--One of the few maidens who declined the attentions of
Apollo.

Menelaüs (Gr.)--His wife, Helen, was wooed by Paris, and they eloped to
Troy, causing the Trojan War. Later, she returned to Menelaüs at
Sparta, where they reigned in splendor.

Metis (Gr.)--She was the first love of Jupiter.

Neptune (Ro.); Poseidon (Gr.)--Although married to Amphitrite, he had
many extra-marital loves.

Orithyia (Gr.)--A nymph who was loved by Boreas, the north wind. Since
is was difficult for him to breathe gently and to sigh like a lover, he
finally let our his true character, and swept her away with great
speed.

Pan (Gr.); Faunua (Ro.)--He made love to the nymphs, and fell in love
with one whose name was Syrinx. He made a musical instrument of
reeds, and named it after her.

Pandemos (Gr.)--Another name for Aphrodite or Venus; the goddess of
vulgar love.

Paris (Gr.)--He fell in love with Helen, and his eloping with her started
the Trojan War.

Pelops (Gr.)--He fell in love with Hippodamis, daughter of King Oenomaüs, who ruled that none could win her without besting him in a
chariot race.

Phaon (Gr.)--He used a salve which possessed magical properties that

161

LOVE (cont.)

Phaon (cont.)--made the women of Lesbos wild for love of him.

Polyphemus (Gr.)--He fell in love with Galatea, spoiling her happiness with her lover, Acis.

Psyche (Gr.)--In love with Cupid; lost him; visited the Lower World to find him. They ascended to the heavenly abodes where Jupiter gave her ambrosia to drink, and made her an immortal.

Pyramus (Gr.)--The handsomest youth in Babylonia, fell in love with Thisbe, the fairest maiden. Theirs was probably the original Romeo and Juliet story.

Scylla (Gr.)--Daughter of King Nisus, who betrayed him to his enemy, Minos II, with whom she had fallen violently in love.

Stheneboea (Gr.)--Daughter of Iobates; enamored of Bellerophon.

Venus (Ro.); Aphrodite (Gr.)--She was the goddess of love and beauty, and conquered every heart.

Zephyrus (Gr.)--The west wind, mild and gentle; lover of Flora.

LOVE UNREQUITED

Anaxerete (Gr.)--A Cyprian maiden who caused the worthy Iphis to hang himself because she spurned him.

Anteros (Gr.)--A god who avenged unrequited love.

Atalanta (Gr.)--She long rejected all lovers.

Clytie (Gr.)--A water-nymph in love with Apollo, unrequited.

Daphnis (Gr.)-- *See* Piplea.

Echo (Gr.)--A talkative nymph, loved by Pan, but she loved the satyr, Marcissus, who did not return her love.

Glaucus (Gr.)-- *See* Scylla.

LOVE UNREQUITED (cont.)

Iphis (Gr.)-- *See* Anaxerete.

Lyde (Gr.)-- *See same under* LOVE.

Narcissus (Gr.)-- *See* Lyde *under* LOVE. He was a handsome satyr for whose love unrequited Echo faded away.

Pan (Gr.); Faunus (Ro.)-- *See* Echo *above. See* Lyde *under* LOVE.

Phaedra (Gr.)--She became enamored of Hippolytus, but his repulsing her caused her to hang herself.

Phaon (Gr.)--Sappho loved him, and leaped from the Leucadian rock because her love was unrequited.

Phoebus (Gr.); Apollo (Gr.)--Struck by one of Cupid's gold-tipped arrows, he fell in love with the nymph Daphne. She fled from him, and when she grew tired she called upon her father, Peneüs, to save her. He changed her into a laurel tree.

Piplea (Gr.)--A maiden loved by Daphnis, but kidnapped by robbers. He regained Piplea, but was susceptible to the wiles of other maidens. One Naiad, unrequited, struck him blind. He wandered awhile, then called on his father, Mercury, who transported him to heaven, leaving Piplea alone.

Pomona (Ro.)--A nymph who spurned all offers of love made her by Pan and mano other Fauns and Satyrs. Assuming all kinds of disguises, Vertumnus wooed her, but did not win her until he dropped al disguises and stood before her a comely youth.

Sappho (Gr.)--Poetess of Lesbos; she leaped from the Leucadion rock because of her love unrequited for Phaon.

Scylla (Gr.)--The fair virgin, who rejected the infatuation of Glaucus.

Syrinx (Gr.)--She ran away when Pan tried to press his love.

Vertumnus (Gr.)-- *See* Pomona.

LOVELINESS *See also* BEAUTY

Danae (Gr.)--Daughter of Acrisius; unsurpassed in loveliness.

LOWER WORLD *See also* ELYSIAN FIELDS; HADES; STYX; UNDER WORLD

Hades (Gr.); Pluto (Class.)--The grim god of the Lower World; husband of Persephone, whom he had carried off from the upper world.

Hercules (Ro.); Alcides (Gr.)--For his Twelfth Labor, he had to fetch the monster, Cerberus, from the Lower World.

Mercury (Ro.); Hermes (Gr.)--He was a messenger of the gods, and conducotr of souls to the Lower World.

Orpheus (Gr.)--He was allowed to take his wife, Eurydice, away from the Lower World, provided he did not turn to look at her. After his death his shade went for a second time to Hades, to rejoin his wife.

Protesilaüs (Gr.)--Slain in the Trojan War by Hector. His wife, Laodamia, implored the gods to let her converse with him for three hours. Mercury led him back to the Upper World, and when he died a second time, she died with him.

Psyche (Gr.)--Visited the Lower World in search of Cupid. Later, the two ascended to the heavenly abodes, where she was made an immortal.

Theseus (Gr.)--He went with his close friend, Pirithoüs, to the Lower World, to assist in kidnapping Pluto's wife, Proserpina. He was one of few mortals who visited the Lower World, and returned.

Ulysses (Gr.); Odysseus (Gr.)--During his many wanderings, he was warned by Circe, the sorceress at the Aeaean Isle, to visit the Lower World to consult the blind prophet, Tiresias, to learn the way home.

LOYALTY

Cephalus (Gr.)--Married to Procris, who could not believe in his loyalty. *See same under* HUNTER.

164

LOYALTY (cont.)

Penelope (Gr.)--Married to Ulysses, she was remarkable for her loyalty to him during his twenty years of wanderings.

LUCK

Hermes (Gr.); Mercury (Ro.)--God of luck, cunning, trickery, etc.

LUTE

Linus (Gr.)--Teacher of Hercules, who when chastised, killed his master with a lute.

LYRE *See also* MUSIC

Amphion (Gr.)--He was so skillful a musician that when he played his lyre, stones moved of their own accord and took their places in the wall he was building, to help fortify Thebes.

Apollo (Gr.); Lycius (Gr.)--He took part in music contests on the flute and the lyre.

Diana (Ro.); Artemis (Gr.)--When weary of the chase, she turned to music, for the lyre, the flute and song were dear to her.

Erato (Gr.)--The Muse who presided over lyric and love poetry. She wore a thin garment and held a lyre.

Hermes (Gr.); Mercury (Ro.)--He was the first of inventors, fashioning a lyre from a tortoise shell.

Orpheus (Gr.)--His father gave him a lyre, and taught him how to play it, and he became famous as a musician.

MADNESS *See also* INSANITY

Alcmaeon (Gr.)--After destroying the city of Thebes, he returned to Argos and put his mother to death. In consequence, he was driven

Alcmaeon (cont.)--mad by the Furies.

Athamas (Gr.)--He became mad, murdered his son, Learchus, and persecuted his wife, Ino, until, with another son, Melicertes, she threw
herself into the sea.

Dionysus (Gr.); Liber (Ro.)--The god of wine. Juno struck him with madness, and sent him wandering through various parts of the earth.

Discord (Gr.); Eris (Gr.)--In the chamber of the Furies, she is mad.

Erinnyes (Gr.); Furies, The (Gr.)--The avenging spirits, Alecto, Megaera
and Tisiphone, who brought retribution upon offenders of piety,
hospitality, etc. These snaky-haired women pursued their victims
and inflicted madness.

Furies, The (Gr.)-- *See* Erinnyes. After Orestes killed his mother, they
drove him mad.

Hercules (Ro.); Alcides (Gr.)--In the prime of his manhood, he was driven
mad by Juno. Minerva struck him with a stone which plunged him
into a deep sleep, from which he awoke in his right mind. Later, in
a fit of madness, he killed his friend, Iphitus; for this he was condemned to spend three years as a slave to Queen Omphale.

Ino (Gr.)-- *See* Athamas.

Lichas (Gr.)--After he had carried a poisoned robe to Hercules, the hero
seized him in a frenzy, and hurled him into the sea.

Medea (Gr.)--A sorceress, who, enraged because her husband tired of her
and wanted to marry Creusa, sent a poisoned robe to the bride, and
killed her own children.

Megaera (Gr.)--Wife of Hercules, whom he renounced, feeling the gods
would be displeased with the marriage since he had slain his children
by Megara during his period of madness.

Minos II (Gr.)-- *See same under* MINOTAUR.

Palamedes (Gr.)--He saw that Ulysses was merely pretending madness, in

MADNESS (cont.)

Palamedes (cont.)--an unsuccessful attempt to avoid going with him into the Trojan War.

MAENADES

Maenades (Gr.)--These were women attendants of Bacchus, who danced and sang.

MAGIC

Circe (Gr.)--A beautiful sorceress, on the island of Aeaea, who feasted those who came there, and then turned them by magic into the forms of beasts.

Hecate (Gr.)--A three-headed goddess with six arms, who represented darkness, terrors, magic, and witchcraft.

Medea (Gr.)--She restored Jason's father, Aeson, to youth with one of her magic potions.

Mercury (Ro.); Hermes (Gr.)--His wand, twined with snakes and sur-mounted by wings, was possessed of magical powers over sleeping, waking and dreams.

MAIDEN

Anaxerete (Gr.)-- *See same under* STONE.

Androgeüs (Gr.)--Son of Minos, who was killed by the Marathonian bull. Because of this, Minos required a penalty of the Athenians--to send seven maidens, and seven youths each year to feed the Minotaur at Crete.

Andromeda (Gr.)-- *See same under* MONSTER.

Diana (Ro.); Artemis (Gr.)--Despising the weakness of love, she imposed vows of perpetual maidenhood upon her nymphs.

167

Hestia (Gr.); Vesta (Gr.)--She scorned the advance of Apollo, Neptune and others, and remained an old maid by choice. *See more under* OLYMPUS.

Marpessa (Gr.)--One of few maidens who declined the attentions of Apollo.

Nymphs (Gr.)--These were inferior divinities of nature represented as beautiful maidens, dwelling in mountains, forests, meadows, waters, etc.

Orpheus (Gr.) The Thracian maidens tried to captivate him in a desert cave, but his music repulsed even their weapons. Finally, in desperation, like maniacs, they tore him limb from limb, and cast his head and lyre into the Hebrus River.

Vesta (Gr.)-- *See* Hestia.

MALE

Priapus (Ro.)--The male generative power personified as a god.

MAN

Epimetheus (Gr.)--Brother of Prometheus who was committed to provide man and all other animals with faculties necessary for their preservation---courage, strength, swiftness, sagacity, claws to one, wings, and shells to others.

Man (Gr.)--He was made a nobler animal by Prometheus, who took some earth, kneaded it with water, and molded it in the image of the gods.

Prometheus (Gr.)--Stole fire from heaven for the use of man.

Vulcan (Ro.); Hephaestus (Gr.)--The god of fire, especially of terrestial fire. He took part in the making of the human race.

MARATHONIAN BULL *See* BULL; MINOTAUR

MARRIAGE *See also* NUPTIALS; WEDDING

Demeter (Gr.); Ceres (Ro.)--Goddess of the fruitfulness of mankind; guardian of civil life, especially of marriage.

Dione (Gr.)--A nymph; goddess of women and marriage.

Eurytion (Gr.)--One of the Centaurs, who became intoxicated at the marriage feast of Pirithoüs and Hippodamia, causing a fight in which some guests were killed.

Hymen (Gr.)--A handsome youth of divine descent; the personification of the wedding feast and leader of the nuptial chorus; the god of marriage.

Iobates (Gr.)--Although his daughter, Antea, was already married to Proetus, King Iobates gave her in marriage to Bellerophon, and made him successor to the throne.

Jocasta (Gr.)--Queen of Thebes, mother of Oedipus, who had been cast out by his father, Laiüs. Years later, when he returned to Thebes and conquered the monster, the Sphinx, the grateful Thebans gave him in marriage to their Queen.

Medea (Gr.)--Wife of Jason. He grew tired of her, and wanted to marry Creusa.

Polynices (Gr.)--After his brother, Eteocles, refused to give him his turn as ruler of Thebes, he fled to Adrastus, King of Argos, who gave him his daughter in marriage, and an army to enforce his claim to the kingdom.

Tereus (Gr.)--King of Thrace, cruel husband of Procne, who grew tired of her, plucked out her tongue to insure her silence, then married her sister, Philomela.

MARSH

Hydra (Gr.)--A water-serpent that lived in the marsh of Lerna, and ravaged the country of Argos.

Oracles (Gr. and Ro.)--These mediums through which the gods revealed

MARSH (cont.)

Oracles (cont.)--hidden knowledge, lived near cavernous spots, sheer abysms, deep and melancholy streams, and baleful marshes.

MASK

Melpomene (Gr.)--The Muse of tragedy, who held a tragic mask.

Thalia (Gr.)--Daughter of Jupiter and Mnemosyne; the Muse of comedy, who carried a shepherd's staff and a comic mask.

MATHEMATICS

Mercury (Ro.); Hermes (Gr.)--He was forerunner of mathematicians and astronomers.

MECHANICAL

Daedalus (Gr.)--A famous artificer; uncle of Perdix. Builder of the labyrinth to contain the Minotaur.

Perdix (Gr.)--He had been placed in the care of his uncle Daedalus, to learn the mechanical arts. He imitated the spine of a fish in iron, and thus invented the saw.

MEDICINE *See also* HEALING

Aesculapius (Ro.)--God of medicine, with skill so great he could sometimes restore the dead to life. His worhip was introduced in Rome around 293 B.C., in response to an oracle who was promising relief from the plague.

Asclepius (Gr.)--God of mediciene. *See* Aesculapius.

MEMORY

Mnemosyne (Gr.)--A Titaness; goddess of memory.

170

MEMORY (cont.)

Muses, The (Gr.)--Patronesses of memory.

MERMAID *See also* NAIADS; NEREIDS

Amphitrite (Gr.)--One of the fifty fair mermaid daughters of Nereus and Doris; the wife of Neptune, and with him founder of the younger dynasty of waters.

Cassiopeia (Gr.)--She had offended Neptune. *See same under* NYMPHS.

Galatea (Gr.)--A sea-nymph; one of the many daughters of Nereus and Doris.

Nereids (Gr.)--The fifty mermaid daughters of Nereus and Doris.

Panope (Gr.)--One of the most famous of the mermaid daughters of Nereus and Doris.

Thetis (Gr.)--A famous Nereid who, with her sister, Eurynome, cared for the young Vulcan for nine years. Her son, by Peleus, was Achilles.

MESSENGER

Hermes (Gr.); Mercury (Ro.)--Swift of foot, he was herald and messenger of the gods.

Iris (Gr.)--As the fleet-footed messenger of Hera, she bore commands to other gods, as well as to mortals.

Jupiter (Ro.); Jove (Ro.); Zeus (Gr.)--His special messenger was the eagle.

Mercury (Ro.)-- See Hermes.

Rhoecus (Gr.)--The dryad of an oak tree, in love with this youth, sent her messenger, a bee, to remind him to be constant.

METAL WORKING

Hephaestus (Gr.); Vulcan (Ro.)--God of fire, and of arts dependent on fire, such as metal working.

Vulcan (Ro.)-- *Same as* Hephaestus. He was the blacksmith of the gods, and the finest artificer of metal among them.

MINOTAUR *See also* BULL

Aegeus (Gr.)--King of Athens. It was he who sent Androgeüs, the son of Minos, against the Marathonian bull, which killed the young man.

Androgeüs (Gr.)--Son of Minos II, who lost his fight against the Marathonian bull.

Cretan Bull (Gr.)-- *Same as* Marathonian Bull.

Daedalus (Gr.)--The famous artificer, who built a labyrinth to confine the monster, the Minotaur.

Hercules (Ro.); Alcides (Gr.)--For his Seventh Labor, he overcame the bull which had been terrorizing the people of Crete. He rode it through the waves to Marathon, Greece, where it was slain by Theseus.

Labyrinth (Gr.)--The maze in which Daedalus was able to confine the Minotaur.

Marathonian Bull (Gr.)--Father of the Minotaur by Pasiphaë.

Minos II (Gr.)--Because he refused to kill the handsome bull sent him by Neptune for sacrifice, the infuriated god not only drove the bull wild, but caused Mino's wife, Pasiphaë, to fall into a frenzy of love for it. She gave birth to the Minotaur. After he lost his son, Androgeüs, Minos exacted a penalty--requiring the Athenians to send seven youths and seven maidens to Crete each year, to feed the monster, the Minotaur.

Minotaur (Gr.)--He was a bull-headed, man-bodied monster, son of the Marathonian Bull and Pasiphaë, the wife of King Minos II.

MINOTAUR (cont.)

Neptune (Ro.); Poseidon (Gr.)--He answered the prayer of King Minos II, and sent a bull for sacrifice. *See* Minos II.

Pasiphaë (Gr.)--Wife of Minos II, whom for spite, Neptune had driven into a passion for the Cretan Bull.

Poseidon (Gr.)-- *See* Neptune.

Theseus (Gr.)--The Attic hero; son of Aegeus; after Hercules rode the Cretan Bull to Greece, Theseus killed it.

MIRTH

Comus (Gr. and Ro.)--The god of festive joy, drunkenness and mirth.

MISTAKEN IDENTITY

Cephalus (Gr.)--A young hunter who thought his wife, Procris, spying on him from behind some bushes, was a wild beast; he hurled a javelin and killed her.

Pentheus (Gr.)--Angered by noises of an orgy in the woods, he plunged through to stop them. Some women there, including his mother, Agave, and his sisters, Autonoë and Ino, mistaking him for a wild boar, rushed him and tore him to pieces.

MISTRESS

Apollo (Gr.)--Although married, he had many love affairs.

Jupiter (Ro.); Zeus (Gr.)--Had many loves, of whom Juno was jealous.

Mars (Ro.); Ares (Gr.)--His loved one and mistress was Aphrodite. Their daughter was Harmonia.

Neptune (Ro.); Poseidon (Gr.)--Had many mistresses.

MOCKERY

Momus (Gr.)--The god of adverse criticism, blame and mockery.

MODESTY

Artemis (Gr.); Diana (Ro.)--A virgin goddess; the ideal of modesty, grace and maidenly vigor.

Icarius (Gr.)--A Spartan prince; father of Penelope. After his daughter had married Ulysses and gone to Ithaca, he erected a statue to Modesty on the spot where they had parted.

MONSTER *See also* DRAGON; GIANT; WITCH

Aloadae (Gr.)--These were Otus and Ephialtes, monster sons of Neptune and Iphimedia, named after her mortal husband, Aloeus. The monsters represented the unregulated forces of vegetation, since they grew at the rate of three cubits in height and one in breadth each year. Beside their stature, they were reowned for their strength and courage.

Andromeda (Gr.)--An Ethiopian maiden whom Perseus rescued from a horrible sea-monster. She married him and they had three sons.

Ärgus (Gr.)-- See same under HEIFER.

Briareus (Gr.)--A monster with 100 hands; one of the shadowy giants assigned to guard the descent to Hades.

Cassiopeia (Gr.)--Because she had offended Neptune, he sent a monster to ravage the land. It was killed by Perseus.

Cerberus (Gr.)--A three-headed dog with a serpent-tail, and neck bristling with snakes, which guarded the gate to the Under World. He was friendly to the spirits entering, but antagonistic to those who would depart.

Charybdis (Gr.)--A whirlpoo monster off the coast of Sicily, which helped Scylla guard the strait of Messina.

Chimaera (Gr.)--A fire-breathing monster which created great havoc. The fore part of his body was part lion, part goat, and the hind part, ad dragon. He was finally destroyed by Bellerophon.

Coroebus (Gr.)--A young man who destroyed a monster that for a season had been killing the children. It had been sent by Apollo.

Cottus (Gr.)--A 100-handed monster known as "The Striker."

Cyclopes (Gr.)--A race of men of gigantic size whose appearance was made more forbidding by their having one enormous eye set in the center of their foreheads, which made them look more like monsters than men.

Daedalus (Gr.)--The magician who built the labyrinth to contain that monster, the Minotaur.

Echidna (Gr.)--A monster; half-serpent, half-woman; mother of the Sphinx, the Chimaera, and other monsters.

Gaea (Gr.); Tellus (Ro.)--The wife of Uranus, and from their union came the Titans, the 100-handed monsters, and the Cyclopes.

Geryon (Gr.)--A monster with three bodies, six arms, six legs and a pair of monstrous wings.

Giants, The (Gr.)--A novel race of monsters, creatures more akin to men than the Titans. Clothed in skins of beasts, they were armed with rocks and the trunks of trees. Their bodies and lower limbs were of snakes.

Gorgons (Gr.)-- *See same under* GORGONS.

Gyges (Gr.)--One of the Hecatonchires, called the "Vaulter," or the "Crippler;" also known as Centimanus, the 100-handed.

Harpies (Gr.)-- *See same under* HARPIES.

Hecatonchires (Gr.)--Hundred-handed monsters, named Briareus, the Strong; Cottus, the Striker, and Gyges, the Crippler.

Hippolytus (Gr.)--He was killed when his horses were frightened by a sea-monster, and his chariot was dashed to pieces along the shore.

Hydra (Gr.)--A water-serpent that ravished the country of Argos. It had nine heads, any one of which would be succeeded by two if it were cut off, and remained uncauterized.

Laomedon (Gr.)--King of Troy, who reneged on a promise to reward Hercules for rescuing his daughter, Hesione, from a sea-monster.

Medusa (Gr.)--One of the Gorgons, most terrible of the three monsters, whose hair had been her chief glory. Because she had dared to vie in beauty with Minerva, the goddess changed her ringlets into hissing serpents.

Mezentius (Gr.)--King of the Etruscans, a monster of cruelty, who invented unheard of torments to gratify his vengeance.

Minotaur, The (Gr.)--A bull-headed, man-bodied monster; a terror to the people of Crete until Daedalus constructed a labyrinth to contain him.

Scylla (Gr.)--Because the enchantress, Circe, did not want the rivalry of Scylla over the sea-green god Glaucus, she transformed the virgin into a monster, hideously shaped, with twelve arms, twelve feet, six heads with sharp rows of teeth, and the yelp of a dog.

Sphinx, The (Gr.)--A monster with the body of a lion and the upper torso of a woman. She lay crouched on the top of a rock, to arrest all travelers and ask them a riddle.

Talus (Gr.)--A giant of living brass, who guarded the domain of King Minos in Crete. When voyagers neared the coast he was protecting, he fired himself red-hot and embraced them as they landed. In his body he had only one vein, and he plugged it on the crown of his head with a nail.

Typhon (Gr.)--A monster whose destiny was to dispute the reign of Jupiter. From his neck their spred 100 dragon-heads, from whose eyes shot fire. From his black-tongued mouth came sounds of hissing snakes, bellowing bulls, roaring lions, barking dogs, and various

MONSTER (cont.)

Typhon (cont.)--pipings and screams. But he still had to quail before the thunderbolt of Jupiter.

MOON

Artemis (Gr.); Diana (Ro.)--A virgin goddess, identified with the chaste brilliance of the moon. Another title for her was Munychia. She is not to be confused with the ancient Greek divinity, Selene.

Cynthia (Gr.); Diana (Ro.)--Goddess of the moon; also known as Luna.

Diana (Ro.); Artemis (Gr.)--Goddess of the moon, of the bright heavens, and the bright day. Another name for her was Phoebe, the shining one.

Endynion (Gr.)--A handsome youth, loved by Diana. She visited him again and again, until her absence from her station in the sky was noted by the Olympians. Then Jupiter took charge, and gave Endymion a choice of death in any manner, or perpetual youth united with perpetual sleep. He chose the latter, and still sleeps in the Carian Cave, and Diana still slips from her nocturnal course to visit him.

Hecate (Gr.)--A three-headed goddess, with six arms which carried a torch and spear. She combined the characters of moon goddess, earth goddess, and Under World goddess.

Hilaira (Gr.)--Daughter of Apollo; sometimes called, the cheerful or the moon.

Luna (Ro.)--The Moon, worshipped by the Romans.

Phoebe (Gr.)--The shining one; another name for Diana.

Selene (Gr.)--An ancient goddess of the moon, frequently identified with Artemis or Hecate, but more ancient than either. Her emblem was the crescent.

MORNING

Aurora (Ro.); Eos (Gr.)--The rosy-fingered goddess of the Morn; mother of the stars.

Eos (Gr.)-- *Same as* Aurora.

Phosphor (Gr.)--The morning star.

MORTAL

Electra (Gr.)--One of the Pleiades, who left her place that she might not witness the ruin of Troy. She became a comet; her hair floating wildly behind her, ranging the expanse of heaven. Some say she is Merope, who was vested with mortality when she married the mortal Sisyphus, King of Corinth.

Juno (Ro.); Hera (Gr.)--The deity of light and the sky. She was hostile to all the offspring of her husband, Jupiter, and their mortal mothers.

Pentheus (Gr.)--He was a mortal brought under the influence of his cousin, Bacchus, but he had no respect for the new worship of Bacchus, and forbade the rites.

MOTHER

Alcmaeon (Gr.)--When his mother, Eriphyle, accepted a bribe from Polynices to continue the war against Thebes, he became a leader of the Epigoni. After destroying the city, he returned to Argos and put his mother to death. In consequence he was driven mad by the Furies.

Cybele (Ro.); Rhea (Gr.)--Mother of the gods. By Cronus, she gave birth to Ceres, Juno, Jupiter, Neptune, Pluto, and Vesta.

Dindymene (Gr.)--Worshipped as the Great Mother; another name for Cybele, or Rhea.

Eos (Gr.); Aurora (Ro.)--Mother of the stars and of the morning and evening breezes.

Euryalus (Gr.)--A young Trojan soldier who, when he wanted to cross

MOTHER (cont.)

Euryalus (cont.)--enemy lines to seek Aeneas, asked Iulus to take care of his mother.

Lucifer (Ro.); Phosphor (Gr.)--The morning star; son of Aurora and Cephalus. By his torch, this brilliant star heralded the coming of his goddess mother.

Magna Mater (Ro.); Rhea (Gr.); Cybele (Ro.)—The great mother of the gods.

Oedipus (Gr.)--When he returned home and found Thebes scourged by the monster Sphinx, he guessed the Sphinx's riddle and caused her to kill herself. The Thebans were so grateful they gave him their queen, Jocasta, in marriage. Unknowingly, he bacame the husband of his mother.

Orestes (Gr.)--He avenged his father's murder by slaying his mother, Clytemnestra, and her lover, Aegisthus.

Rhea (Gr.)-- *See also* Cybele. In Phrygia, Rhea became identified with Cybele, whose worship, as mother of the gods, was introduced at a later period into Rome. Cybele presided over mountain fastness, and was attended by the Corybantes. The Greek mother, Rhea, was attended by the Curetes.

Rhea Silvia (Ro.)--Mother of Romulus and Remus.

MOUNTAIN

Aloadae (Gr.)--The two sons of Neptune and Iphimedia, who when nine years old, tried to dethrone the immortals by piling Mt. Ossa on Olympus, and Mt. Pelias on top of that, to scale the skies. Jupiter killed them with his lightning. They were Otus and Ephialtes.

Arcadia (Gr.)--It was here that Hercules performed his Third Labor by capturing the boar that haunted Mount Erymanthus.

Atlas (Gr.)--He had been holding the heavens on his head and hands as a penalty for warring against Zeus. Perseus came along one day with

Atlas (cont.)--the head of the Gorgon, Medusa. It changed Atlas to stone; his hair became forests, his arms and shoulders cliffs, and his bones rocks, increasing in mass until he became a mountain holding up the heavens.

Cybele (Ro.); Rhea (Gr.)--Her chariot was drawn by lions, and she haunted mountain and forest fastnesses.

Cynthia (Gr.); Diana (Ro.)--Goddess of the moon, born on Mt. Cynthus. She was in love with Endymion, who fed his flock on Mt. Latmos.

Echo (Gr.)--By her chatter she came under the displeasure of Juno, who condemned her to loss of voice except for replying. She may still be heard in caves, rocky hills and mountains.

Ephialtes (Gr.)-- *See* Aloadae.

Ganymede (Gr.)--He was seized from the midst of his playfellows on Mt. Ida, by Jupiter disguised as an eagle, to succeed Hebe in heaven as cupbearer to the gods.

Helicon (Gr.)--A mountain in Greece supposed to be the residence of Apollo and the Muses.

Hercules (Ro.); Alcides (Gr.)--For killing his music teacher, Linus, he was sent off to the mountains, to be raised among herdsmen and the cattle. He captured the wild boar which had haunted Mt. Erymanthus. Died on Mt. Oeta.

Latmos (Gr.)--Endymion fed his flocks of sheep on this mountain.

Oedipus (Gr.)--Because his father, King Laiüs, had been told by an oracle that he would be killed by his son, he sent the new-born Oedipus off with a herdsman to die of exposure on Mt. Cithaeron.

Oreads (Gr.)--These were the immortal nymphs of mountains, hills and grottoes.

Otus (Gr.)-- *See* Aloadae.

Pan (Gr.); Faunus (Ro.)--A god of the woods and fields, he wandered on

MOUNTAIN (cont.)

Pan (cont.)--the mountains, mainly in a range (Maenalus) in Arcadia, which was sacred to him.

Parmassus (Gr.)--Deucalion and his wife, Pyrrha, were the only two survivors of a flood sent by Neptune. They found refuge at the top of Mount Parnassus.

Psamanthe (Gr.)--Mother of one of the two Linuses in mythology. This one was brought up by shepherds in the mountains. But in his youth he was torn to pieces by dogs.

Tmolus (Gr.)--A mountain god.

Zeus (Gr.); Jupiter (Ro.)--Sovereign of the World; his palace was at the summit of the ideal mountain, Olympus. The loftiest trees and the grandest mountains were dear to him.

MOURNING *See also* GRIEF

Cyparissus (Gr.)--A boy who killed a pet stag accidentally. In his grief he begged Apollo to allow him to mourn forever. The god changed him into a cypress tree, associated with mourning.

MOUSE

Apollo (Gr.)--He was also called Sminthian, or the mouse-god, since he was regarded as both the protector and the destroyer of mice. In the Troad, mice were fed in his temple; elsewhere he was honored for freeing the country of them.

MURDER *See also* SLAIN; VENGEANCE

Absyrtus (Gr.)--His sister, Medea, eloped with Jason, and in order to delay the pursuit of her father, she tore Absyrtus to pieces and scattered his body along their line of flight.

Achilles (Gr.)--He was in the temple of Apollo when Paris shot a poisoned arrow which fatally wounded him in the heel.

181

MURDER (cont.)

Acrisius (Gr.)-- *See same under* GAMES.

Aëdon (Gr.)--In an attempt to murder her oldest nephew, she killed her own son, Itylus, by mistake.

Aegisthus (Gr.)--He was in a plot with Clytemnestra to murder her first husband, Agamemnon. He had already killed Agamemnon's father, Atreus, while reviving a treacherous feud his own father, Thyestes, had had with Atreus.

Aeneas (Gr.)–To avenge his friend, Pallas, he thrust his sword through Turnus.

Agamemnon (Gr.)–Murdered by his wife, Clytemnestra.

Agave (Gr.)--A mortal; mother of Penetheus, *which see.*

Alcmaeon (Gr.)--After his mother, Eriphyle, had accepted a bribe (the necklace of Harmonia) to continue the war against Thebes, he helped to destroy the city, then returned to Argos to put his mother to death.

Apollo and Artemis (Gr.)--Two offspring of Latona. They killed thirteen of Niobe's fourteen children, because her pride in them caused her to boast of her superiority over the goddess, Latona, who only had the two.

Athamas (Gr.)--He became mad; murdered his son, Learchus, and persecuted his wife, Ino.

Atreus (Gr.)--During family feuding, he and his brother, Thyestes, murdered their brother, Chrysippus. Later, Atreus killed three sons of his faithless brother, Thyestes, and served them at a banquet of feigned reconciliation.

Clytemnestra (Gr.)-- *See* Aegisthus.

Daedalus (Gr.)--He murdered his nephew, Talus. This was Talus, the inventor.

182

Danaides (Gr.)--These fifty daughters of Danaüs were commanded by their father to murder their husbands on their wedding night. Hypermestra is the only one who abstained. The other forty-nine were condemned to spend eternity in Hades, trying to fill a perforated vessel with water. These probably represent the springs of Argolis, whose waters run off quickly into the dry, porous soil.

Electra (Gr.)--Daughter of Agamemnon and Clytemnestra. She and her brother, Orestes, avenged their father by killing both their mother and her paramour, Aegisthus.

Furies, The Three (Gr.)--They lived in the Infernal Region, and visited earth often to punish perjury, murder, treachery, etc.

Hector (Gr.)--During the Trojan War, he fatally wounded Patroclus with his spear. This brought Achilles into the fight to avenge his friend. He struck the Trojan in a vulnerable part of his neck and killed him, then in further vengeance, he tied a cord to Hector's body and dragged him behind his chariot back and forth in front of the gates of Troy.

Hercules (Ro.); Alcides (Gr.)--He murdered his music teacher by striking him with a lute. He was married to Dejanira. When Nessus tried to kidnap her while carrying her across a river, Hercules shot him in the heart with an arrow. In the prime of his manhood, he was driven insane by Juno; killed his children, and would have slain his father, Amphitryon, had not Minerva knocked him unconscious with a stone. He woke up in his right mind. To obtain the girdle of Hippolyta, Queen of the Amazons, as his Ninth Labor, Hercules killed her. In another fit of madness, Hercules killed his friend, Iphitus, for which he was condemned to spend three years as a slave to Queen Omphale. *See also* Lityerses.

Hippolyta (Gr.); Antiope (Gr.)-- *See also* Hercules. Another Antiope was wooed by Jupiter and bore him two sons, Amphion and Zethus. She fell into the hands of her uncle Lycus, the usurping King of Thebes. who, with his wife, Dirce, treated her with extreme cruelty. When doomed to be dragged to death tied behind a running bull, she reached her sons. They came and killed Lycus; tied Dirce's hair to the bull, and let her die by her own device.

183

Ibycus (Gr.)--A poet, murdered by two robbers in a grove of Neptune. A flock of cranes who witnessed the murder, flew overhead at a music festival and caused the murderers to reveal themselves through their surprised recognition of the cranes.

Iphitus (Gr.)--A friend of Hercules. *See also* Hercules.

Jupiter (Ro.); Jove (Ro.); Zeus (Gr.)--He ruled as Sovereign of the World for several eons; then, tiring of the fraud, violence, wars and frightful conditions of the earth, he proceeded to drown all its inhabitants, saving only one couple, Deucalion and his wife, Pyrrha. Jupiter was always lashing his enemies with his lightning and punishing with his thunderbolts.

Linus (Gr.)-- *See* Hercules.

Lityerses (Gr.)--King of Phrygia, who induced strangers to enter a contest with him in picking corn. If the king won, he cut off their heads. One day, Daphnis was about to lose his head when Hercules arrived and cut off the king's, and threw his body into the River Meander.

Lycus (Gr.)--Usurping king of Thebes. *See also* Hippolyta.

Medea (Gr.)--A sorceress who made her art an instrument of revenge. She told the daughters of Pelias, the usurping King of Iolcus, that by cutting him up and boiling the pieces, he could be restored to youth. After her husband, Jason, tired of her, she sent a poisoned robe to his new bride; killed her own children; set fire to the palace and fled to Athens.

Medusa (Gr.)--Perseus cut off her head, carried it in a pouch to Minerva, who bore it afterwards on her shield. This Gorgon's head changed to stone all who looked at it.

Myrtilus (Gr.)--He was thrown into the sea by Pelops, after he had accepted a bribe to remove a bolt from King Oenomaüs's chariot wheel.

Niobe (Gr.)-- *See Niobe under* CHILDREN.

Orestes (Gr.)--Son of Agememnon and Clytemnestra, who avenged his father's murder by slaying both his mother, and her lover, Aegisthus.

MURDER (cont.)

Pallas (Gr.)--A young warrior who was felled by the lance of Turnus. Aeneas came along, and to avenge Pallas thrust his sword through Turnus.

Pentheus (Gr.)--He had no respect for the new worship of his cousin, Bacchus. Angered by the noise of a Bacchanalian orgy, he plunged through the woods to the space where it was being held. There, some women, including his mother, Agave, and his sisters, Autonoë and Ino, mistook him for a wild boar and tore him to peices.

Perdix (Gr.)--An ingenius scholar and inventor. His uncle Daedalus was so envious of him that he pushed him off a tower to his death.

Periphetes (Gr.)--A ferocious savage; son of Vulcan, who always went armed with an iron club. All stood in terror of him, except Theseus, who felled him with many blows.

Polyphemus (Gr.)--One of the giant Cyclopes with one eye, who found two of Hercules' men in his cave and dashed their brains out against the wall. He then devoured them with relish.

Semele (Gr.)--She asked for proof that it was Jupiter himself who had come as her lover. He appeared the next time in a full suit of armor, with thunder and lightnings. Her mortal frame could not endure the splendors of the immortal radiance, and she was consumed to ashes.

Thyestes (Gr.)-- See Aegisthus and Atreus.

Turnus (Gr.)-- See Pallas.

MUSES

Camenae (Ro.)--The nymphs of fountains and springs in ancient Rome; later identified with the Greek Muses.

Calliope (Gr.)--The "beautiful-voiced;" Muse of epic poetry, eloquence and rhetoric; loved by Apollo, and by him the mother of Orpheus. Her symbols were the stylus and tablet.

Clio (Gr.)--The Muse of History, holding a roll of papyrus unfolded on

Clio (cont.)--on her lap. Her symbols: the trumpet and clepsydra (water clock).

Egeria (Ro.)–Sometimes associated with Carmenta, leader of the fountain-nymphs; later identified as the Muse who sang of both the future and the past.

Erato (Gr.)--A Muse of lyric and love poetry.

Euterpe (Gr.)--A Muse of music and of lyric poetry; her symbol, the flute.

Helicon (Gr.)--A mountain in Greece, reputed to be the residence of Apollo and the Muses.

Melpomene (Gr.)--The Muse of Tragedy. She holds a tragic mask, and the club of Hercules.

Mnemosyne (Gr.)–A Titan goddess of memory; mother of the nine Muses, by Jupiter.

Musagetes (Gr.)–The name given Apollo as leader of the Muses.

Muses, The Nine (Gr.)--All were the daughters of Jupiter and Mnemosyne. They presided over song and prompted the memory. Each was assigned patronage in literature, art or science. *See also* Calliope; Clio; Euterpe; Melpomene; Polyhymnia; Terpichore; Thalia and Urania.

Polyhymnia (Gr.)--The Muses of heroic hymns; later the Muse of Mimic Art; represented in an attitude of meditation with a finger on her mouth.

Terpsichore (Gr.)--The Muse of choral dance, song and lyric poetry. Her symbol: the cithara, a form of lyre.

Thalia (Gr.)--The Muse of Comedy. She carried the shepherd's staff and the comic mask.

Urania (Gr.)--The Muse of Astronomy. Her symbols were a celestial globe and a compass.

MUSIC *See also* LUTE; LYRE; SYRINX

Amphion (Gr.)-- *See same under* LYRE.

Apollo (Gr.)--God of music and poetry. He entered many music contests on the flute and lyre.

Calliope (Gr.)--The "beautiful-voiced;" mother of Orpheus.

Chiron (Gr.)--A centaur, skilled in riding, music and the art of healing.

Diana (Ro.)--Goddess of the moon; a huntress. When weary of the chase, she turned to music, for the lyre, the flute, song and dancing were dear to her.

Eurydice (Gr.)--A nymph who was married to Orpheus. After she died and went to Hades, he descended and so pleased Pluto with his music that the god allowed him to lead Eurydice back to earth, on condition that he not look back. He turned and she vanished.

Euterpe (Gr.)--The Muse of Music and of lyric poetry.

Hercules (Ro.)--He was trained in music by Linus.

Hermes (Gr.); Mercury (Ro.)--Famous for swiftness, he was also an inventor, fashioning a lyre from a tortoise shell, and a reed-pipe called the syrinx.

Io (Gr.)--She was held captive by the 100-eyed creature, Ärgus, until Mercury came to play on his pipes and tell stories until all the eyes were asleep.

Linus (Gr.)--A legendary musician and teacher of Hercules, who killed him by striking him with a lute.

Marsyas (Gr.)--He found a flute, and could make such a ravishing music on it that he challenged Apollo to a music contest. The god won, of course, and punished Marsyas by flaying him alive.

Midas (Gr.)--For deciding against Apollo in a music contest with Pan, the god changed Midas's ears into those of an ass.

Minerva (Ro.); Athena (Gr.)--She invented the flute; rejoiced in martial

MUSIC (cont.)

Minerva (cont.)--music.

Olympus (Gr.)--In this heaven of the Greek gods, they feasted on ambrosia and nectar; listened to Apollo playing on his lyre, and the Muses singing in response.

Orpheus (Gr.)--Given a lyre by his father, Apollo, who taught him to play it, he became famous as a musician, and could charm even wild beasts with his music.

Pan (Gr.); Faunus (Ro.)--He led the dances of the wood-nymphs, who played on the syrinx, or "Pan's pipes," fabled to be his invention, which he played himself in a masterly way.

Phoebus (Gr.); Apollo (Gr.)--He was a patron of music and of poetry.

Syrinx (Gr.)--She ran away from Pan, and when he tried to seize her along the bank of a stream, he held a handful of reeds. His windy sighs made a sweet sound, so he broke the reeds into unequal lenths, fastened them together and so made the "Syrinx" in her honor.

Triton (Gr.)--Trumpeter of the ocean. By his blast on a long conch seashell, he could stir up or calm the waves.

MYRMIDONS See also COMPANION

Myrmidons (Gr.)--These were soldiers of Achilles. The army had been created by Jupiter for Achilles' grandfather, Aeacus.

N

NAIADS See also HORN; NYMPHS

Acis (Gr.)--He was the son of a Naiad by Faunus. Killed by the Cyclops Polyphemous, his blood became a stream which still bears his name.

Naiads (Gr.)--These were the beautiful nymphs of fresh water. They lived in, and gave life to rivers, lakes, streams and fountains, and main-

NAIADS (cont.)

Naiads (cont.)--tained an intimate association with deities of the earth. They kept the waters sacred.

Oreads (Gr.)--They, as well as the Naiads, were immortal.

NAME *See also* EPITHET; PATRONYM

Aecides (Gr.)--This was the name given Achilles, after his grandfather, Aeacus.

Moeragetes (Gr.)--This name was applied to Zeus as leader of the Fates.

Pelasgus (Gr.)--A division of the Greek people derived their name, Pelasgic, from him.

Scamandrius (Gr.)--A nickname used by Hector for his son Astyanax.

Zeus (Gr.)--His Greek name signified radiant light of heaven.

NATURE

Ceres (Ro.); Demeter (Gr.)--Goddess of harvest festivals, and of agriculture in general. She was associated with the alternate death and life in nature, which simulated the resurrection and immortality of man.

Faunus (Ro.); Pan (Gr.)--A rural deity, worshipped as the god of animal life, fields and fruitfulness. He was a patron of husbandry, and the secret lore of nature.

Light (Gr.)--He sprang from the prime elements of Nature, Night and Darkness.

Night (Gr.); Nyx (Gr.)--A prime element of Nature; mother of the Fates, Nemesis, and others.

Pan (Gr.); Faunus (Ro.)--A god of woods and fields; the personification of nature.

NAVIGATION *See also* PILOT

Athena (Gr.); Minerva (Ro.)--She presided over the useful and ornamental arts; agriculture and navigation.

NECKLACE

Alcmaeon (Gr.)–Son of Amphiaraüs and Eriphyle, she who accepted a bribe of the necklace of Harmonia from Polynices to continue the war against Thebes.

Callirrhoe (1) (Gr.)--Wife of Alcmaeon, and the cause of his death through her coveting the necklace of Harmonia.

Eriphyle (Gr.)--She who was bribed by Polynices with Harmonia's necklace. She was slain by her son, Alcmaeon, to avenge the death of his father.

Harmonia (Gr.)--When she married Cadmus, the gods left Olympus to honor the occasion with their presence. Vulcan presented to the bride a necklace of unsurpassed brilliance which he had forged himself. But disaster hung over the family, and the necklace carried bad luck to all who wore it.

Polynices (Gr.)--He gave the fated necklace of Harmonia to Eriphyle.

NECTAR

Hebe (Gr.); Juventas (Ro.)–Though ranked as one of the lesser gods, she poured the nectar that the gods quaffed in Olympus.

Olympus (Gr.)--The heaven of the Greek gods. In the great hall of Jupiter the gods feasted each day on ambrosia and nectar.

NEEDLEWORK

Athena (Gr.); Minerva (Ro.)--The virgin goddess; presided over the useful and ornamental arts, including spinning, weaving and needlework.

NEREIDS

Amphitrite (Gr.)--One of the fifty fair mermaid daughters of Nereus and Doris; wife of Neptune.

Galatea (Gr.)--One of the most famous of the sea-nymph daughters of Nereus and Doris.

Nereids (Gr.)--These daughters of Nereus and Doris lived below the waters in a great shining cave. They were also attendants of Neptune.

Panope (Gr.)--One of the better-known daughters of Nereus, the old man of the sea, and Doris.

Pasithea (Gr.)--A Nereid.

Thetis (Gr.)--Another famous daughter of Nereus and Doris. When Vulcan was cast out of heaven, this sea-goddess and her sister, Eurynome, took him in and cared for him nine years.

NIGHT

Cimmerian (Gr.)--Pertaining to a fabulous land at the limits of the world, where no sunshine ever falls, and deadly night spreads over miserable mortals.

Cupid (Ro.); Eros (Gr.)--The god of love, worshipped Psyche, but visited her only at night.

Dagon (Gr.)--The fish-god who swam nightly through subterranean waters, and appeared eastward again at daybreak.

Death (Gr.); Thanatos (Gr.)--Twin brother of Sleep; son of Night; brother of Dreams. All dwell in subterranean darkness. Night brings to mortals solace and can lull the eyes of Jove, himself. Death closes forever the eyes of man.

Fates, The (Gr.)--Three daughters of Night, named Clotho, Lachesis and Atropos, goddesses who were to determine the course of human life.

Light (Gr.)--In early Greek myths, Night and Darkness were the prime elements of Nature, and from them sprang Light.

NIGHT (cont.)

Mors (Ro.); Thanatos (Gr.)--The god of Death; son of Nyx (Night), and brother of Hypnos (Sleep).

Nemesis (Gr.)--An ancient goddess; daughter of Night. She personified retributive justice.

Night (Gr.); Nyx (Gr.); Nox (Ro.)--A prime element of Nature; mother of the Fates, Nemesis, and others.

Nyx (Gr.); Nox (Ro.)--Mother of the Fates, Thanatos (Death), Somnus (Sleep), Dreams, Momus (Mockery), Care, the Hesperides and Nemesis.

Vesper (Gr.)–*Same as* Hesper, of the evening star of Venus.

NOBILITY

Cresphontes (Gr.)--King of Messenia; killed by rebellious noblemen.

NUPTIALS *See also* MARRIAGE; WEDDING

Hymen (Gr.)–A youth of divine descent. *See same under* MARRIAGE.

NURSE

Beroë (Gr.)--The aged nurse of Semele, future mother of Bacchus.

Demeter (Gr.)--Employed as Demophoön's nurse, she placed him nightly in a fire to immortalize him.

Demophoön (Gr.)-- *See* Demeter.

Euryclea (Gr.)--The old nurse of Ulysses, who, upon his return in disguise, recognized him by a scar left long before by a boar.

Hyades (Gr.)--Nymphs; daughters of Atlas, and nurses of Dionysus.

Semele (Gr.)--Jealous of Jupiter's interest in Semele, Juno assumed the

NURSE (cont.)

Semele (cont.)—form of her aged nurse to cast doubts about the god. The next time Jupiter had to appear in full regalia with lightning, etc., and Semele was consumed to ashes.

NYMPHS *See also* NAIADS; NEREIDS; OREADS

Aegle (Gr.)--One of the four daughters of Atlas, known as the Hesperides, who guarded the tree of the golden apples.

Alpheüs (Gr.)--A god of the river, who pursued the nymph, Arethusa.

Apollo (Gr.)—God of the sun, poetry and music. He had numerous love affairs, and made love to nymphs as well as to mortal maidens.

Arethusa (Gr.)--A woodland nymph; daughter of Atlas. While bathing in a brook she was surprised by Alpheüs, ran from him until exhausted; called to Diana for help, and was changed by her into a fountain. This plunged into an abyss to come out in Sicily, with Alpheüs still in pursuit.

Aruns (Gr.)– *See same under* WARRIOR.

Atlas (Gr.)--A giant, and the father of the three classes of nymphs: By his first wife, Pleione, he had the Pleides; by his second wife, Aethra, the Hyades; by his third, Hesperis, the Hesperides.

Boreas (Gr.); Aquilo (Ro.)--God of the north. He tried to woo the nymph Orithyia, with gentle breathing and sighing, but finally had to act out his true self by seizing her and carrying her away.

Callirrhoe (Gr.)--An ocean nymph; wife of Chrysaor.

Callisto (Gr.)--A nymph attendant upon Artemis, and mother of Arcas, by Jupiter.

Calypso (Gr.)—A sea-nymph on the island of Oxygia, who persuaded Ulysses to remain with her seven years.

Camenae (Ro.)—Nymphs of.fountains and springs in ancient Rome; later, identified in some way with the Greek Muses.

Carmenta (Ro.)--Leader of the fountain nymphs.

Cassiopeia (Gr.)--Wife of Cepheus, who offended Neptune by boasting that she was more beautiful than his attendants, the mermaids. In revenge, he sent a monster to ravage the land, which King Cepheus was unable to appease. Perseus arrived and killed it.

Clytie (Gr.)--A water-nymph in love with Apollo, unrequited. She pined, and sat on the ground for nine days, with only the dew as sustenance. Her eyes were constantly fixed on the sun-god as he drove across the sky. At last her limbs took root, and her face became a sun-flower, turning on its stem to follow the journeying sun.

Crocale (Gr.)--The most skillful of the nymphs who attended Diana.

Cyane (Gr.)--A Sicilian nymph who found Proserpina's girdle floating in the Anapus River.

Cyrene (Gr.)--A water-nymph loved by Apollo; mother of Aristaeus; sister of Daphne.

Daphne (Gr.)--A graceful nymph; daughter of the river-god, Peneüs. Because her heart had been pierced with one of Cupid's lead-tipped arrows, she repelled love. Running from Apollo, she appealed to a woodland divinity, and was transformed into a laurel tree. Apollo embraced it and declared it sacred.

Diana (Ro.); Artemis (Gr.)--Goddess of the moon. Despising the weakness of love, she imposed upon her nymphs vows of perpetual maidenhood.

Dione (Gr.)--A nymph; mother of Aphrodite, by Jupiter.

Doris (Gr.)--A nymph; daughter of Oceanus; wife of the genial old man of the sea, and mother of the fifty fair Nereids.

Dryads of Hamadryads (Gr.)--These were wood-nymphs. Each nymph's life begins and ends with a particular tree.

Dryope (Gr.)--A playmate of the wood-nymphs; loved by Apollo. Once when she was gathering flowers for the altar of the nymphs, she

Dryope (cont.)--plucked a purple blossom from a lotus plant, which happened to be the transformed nymph, Lotis. The displeasure of the nymph caused Dryope to spur forth branches and leaves and to change into a lotus tree.

Egeria (Ro.)--Associated with Carmenta, leader of the fountain nymphs; goddesses of prophecy and healing; later identified with the Greek Muses.

Electra (Gr.)--One of the daughters of Atlas; a nymph of Diana's train; one of the Pleiades, but left her place to become a comet.

Erytheia (Gr.)--A nymph; daughter of Atlas.

Eunice (Gr.)--One of the sleepless nymphs.

Eurydice (Gr.)--A nymph loved by Aristaeus; but beloved by Orpheus, whom she married. See *same under* HADES.

Galatea (Gr.)--One of the sea-nymph daughters of Nereus and Doris.

Golden Apples, The (Gr.)--These were a wedding present to Hera from the Earth goddess, Gaea. They were guarded by the nymphs (Hesperides), with the aid of a dragon.

Hamdryads (Gr.);--Dryads, female, and of the lesser gods of earth; wood-nymphs.

Helice (Gr.)--An Arcadian nymph confused with Callisto. (b)-Also a Cretan nymph, one of the nurses of the infant, Zeus.

Hesperides (Gr.)--The four nymphs fabled to be the daughters of Atlas and Hesperis. They were Aegle, Arethusa, Erytheia and Hestia.

Hippolytus (Gr.)--Killed in a chariot accident, he was restored to life by Aesculapius, and placed in Italy under the protection of the nymph, Egeria.

Hyades (Gr.)--Nymphs; daughters of Atlas, and nurses of Dionysus. They were placed by Zeus in the heavens.

195

Hyale (Gr.)--A nymph, attendant to the chaste Diana.

Hylas (Gr.)--A lad who attended Hercules on the expedition of the Argo-nauts. He tried to draw water from a spring, and was drawn down in-to the depths by the Naiads. They held him captive, and he became numbered among the Blessed.

Idaea (Gr.)--A nymph; wife of the river-god, Scamander.

Jupiter (Ro.); Zeus (Gr.)--When his mother, Rhea, concealed him on the island of Crete, he was nurtured by the nymphs Adrasta and Ida, and fed on the milk of the goat, Amalthea.

Juturna (Ro.)--A water-nymph; goddess of springs and brooks, whose pool in the Forum was sacred.

Lotis (Gr.)--A nymph who was transformed into a lotus plant.

Maia (Gr.)--Originally a mountain nymph; mother of Hermes (Mercury) by Jupiter; later identified as one of the daughters of Atlas.

Malis (Gr.)--One of the sleepless nymphs.

Melic Nymphs (Gr.)--The fearsome maidens of the ashen spear.

Naiads (Gr. and Ro.)--These were nymphs who lived in, guarded and gave life and perpetuity to rivers, streams, lakes and fountains of fresh water, and kept them sacred. Although immortal, they maintained an intimate association with deities of earth. It was the Naiads who consecrated the horn which became the Cornucopia.

Narcissus (Gr.)--A handsome satyr for whose unrequited love Echo faded away, leaving nothing but her voice. Being self-conceited, he also shunned the other nymphs. Nemesis punished him by causing him to fall in love with his own reflection. He pined for it until he died. The water-nymphs mourned for him, and their cries were repeated by Echo.

Nycheia (Gr.)--One of the sleepless nymphs (she with "the April eyes"'); the dread goddesses of the country people.

Nymphs (Gr.)--Any of the minor, female divinities of nature, represented as beautiful maidens, living in mountains, forests, meadows, waters, groves, fountains, etc., usually restricted to a single tree, spring, mountain, or the like. They were of several classes:

    Dryads--Nymphs of the woods.

    Hamadryads--Wood-nymphs.

    Naiads--Nymphs of fresh water.

    Nereids--Nymphs of the sea.

    Oceanides--The offspring of Oceanus and Tethys. 3000 in numbers.

    Oreads--Nymphs of mountains and hills and grottoes.

Oenone (Gr.)--A nymph whom Paris had married when a youth and abandoned for the fatal beauty of Helen.

Oreads (Gr.)--Immortal nymphs of the mountains, hills and grottoes. Echo was a beautiful Oread.

Orithyia (Gr.)--*See* Boreas.

Pan (Gr.); Faunus (Ro.)--Son of Mercury and a Dryad. He made love to the nymphs, but frequently to no avail, for he was not prepossessing, having the horns, ears and legs of a goat. But he had one son by a nymph--the jovial Silenus. He fell in love with another nymph, Syrinx, and wooed her, but she ran away to a riverbank, where the water-nymphs changed her into a tuft of reeds. When he sighed the air through the reeds produced a melody, giving him the idea for making the instrument, the Syrinx. At one time he loved the nymph, Echo, but she wanted Narcissus, and he, in turn, loved only Lyde, making a circle of unrequited love.

Phaëton (Gr.)--The son of Apollo and the nymph Clymene.

Pleiades (Gr.)--These seven daughters of Atlas, and the nymphs, Pleione, were nymphs of Diana's train, and they still fly before Orion in the heavens.

Pomona (Ro.)--A beautiful Hamadryad, guardian of fruit groves, especially apple orchards. She spurned all of Pan's offers of love, as well as those of other Fauns and Satyrs. Vertumnus finally won her.

NYMPHS (cont.)

Protesilaüs (Gr.)--An admirable Greek, slain by Hector. The nymphs planted elm trees around his grave, which flourished only until they were high enough to command a view of Troy.

Salmacis (Gr.)--A nymph of a fountain in ancient Caria. Its waters were supposed to render effeminate all who drank them.

Styx (Gr.)--A nymph of the river Styx of the Lower World; the daughter of Oceanus and Tethys.

Syrinx (Gr.)--A nymph of whom Pan tried to press his love. *See* Pan.

Uranus (Gr.)--From his blood sprang the Furies, the Giants and the Melic nymphs.

O

OATHS

Styx (Gr.)--It was by this nymph of the Lower World that the most solemn oaths were sworn.

OBLIVION

Elysian Fields (Gr.)--The souls of the guiltless were sent here. In the Fields flowed the River Lethe, from which the souls of those who were to return to earth in other bodies drank oblivion of their former lives.

Lethe (Gr.)--A river in Hades, a drink of which brought forgetfulness of the past.

OCEAN *See also* SEA

Callirrhoë (Gr.)--An ocean nymph; wife of Chrysaor.

Callisto (Gr.)--A nymph attendant upon Artemis. She was changed into a bear by Juno, and Jupiter placed her and her son, Arcas, in

Callisto (cont.)--the heavens as the Great and Little Bears. The gods of the ocean, Tethys and Oceanus, did not allow the two into their waters; consequently, the Bear constellations move around the pole, but never sink beneath the ocean as do the other stars.

Eos (Gr.); Aurora (Ro.)--Goddess of the Morn. Saffron-robed, she rises from the Ocean to bring light to gods and men.

Glaucus (Gr.)--One of the lesser powers of the Ocean.

Oceanides (Gr.)--These were the offspring of Oceanus and his sister-wife Tethys. Nymphs of the ocean, they were 3000 in number.

Tethys (Gr.)--Married to her brother, Oceanus, she lived with him in their palace in the remote west beyond the sea.

OFFSPRING

Abas (Gr.)--Son of Hypermnestra and Lynceus, from whom sprang the royal house of Argos.

Acis (Gr.)--Son of Faunus and a Naiad. Killed by the Cyclops Polyphemous.

Actaeon (Gr.)--Son of Autonoë and Aristaeus, who was transformed into a stag by Diana.

Adonis (Gr.)--Son of Cinyras and Myrrha, a young shepherd with whom Aphrodite fell in love. He was killed by a wild boar.

Aeacus (Gr.)--Son of Jupiter and the nymph, Aegina; famed for his justice on earth.

Aeneas (Gr.)--A Trojan prince; son of Aphrodite and Anchises.

Aepytus (Gr.)--Third son of Merope and Cresphontes.

Aërope (Gr.)--Daughter of Cepheus.

Agamemnon (Gr.)--Son of Aërope and Atreus.

OFFSPRING (cont.)

Aglauros (Gr.)--Daughter of Cecrops; personification of the dew.

Ajax the Less (Gr.)–Son of Oileus.

Alcides (Gr.); Hercules (Ro.)--Son of Alcmene and Jupiter, although Alcmene was married to Alcaeus.

Aloadae (Gr.)--They were Otus and Ephialtes, sons of Iphimedia and Neptune.

Aloeus (Gr.)--Son of Canace and Poseidon.

Alphenor (Gr.)--Son of Niobe and Amphion.

Amphiaraüs (Gr.)--Son of Oicles and Hypermnesta; a soothsayer.

Amphion (Gr.)--Son of Antiope and Jupiter.

Amphitrion (Gr.)--Daughter of Alcaeus.

Andromeda (Gr.)--Daughter of Cassiopeia and Cepheus; she was rescued from a sea-monster by Perseus.

Antaeus (Gr.)--Sone of Gaea and Neptune.

Antigone (Gr.)--Faithful daughter of Jocasta and Oedipus. She was buried alive.

APOLLO (Gr.)--His numerous offspring:
Aesculapias--by Princess Coronis.
Aristaeus--by Cyrene.
Heliades--by Clymene.
Linus--by Psamanthe.
Orpheus--by Calliope.
Phaëton--by Clymene.

Ariadne (Gr.)--Daughter of Pasiphaë and King Minos II. She led Theseus out of the labyrinth by a thread.

Astyanax (Gr.)–Young son of Andromache and Hector.

OFFSPRING (cont.)

Atalanta (Gr.)--Daughter of Schoeneus.

Ate (Gr.)--Daughter of Zeus.

Athena (Gr.); Minerva (Ro.)--The virgin goddess, who sprang from the brain of Jove agleam with the paraphenalia of war.

ATLAS (Gr.)--Son of Clymene and Iapetus. *His offspring include:*
Arethusa--a daughter.
Hesperides, The--Nymphs by his third wife, Hesperis.
Hyades, The--Nymphs by his second wife, Aethra.
Maia--Daughter by his fourth wife, Sterope I.
Pleides, The--Nymphs by his first wife, Pleione.

Atreus (Gr.)--Son of Hippodamia and Pelops. He became King of Mycena.

Atreidae (Atrides (Gr.)--Sons, Agamemnon and Menelaus, of Atreus.

Bellerophon (Gr.)--Son of Glaucus, King of Corinth.

Boreas (Gr.)--Son of Aeolus.

Cadmus (Gr.)--Son of Agenor, of Phoenicia.

Calaïs (Gr.)--Son of Orithyia and Boreas.

Calliope (Gr.)--*See* Muses.

Camilla (Gr.)--Daughter of Metabus.

Castor (Gr.)--Son of Leda and Tyndareus, King of Sparta. *See* Jupiter, for Castor's twin brother, Pollux.

Cereberus (Gr.)--Son of Echidna and Typhon.

Ceres (Ro.); Demeter (Gr.)--Daughter of Rhea and Cronus.

Ceto (Gr.)--Married to Phorcys; their offspring were the Gorgons, the Graea, the Sirens and Scylla.

Chloris (Gr.); Flora (Ro.)--Daughter of Niobe and Amphion.

Chrysippus (Gr.)--Son of Hippodamia and Pelops. Brother of Atreus and Thyestes.

Clymene (Gr.)--Daughter of Minyas.

Clytemnestra (Gr.)--Daughter of Leda and Tyrndareus.

Cronus (Gr.); Saturn (Ro.)--A Titan; son of Gaea and Uranus.

Cupid (Ro.); Eros (Gr.)--Son of Venus (Ro.); Aphrodite (Gr.), and Mars (Ro.); Ares (Gr.).

Cyclopes (Gr.)--Sons of Gaea and Uranus.

Danaë (Gr.)--Daughter of Acrisius.

Danaides (Gr.)--The fifty daughters of Danaüs.

Daphne (Gr.)--Daughter of the river-god, Peneüs.

Därdanus (Gr.)--Son of Electra and Zeus the true founder of the Trojan Race.

Demophoön (Gr.)--Son of Theseus and Phaedra.

Deucalion (Gr.)--Son of Prometheus.

Diomede (Gr.)--Son of Tydeus.

Electra (Gr.)--Daughter of Clytemnestra and Agamemnon.

Electryon (Gr.)--Son of Andromeda and Perseus.

Epaphus (Gr.)--Son of Io and Zeus.

Erechtheus (Gr.)--Son of Gaea and Hephaestus; inventor of the four-wheeled chariot.

Eros (Gr.)-- *See* Cupid.

OFFSPRING (cont.)

Erysichthon (Gr.)--Son of Cecrops.

Etocles (Gr.)--Faithless son of Jocasta and Oedipus.

Galatea (Gr.)--Daughter of Doris and the sea-god, Nereus.

Geryon (Gr.)--Son of Callirrhoë and Chrysaor. He was a monster.

Graeae, The (Gr.)--Three daughters of Ceto, and the sea deity, Phorcys.

Hades (Gr.)--Son of Rhea and Cronus.

Harmonia (Gr.)--Daughter of Aphrodite and Mars.

Harpies (Gr.)--Offspring of Thaumas; goddesses of storm and death.

Hector (Gr.)--Noblest son of Hecuba and Priam.

Helen (Gr.)--Daughter of Tyndareus.

Helenus (Gr.)--Son of Hecuba and Priam.

Helle (Gr.)--Daughter of Nephele and Athamas.

Hellen (Gr.)--Son of Pyrrha and Deucalion of Thessaly.

Hephaestus (Gr.); Vulcan (Ro.)--Son of Hera and Zeus.

Hercules (Ro.)-- *See* Jupiter.

Hermaphroditus (Gr.)--Son of Aphrodite and Hermes.

Hermes (Gr.); Mercury (Ro.)--Son of Maia and Zeus.

Hermione (Gr.)--Daughter of Helen and Menelaüs.

Herse (Gr.)--Daughter of Cecrops. Personification of the dew.

Hesione (Gr.)--Daughter of Hecuba and Laomedon.

Hesperides (Gr.)--Four nymph daughters of Hesperis and Atlas.

OFFSPRING (cont.)

Hestia (Gr.); Vesta (Ro.)--First-born child of Rhea and Cronus.

Hippodamia (Gr.)--Daughter of Oenomaüs, king of Elis.

Hippolytus (Gr.)--Son of Antiope (Hippolyta), Queen of the Amazons, and Theseus.

Hymen (Gr.)--Son of Venus and Bacchus; the god of marriage.

Iacchus (Gr.)-- *See* Bacchus under Jupiter.

Icarus (Gr.)--Son of Daedalus, the artificer.

Iloneus (Gr.)--Son of Niobe and Amphion. Killed by Apollo.

Inachus (Gr.)--Son of Tethys and her brother, Oceanus.

Ino (Gr.)--Daughter of Cadmus.

Iole (Gr.)--Daughter of King Eurytus of Oechalus.

Iphigenia (Gr.)--Daughter of Clytemnestra and Agamemnon.

Ismenos (Gr.)-- *Same as* Iloneus.

Itylus (Gr.)--Son of Procne and Tereus, King of Thrace.

Iulus (Ro.)--Son of Lavinia and Aeneas; founder of Alba Longa, the cradle of Rome.

Jocasta (Gr.)--Married her son, Oedipus.

JUNO (Ro.); Hera (Gr.)--Daughter of Rhea and Cronus. Brought up by Tethys and Oceanus.

JUPITER (Ro.); Jove (Ro.); Zeus (Gr.)--*His many offspring by his various loves:*
Aeacus--by Aegina.
Aglaia (One of three Graces)--by Eurynome.
Amphion--by Antiope.

OFFSPRING (cont.)

JUPITER (cont.)--offspring:

Aphrodite--by Dione.
Apollo--by Latona.
Arcas--by Callisto.
Ares--by his wife, Juno.
Artemis--by Latona.
Athena--by Metis.
Bacchus--by Semele.
Charites--by Eurynome. Same as the Three Graces.
Dardanus--by Electra.
Diana--by Latona. Same as Artemis.
Epaphus--by Io.
Euphrosyne (One of the Three Graces---by Eurynome.
Fortuna--First-born daughter of Jupiter.
Hebe--by Hera.
Helen--by Leda.
Hercules--by Alcmene.
Horae (goddesses of the hours, seasons)--by Themis.
Mars (Ares)--by Juno.
Mercury--by Maia.
Minos--by Europa.
Muses, The Nine--by Mnemosyne.
Pelasgus--by Niobe.
Perseus--by Danaë.
Phoebus (Apollo)--by Latona.
Pollux--by Leda.
Proserpina--by Ceres.
Prometheus--by Themis.
Rhadamanthus--by Europa.
Sarpedon--by Europa.
Sarpedon (another)--by Laodamia.
Thalia--by Eurynome' (One of the Three Graces.)
Venus--by Dione.
Vulcan--by Juno.
Zethus--by Antiope.

Kronos (Gr.)--Son of Gaea and Uranus

Labdacus (Gr.)--Son of Polydorus.

OFFSPRING (cont.)

Laïus (Gr.)--Son of Labdacus.

Lampetia (Gr.)--Daugther of Helios.

Linus (Gr.)--Handsome son of Psamanthe and Apollo; a legendary musician.

Laodice (Gr.)--Daughter of Clytemnestra and Agamemnon.

Lucifer (Ro.); Phospher (Gr.)--Son of Aurora and Cephalus; the morning star.

Maia (Gr.)--Daughter of Sterope.

Mars (Ro.); Ares (Gr.)--Son of Juno and Jupiter.

Medea (Gr.)--Daughter of Hecate and Aeëtes, King of Colchis. She was a sorceress.

Medusa (Gr.)--One of the three Gorgons (with Euryale and Stheno); daughters of Ceto and Phorcys.

Meleager (Gr.)--A hero, son of Queen Althaea and King Oeneus, of Calydon.

Memnon (Gr.)--Son of Eos (Aurora) and King Tithonus, of Aethiopia.

Menelaüs (Gr.)--Son of Aërope and Atreus. The cause of the Trojan War was when Paris came to Greece and made love to Menelaüs wife, Helen.

Mercury (Ro.); Hermes (Gr.)--Son of Maia and Jupiter.

Merope (Gr.)--Daughter of Oenopion.

Metis (Gr.)--Daughter of Tethys and Oceanus. She was the first love of Jupiter.

Minerva (Ro.); Athena (Gr.)--Daughter of Jupiter, who sprang full-grown and fully-armed from his brain.

Muses, The (Gr.)--The nine daughters of Mnemosyne (Memory) and Jupiter. They were:

Calliope--Muse of epic poetry.
Clio–Muse of History.
Erato–Muse of love poetry.
Euterpe–Muse of lyric poetry.
Melpomene--Muse of tragedy.
Polyhymnia--Muse of sacred poetry.
Terpsichore--Muse of choral dance and poetry.
Thalia--Muse of comedy.
Urania--Muse of astronomy.

Naiads (Gr. and Ro.)--Daughters of Jupiter.

Neleus (Gr.)--Son of the Princess Tyro and Neptune.

Nereids (Gr.)--The 50 daughters of Doris and Nereus.

NEPTUNE (Ro.); Poseidon (Gr.)--*Offspring of his many loves:*

Aloadae, The--by Iphimedia.
Aloeus–by Canace.
Antaeus--by Gaea.
Arion--by Ceres.
Arne--Through him Neptune became the forefather of the Boeotians.
Belus and Angenor–by Libya.
Neleus–by Princess Tyro.
Pelias–by Princess Tyro.
Procrustes
Proserpina--by Ceres.

Nereus (Gr.)--Son of Mother Earth and Pontus.

Niobe (Gr.)--Daughter of Tantalus, king of Phrygia.

Oceanides (Gr.)--The 3000 offspring of Tethys and Oceanus.

Oedipus (Gr.)--Son of Jocasta and Laïus, King of Thebes.

Oenomaüs (Gr.)--Son of Mars.

Orestes (Gr.)–Son of Clytemnestra and Agamemnon.

Orion (Gr.)–Son of Neptune.

Orithyia (Gr.)--Daugther of Erectheus.

Orpheus (Gr.)--Son of Calliope and Apollo.

Otus (Gr.)--One of two sons (with Ephialtes), of Iphimedia and Neptune.

Pan (Gr.); Faunus (Ro.)–Son of a Dryad and Mercury.

Pandion (Gr.)--Son of Erichthonius, and a special ward of Minerva, who raised him in her temple.

Pandrosos (Gr.)--Daughter of Cecrops; personification of the dew.

Panope (Gr.)--One of the fifty fair daugthers–the Nereids–of Doris and Nereus.

Paphos (Gr.)–Son of Cupid and Psyche. The city was named after him.

Paris (Gr.)--Son of Hecuba and King Priam of Troy.

Parthenopaeus (Gr.)--Son of Atlanta and Mars; an ally with Adrastus in the Seven against Thebes.

Pelasgus (Gr.)–Son of Niobe and Jupiter.

Pelias (Gr.)–Son of Tyro (Princess), and Neptune.

Pelops (Gr.)--Son of Tantalus, who was served roasted at his father's banquet table; he was restored to life by the gods.

Penelope (Gr.)–Daughter of Icarius.

Pentheus (Gr.)–Son of Agave.

Periphetes (Gr.)–A son of Vulcan.

Perseus (Gr.)--Son of Danaë and Jupiter.

Persephone (Gr.); Proserpina (Ro.)--Daughter of Ceres and Jupiter; Queen of Hades.

Phaedra (Gr.)--Daughter of Pasiphaë and Minos I.

Phaëthusa (Gr.)--Daughter of Helios, who with her sister, Lampetia, guarded their father's flock on Thrinacia.

Phaëton (Gr.)--Son of the nymph, Clymene and Apollo.

Phantasus (Gr.)--Son of Somnus.

Philoctetes (Gr.)--Son of Poeas; close friend of Hercules.

Philomela (Gr.)--Daughter of Pandion.

Phoebe (Gr.)--Mother of Latona.

Phoebus (Apolloa) (Gr.)--Son of Latona and Jupiter.

Phorcys (Gr.)--Son of Pontus.

Phoroneus (Gr.)--Son of Inachus.

Phosphor (Gr.)--Son of Aurora and the hunter, Cephalus.

Phrixus (Gr.)--Son of Nephele and Athamus.

Pierides (Gr.)--Daugthers of Pierus. Defeated in a contest with the Muses, they were changed into magpies.

Pleasure (Gr.)--The daughter born to Psyche and Cupid.

Pleiades (Gr.)--The seven daughters of Pleione and Atlas.

Pleisthenes (Gr.)--Son of Atreus.

Plutus (Gr.)--Son of Demeter and Iasion; the god of wealth.

Polites (Gr.)--Son of King Priam and Hecuba.

Pollux (Gr.)--Son of Leda and Jupiter.

Polydorus (1), (Gr.)--Only son of Harmonia and Cadmus.

Polydorus (2), (Gr.)--Son of Priam and Hecuba.

Polydorus (3), (Gr.)--Son of Hippomedon.

Polynices (Gr.)--Son of Jocasta and Oedipus.

Polyxena (Gr.)--Daughter of Hecuba and King Priam; sacrificed on the tomb of her father.

Portumnus (Ro.); Palaemon (Gr.)--Son of Leucothea; god of ports and shores.

Priam (Gr.)--Son of Laomedon; King of Troy.

Priapus (Ro.)--According to one myth, he was the son of Aphrodite and Dionysus.

Procne (Gr.)--Daughter of Pandion. Her husband, Tereus, had her tongue plucked out to insure her silence.

Procris (Gr.)--Daughter of Erechtheus.

Prometheus (Gr.)--Son of Clymene and the Titan, Iapetus. He stole fire from heaven for man.

Proserpina (Gr.)--Daughter of Ceres and Jupiter; wife of Pluto.

Pylades (Gr.)--Son of Strophius, King of Phocis.

Pyrrha (Gr.)--Daughter of Epimetheus.

Pyrrhus (Gr.)--Son of Achilles.

Rhadamanthus (Gr.)--Son of Europa and Jupiter.

Rhea (Gr.); Cybele (Gr.)--Daughter of Gaea and Uranus. Wife of Cronus, she gave birth to six gods: Demter; Hades; Hera; Hestia; Poseidon

OFFSPRING (cont.)

Rhea (cont.)--and Zeus.

Rhea Silvia (Ro.)--Daughter of Numitor, King of Alba Longa.

Sarpedon (1), (Gr.)--Son of Europa and Jupiter.

Sarpedon (2), (Gr.)--Son of Laodamia and Jupiter.

Scylla (Gr.)--A fair virgin, daugther of the sea-god, Phorcys.

Semele (Gr.)--Daughter of Cadmus, King of Thebes.

Silenus (Gr.)--Son of a nymph and Pan. He became the oldest of the Satyrs.

Silvia (Gr.)--Daughter of Tyrrheus, the king's herdsman.

Sleep (Somnus), (Gr.)--The son of Night, who lived in subterranean darkness.

Stheneboea (Gr.)--Daughter of Iobates.

Styx (Gr.)--Daughter of Tethys and Oceanus.

Telamon (Gr.)--Son of Aeacus, King of Aegina.

Telemachus (Gr.)--Son of Penelope and Ulysses.

Telephus (Gr.)--Son of Auge and Hercules.

Teucer (Gr.)--Son of Hesione and Telamon. or (b)--He was the son of the nymph Idaea and the river-god Scamander.

Thalia (Gr.)--Daughter of Eurynome and Jupiter.

Thanatos (Gr.)--Son of Night.

Thaumas (Gr.)--Son of Gaea and Pontus.

Themis (Gr.)--Daughter of Uranus.

Thersander (Gr.)--Son of Polynices.

Theseus (Gr.)--Son of Aethra and Aegeus, King. One of the older heroes.

Thetis (Gr.)--One of the most famous of the fifty daugthers of Doris and Nereus.

Thyestes (Gr.)--Son of Pelops.

Tisiphone (Gr.)--One of the three Furies, who sprang from the blood of Uranus.

Tithonus (Gr.)--Son of Laomedon, King of Troy.

Triton (Gr.)--Son of Amphitrite and Neptune.

Troilus (Gr.)--Son of Hecuba and King Priam.

Tros (Gr.)--Son of Erichthonius, in the royal line of Troy.

Typhon (Gr.)--Son of Gaea.

Ulysses (Gr.)--Son of Anticlea and Laërtes.

Venus (Ro.); Aphrodite (Gr.)--Daughter of Dione and Jupiter.

Vesta (Ro.); Hestia (Gr.)--One of the three daughters (with Ceres and Juno), of Rhea and Cronus.

Victoria (Ro.); Nike (Gr.)--Daughter of Styx and the Titan Pallas. Goddess of victory.

Vulcan (Ro.); Hephaestus (Gr.)--Son of Juno and Jupiter.

Xuthus (Gr.)--Son of Pyrrha and Deucalion.

Zetes (Gr.)--Son of the north wind, Boreas, and Orithyia.

Zethus (Gr.)--Son of Antiope and Jupiter.

OLIVE

Aristaeus (Gr.)--An Arcadian deity; protector of vine and olive.

Minerva (Ro.); Athena (Gr.)–A virgin goddess, of horticulture and agriculture. The olive tree, created by her, was sacred to her.

OLYMPUS

Diomede (Gr.)--During the Trojan War, Venus tried to rescue her son, Aeneas, but Diomede grazed her palm with his spear, causing her to lose ichor, that life-stream of the gods, and forcing her to return to Olympus.

Hestia (Gr.); Vesta (Ro.)--She scorned the flattering advances of both Neptune and Apollo, and chose to remain an old maid. Zeus granted her a place in his palace, to receive the choicest morsels of the feast in Olympus, and to accept reverence as the oldest and worthiest Olympian divity.

Horae (Gr.)--Goddesses of the hours and seasons, who took charge of the gate of clouds at Olympus, which they opened to permit the passage of Celestials going to and returning from the earth.

Olympus (Gr.)--The heaven of the Greek golds was the summit of an ideal mountain called Olympus.

Pan (Gr.); Faunus (Ro.)--When the birth of Christ was announced to the shepherds, a groan heard through Greece told that Pan was dead, that the dynasty of Olympus was dethroned, and the several deities were to be sent wandering through the cold and darkness.

Saturn (Ro.); Cronus (Gr.)--He had been expelled from Olympus by his sons; had come to the site of the future Rome, formed a society and given them laws. Men called his reign the Golden Age.

Zeus (Gr.); Jupiter (Ro.)–His palace was at the summit of the Olympus mountain.

ORACLE

Acrisius (Gr.)-- *See* Perseus.

Apollo (Gr.)--At Apollo's oracle in Delphi men tried for centuries to seek help from him through his priestess, Pythia.

Asclepius (Gr.); Aesculapius (Ro.)--God of medicine. His worship was introduced in Rome about 293 B. C., in response to an oracle who was promising relief from the plague.

Cadmus (Gr.)--The oracle of Apollo told him to follow a cow, and when she stopped, to build a city on the spot and call it Thebes.

Danaë (Gr.)--An oracle prophesied that her son would cause the death of his grandfather, Acrisius.

Erechtheus (Gr.)--In obedience to an oracle, he sacrificed his youngest daughter, Procris, to save Athens.

Laïus (Gr.)--Being warned by an oracle that he would be killed by his son, he sent the new-born boy, Oedipus, to die in the mountains.

Oedipus (Gr.)--He was also warned that he would cause the death of his father. After he reached his majority, his chariot met another in a narrow pass. In a fight which ensued, Oedipus killed both the charioteer and Laïus, thus unkowingly fulfilling two prophecies.

Oracles (Gr. and Ro.)--These were the mediums through whom the gods revealed hidden knowledge. The most famous oracle of the ancient world was the one at Delphi. Sometimes the Greeks communicated with the ghosts of Hades, through certain oracles of the dead.

Perseus (Gr.)--After an aracle told his grandfather, Acrisius, that he would be killed by this boy, it so happened at an athletic contest when a discus bounded the wrong way.

Phoebe (Gr.)--She bequeathed the Delphic oracle to her grandson, Apollo. (Phoebus)

Phoebus (Gr.)--Through his oracle at Delphi, he told the future of those who consulted him.

ORACLE (cont.)

Psyche (Gr.)--An oracle had told her parents that she was destined to marry no mortal. She became the bride of Cupid, the god of love.

Tityus (Gr.)--He was a giant who not only obstructed the peaceful way to the oracle of Delphi, but insulted the goddess Latona, mother of Apollo and Diana.

OREADS

Echo (Gr.)--Was a beautiful Oread, fond of the woods and hills, and a favorite of Diana.

Oreads (Gr.)--These were nymphs of mountains, hills, and grottoes. Like the Naiads, nymphs of fresh water, and the Dryads, wood-nymphs, they were immortal.

ORGIES

Bechantes (Gr.)--These were women worshipers of Bacchus, who, filled with religious frenzy, followed in his train and indulged in wild orgies.

Cybele (Ro.)--Mother of the gods. She haunted mountain and forest fastnesses, accompanied by a retinue of wild attendants--the Curetes and Dactyls--who celebrated with orgiastic rites and revelries in honor of her and her god lover, Attis.

Pentheus (Gr.)--Annoyed by noise of an orgy, he plunged into the woods to stop it. Some women there mistook him for a wild boar, rushed him and tore him to pieces.

ORNAMENTS

Argus (Gr.)--This 100-eyed creature had been sent by Juno to guard Io (transformed into a heifer), because Io had been a rival for Jupiter. Mercury was sent to set Io free by slaying the monster. Juno took the 100 eyes and scattered them as ornaments on the tail of her peacock, where they remain to this day.

OUTCASTS

Oedipus (Gr.)--He was cast out by his father, Laïus, to be raised by shepherds.

Vulcan (Ro.)--Because he was born lame, his mother, Juno, chagrined by his deformity, cast him from Heaven out of sight of the gods.

OWL

Aloadae (Gr.)--Because they--Otus and Ephialtes--tried to dethrone the immortals, Jupiter killed them with his lightning, and made them atone in Hades by being bound to a pillar with serpents, and tormented by the perpetual hooting of a screech owl.

OXEN

Augeas (Gr.)--King of Elis, who owned a herd of 3000 oxen, whose stalls had not been cleaned out in thirty years. It was the sixth Labor of Hercules to purify these stables in one day.

Eurytion (Gr.)--A giant who, with his two-headed dog, guarded the oxen of Geryon.

Geryon (Gr.)--He was a monster, and rich. He owned thousands of red oxen on Erythea Island, and had them guarded by the giant, Eurytion, and his two-headed dog.

Hercules (Ro.)--Beside his sixth Labor, to clean the stalls of King Augeas's 3000 oxen, his tenth task was to steal the red oxen of Geryon. In order to do so, he had to kill the giant, Eurytion, and his two-headed dog.

P

PAGANISM

Pan (Gr.)--His name seemed to signify all, and it came to be a symbol of the universe, and a personification of nature, as well as representa-

PAGANISM (cont.)

Pan (cont.)--tive of all the Greek gods and of paganism itself.

PALENESS

Adrastus (Gr.)--Witnessing the deaths of his sons-in-law caused him to become permanently pale.

Electra (Gr.)–Left her sisters, the Pleiades, in order not to witness the ruin of Troy. She became a comet. The sight had such an effect on her sisters that they blanched and have been pale ever since.

Harpies, The (Gr.)--Foul creatures whose faces were always pale with hunger.

PALLADIUM

Diomede (Gr.)--He and his friend, Ulysses, entered Troy and carried off the Palladium to Greece.

Palladium (Gr.)--This was the celebrated statue of Minerva, called the Palladium. It was believed to have fallen from heaven, and that the city of Troy could not be taken as long as this statue remained in it.

PANIC

Pan (Gr.); Faunus (Ro.)--Like other gods of the forest, he was dreaded by those who had to pass through the woods at night, for the gloom and loneliness oppressed them and sometimes caused sudden, unreasonable fright, ascribed to Pan, and called panic terror.

Phobos (Gr.)–A goddess who personified panic fear, whichi sometimes puts armies to flight.

PAPYRUS

Clio (Gr.)-- *See same under* MUSES.

PARENTAGE

Oedipus (Gr.)–He was raised by King Polybus and the queen, without knowing his true parents, Laïus and Jocasta.

Phaëton (Gr.)--Son of the nymph Clymene and Apollo. When his friends scoffed at the idea of his being the son of a god, he went directly to Apollo to ask whether he had been truly informed of his parentage.

PASSION

Pasiphaë (Gr.)–The wife of King Minos II, whom Neptune for spite drove into a passion for the Cretan Bull. In consequence, she gave birth to the Minotaur.

PAST

Lethe (Gr.)--A river in Hades, a drink of which brought forgetfulness of the past.

PASTORAL

Arcadia (Gr.)--A mountainous, picturesque district in Greece. Celebrated as the abode of a happy, pastoral people.

Faunus (Ro.)--Patron of the secret lore of nature. His pastoral character became identical, under Greek influence, with that of Pan.

PATRIOT

Hector (Gr.)--A hero at the siege of Troy.

Troilus (Gr.)--A patriot like his brother, Hector, and persistent in the face of overwhelming odds.

PATRON

Diana (Ro.); Artemis (Gr.)–Patroness of temperance.

PATRON (cont.)

Ergane (Gr.)--Patroness of the arts, especially weaving.

Gemini (Gr.)--These were Castor and Pollux; horsemen and patrons of games and equestrian exercises.

Mercury (Ro.); Hermes (Gr.)--Although he was a patron of gamblers and a god of chance, he was also the furtherer of lawful industry.

Neptune (Ro.); Poseidon (Gr.)--He created the horse and was the patron of horse races.

Orthia (Gr.); Diana (Ro.)--Patroness of temperance in all things, and guardian of civil rights.

Phoebus (Apollo) (Gr.)--A patron of music and poetry.

Vulcan (Ro.); Hephaestus (Gr.)--The god of fire; founder of wise customs and the patron of artificers.

PATRONYM *See also* EPITHET; NAME

Aecides (Gr.)--The patronym given Achilles, since he was the grandson of Aeacus.

Alcides (Gr.)--Patronym given Hercules, as son of Alcaeus.

Aloadae (Gr.)--Two sons, (Otus and Ephialtes) of Iphimedia and Neptune; named after Iphimedia's mortal husband, Aloeus.

Atrides (Gr.)--Patronym given Agamemnon and Menelaüs, as sons of Atreus.

Dioscuri (Gr.)--Sons of Jove (Castor and Pollus).

Lycius (Gr.)--Another name given Apollo; the wolf-god.

Minoïd (Gr.)--Patronym given Ariadne, daughter of King Minos.

Moerae (Gr.)--The Fates.

PATRONYM (cont.)

Moeragetes (Gr.)--Zeus, leader of the Fates.

Musagetes (Gr.)--Name of Apollo as leader of the Muses.

Nereids (Gr.)--The fifty mermaid daughters of Doris and Nereus.

Parcae (Ro.)–The Fates, corresponding to the three Moerae of the Greeks.

Pelides (Gr.)–Patronym of Achilles, being the son of Peleus, by Thetis.

Poenae (Gr.)--A title used sometimes for the Furies.

Scamandrius (Gr.)--A name used by Hector for his son, Astyanax.

Semnae (Gr.)--The three Furies.

Teucri (Gr.)--The Trojans, so named from Teucer, the first king of Troy.

Tydides (Gr.)--Patronym for Diomede, as the son of Tydeus.

Tyndaridae (Gr.)–Patronym of Castor and Pollus; as sons of Tyndareus.

Tyndaris (Gr.)--Patronymic given Helen and Clytemnestra, daughters of Tyndareus.

PEACE

Bacchus (Gr.)–A lawgiver and lover of peace.

Phoebus (Apollo) (Gr.)–Although he was a god of life and peace, he did not shun the weapons of war.

PEASANT

Baucis (Gr.)--An old Phrygian peasant women. *See same under* LAKE.

Dyrads (Gr.)--Wood-nymphs, who at times assumed the forms of peasant girls, or shepherdesses.

PENANCE

Cadmus (Gr.)--For killing a dragon sacred to Mars, he had to serve penance to this god for eight years.

Hippomenes (Gr.)--Venus helped him to win Atalanta for his wife. When the couple forgot to pay due honor to Venus, she had Cybele transform them into lions to pull this goddess's chariot wherever she wished to go.

Tantalus (Gr.)--He ridiculed the omnisciene of the gods, and for this he was doomed to stand in a pool of water, but parched with thirst. Trees of fruit above his head were whirled away when he tried to seize them.

PERFECTION

Pandora (Gr.)--She was beautiful, and the first woman endowed by immortals with heavenly graces. Every god and goddess contributed something to her perfection: one gave her beauty, another persuasive charm, a third the talent for music, etc., then named her Pandora, "the gift of the gods."

PERJURY

Furies, The (Gr.)--Often they visited earth to punish murder, treachery and perjury, among other duties.

PERSECUTORS

Furies, The (Gr.)--They were sometimes called Erinnyes, the persecutors.

Ino (Gr.)--Her husband, Athamas, so persecuted her that she jumped from a cliff into the sea.

Latona (Ro.)-- *See same under* WANDERING.

PERSONATION *See also* PERSONIFICATION

Icelus (Gr.)--Son of Somnus; producer of dreams. He personated birds, beasts and serpents.

Morpheus (Gr.)--An expert in making himself into the counterfeit forms of man.

Phantasus (Gr.)-- *See same under* ROCK.

PERSONIFICATION *See also* PERSONATION

Adonis (Gr.)--He personified spring-time.

Aether (Gr.)--A personification of the sky.

Aglauros (Gr.)--With her sisters, Herse and Pandrosos, personifications of the dew.

Charis (Aglaia) (Gr.)--Youngest of the three Graces; the personification of grace and beauty.

Deimos (Gr.)--Son of Mars; the personification of terror, or dread.

Dike (Gr.)--Personification of justice.

Doris (Gr.)--A sea-goddess , often a personification of the sea.

Harpies, The (Gr.)--Goddesses of storm and death; originally, they were the personifications of devasting winds.

Hebe (Gr.)--Cupbearer of the gods; she was youth personified as a goddess.

Himeros (Gr.)--Personification of tender desire.

Hyacinthus (Gr.)--The personification of blooming vegetation of spring, which withers under the heat of summer.

Hygeia (Gr.)--The personification of health.

Hymen (Gr.)--Leader of the nuptial chorus, and personification of the

PERSONIFICATION (cont.)

Hymne (cont.)--wedding feast. The god of marriage.

Nemesis (Gr.)--An ancient goddess, who personified retributive justice.

Pan (Gr.); Faunus (Ro.)--Considered to be a symbol of the universe, and a personification of nature.

Priapus (Ro.)--The male generative power personified as a god.

Proteus (Gr.)-- *See* BEAST.

Titans, The (Gr.)--They were the personification of mighty convulsions of the physical world, of volcanic eruptions and earthquakes.

Uranus (Gr.)--The personified Heaven, took Gaea, the Earth, for his wife.

Victoria (Ro.)--Goddess of victory; personified with wings, and carrying a wreath and palm branch.

PESTILENCE

Chryseïs (Gr.)--She was captured by the Greeks. When the Greek general, Agamemnon, refused to return her for ransom, he offended Apollo, who sent a pestilence upon the Greeks as punishment.

PETRIFIED *See also* ROCK; STONE

Atlas (Gr.)-- *See same under* MOUNTAIN.

Battus (Gr.)--He violated a secrecy he had promised Mercury, and was petrified by the offended deity.

Scylla (Gr.)--Through jealousy, she was changed by Circe into a monster, to infest the shore of Sicily and work evil to mariners, until she was petrified as a reef, not less perilous to seafarers.

PHYSICIAN *See also* MEDICINE

Paean (Gr.)--The family physician of the gods. He healed one of the wounds of Mars.

PILOT *See also* SHIP

Acetes (Gr.)--A fisherman who acquired the pilot's art of steering by the stars. He piloted the ship which carried Bacchus to Naxos.

Palinurus (Gr.)--He was the pilot of the ship in which Aeneas encountered many adventures on his way to Italy.

Ulysses (Gr.) During his ten years of wandering between Troy and Ithaca, he, himself piloted one of his several ships. The pilot on one of the other ships was killed by lightning.

PIPES *See* Io; Pan; *under* MUSIC

PLACES *See also* CITIES; RESIDENCE

Aegina (Gr.)--An island southwest of Athens, where Aeacus had been the righteous king.

Aeolia (Gr.)--King Aeolus.

Arcadia (Gr.)--A mountainous district of Greece inhabited by pastoral people. The god Mercury was born in a cave of Mt. Cyllene in Arcadia. Hercules captured a fierce boar which had haunted Mt. Erymanthus. Apollo spent some of his younger years as a herdsman here.

Athens (Gr.)--King Aegeus; Theseus.

Calydon (Gr.)--In Aetolia, ruled by King Oeneus and Queen Althaea. Diana sent an enormous boar here to lay waste to the fields.

Chios (Gr.)--Its king, Oenopion. Phaon ferried a boat between Chios and Lesbos.

Colchis (Gr.)--Ruled by King Aeëtes, keeper of the Golden Fleece.

PLACES (cont.)

Corinth (Gr.)--Creusa, a princess of.

Crete (Gr.)--Ruled by Minos I; later Minos II.

Cumae (Ro.)--Here in Italy, in a deep cavern, lived a young prophetess, known as the Cumaean Sibyl.

Delphi (Gr.)--Here the most famous oracle of the ancient world revealed hidden knowledge. She held forth on the slopes of Parnassus in Phocis.

Dodona (Gr.)--The prophecies and will of Jupiter were made known by the oracle here, the most ancient in Greece.

Edones (Gr.)--Their King was Lycurgus, who resisted the worhip of Bacchus.

Elis (Gr.)--The land of King Augeas, who owned a herd of 3000 oxen. A later King of Elis was Oenomaüs.

Erebus (Gr.)--A place of nether darkness through which souls passed on the way to Hades.

Euboea (Gr.)--The home of Neptune, near the Greek coast.

Isle of Lemnos (Gr.)--Philoctetes was taken here to recover from a wound accidently caused by one of Hercules' poisoned arrows.

Ithaca (Gr.)--Ulysses' own kingdom.

Laconia (Gr.)--Apollo tended herds here.

Lerna, The Marsh of (Gr.)--Where Hercules destroyed the water-serpent, Hydra.

Libethra (Gr.)--Orpheus was buried here.

Lydia (Gr.)--The domain of Omphale. Hercules spent three years here spinning wool to expiate his crime of killing his friend, Ephitus. The first King of Lydia was Gyges.

225

Marathon, Plain of (Gr.)--From where Pirithoüs tried to take away the herds of Theseus, King of Athens.

Marathon (Gr.)--Hercules rode the Cretan Bull through the waves to Marathon, Greece.

Media (Gr.)--A country in Asia, named after the sorceress, Medea.

Messenia (Gr.)--Polyphontes was the leader of a revolt against Cresphontes, King of Messenia. Aphareus was also a king.

Megara (Gr.)--King Nisus, father of Scylla, who betrayed him to his enemy, Minos II, of Crete.

Mt. Oeta (Gr.)--After he had been poisoned, Hercules was taken here to die.

Mycenae (Gr.)--This is where Hercules brought the golden-horned Cerynean doe.

Naxos (Gr.)--A place haunted by Bacchus.

Nemea, Valley of (Gr.)--Infested by a lion, which Hercules strangled with his hands.

Olympus, Mt. (Gr.)--Its summit was the heaven of the Greek gods.

Orchomensis (Gr.)--A city won by Amphitryon, King of Thebes.

Orchomenus in Boeotia (Gr.)--King Minyas.

Ossa, Mt. (Gr.)--Two giants, Otus and Ephialtes, tried to attack the Olympians by piling Mt. Ossa on Mt. Pelion, and Pelion on Mt. Olympus.

Othyrs (Gr.)--A mountain in Thessaly.

Oxygia (Gr.)--An island where the sea-nymph, Calypso, kept Ulysses for seven years.

Peloponnesus (Gr.)--The southern peninsula of Greece.

Phrygia (Gr.)--Some of its kings were: Bacchus; Midas; Tantalus.

Pylos (Gr.)--The young hunter and Argonaut, Nestor, became King of Pylos.

Scheria (Gr.)--Nausithoüs, King of the Phaeacians, who, after being oppressed by that savage race, the Cyclopes, migrated with his people to the isle of Scheria. Later, he turned the throne over to his son, Alcinoüs.

Scyros (Gr.)--Achilles' mother sent him to the court of King Lycomedes in Scyros, to save him from taking part in the Trojan War. When Ulysses came along, he persuaded Achilles to join his countrymen.

Sicily (Gr.)--King Acestes gave Aeneas a hospitable reception here. Cocalis was also a King of Sicily. One of his daughters scalded Minos II to death here.

Sicyon (Gr.)--The king was Epopeus, with whom Antiope found refuge. This is where the gods were in dispute.

Sparta (Gr.)--When Paris came to Greece, he was received hospitably by King Menelaüs. But when he eloped with Helen, Menelaüs wife, this was the cause of the Trojan War. Later, Paris died of wounds at Troy, and Helen returned to Menelaüs at Sparta, where they resumed their royal splendor.

Taenarus (Gr.)--A cave on the side of this promontory, was the entrance to Hades.

Taurus (Gr.)--The goddess, Artemis, carried Iphigenia to Taurus, where she made her a priestess.

Thebes (Gr.)--This was the birthplace of Hercules. Some of its kings were: Amphion; Amphitryon; Cadmus; Labdacus; Laïus; Lycus; Nycteus.

Thessaly (Gr.)--Ceyx was King of Trachis in Thessaly; and Deucalion. *See also* Labithae *under* CENTAUR.

Thrace (Gr.)--King Diomedes possessed two swift and fearful horses which fed on human flesh. The Thracian maidens tried to captivate

Thrace (cont.)--Orpheus, but his music repulsed them. Finally, they tore him limb from limb. One of the Kings of Thrace was Tereus.

Thrachis (Gr.)-- *See* Thessaly.

Thrinacia (Gr.)—An island where Helios pastured his cattle. Ulysses' men killed some of them for food.

Troy (Gr.)--King of Priam was a wise ruler.

PLAGUE

Aegina (Gr.)—Because Juno was jealous of her, the goddess devastated the island of Aegina with a plague.

Apollo (Gr.)--God of the sun; the stayer of plagues.

Asclepius (Gr.); Aesculapius (Ro.)--His worhip began around 294 B.C., after a plague.

Auge (Gr.)--When a plague afflicted the land (Arcadia), she and her baby, Telephus, were condemned to death, but Hercules rescued the child, and after he had grown to manhood, he found his mother in Mysia.

Pandora (Gr.)--Overcome with curiosity to see what was in the box Jupiter had given her, she lifted the lid, and a multitude of plagues for hapless man escaped.

PLANTS *See also* FLOWERS

Aphrodite (Gr.); Venus (Ro.)--Among plants, the rose, myrtle and apple, were sacred to her.

Circe (Gr.)--Before Ulysses tried to rescue his companions from Circe, Mercury provided him with a sprig of Moly plant to give him the power to resist her sorceries.

Polydorus (2) (Gr.)--He was murdered by many arrows, and from his blood a bush grew.

PLANTS (cont.)

Pyramus (Gr.)--He threw himself on his sword. His blood spurted onto white mulberries, tinging them purple. From that time on, the mulberry has produced only purple berries.

PLEASURE *See* CROSS-ROADS

PLEIADES

Pleiades (Gr.)--These were the seven daughters of Pleione and Atlas; nymphs of Diana's train that still fly before Orion in the heavens. They were Alcyone; Celaeno; Electra; Maia; Merope; Sterope; and Taygeta. Electra left the group to become a comet.

PLENTY

Plenty (Gr.); Ops (Ro.)--The goddess of Plenty; adopted the Cornucopia as her symbol.

PLUNDER

Cacus (Gr.)--A giant who lived in a cave on Mt. Aventine and plundered the countryside.

POET

Alcaeus (Gr.)--A lyric poet; father of Amphitryon.

Elysian Fields (Gr.)--Among those who abided here were Orpheus; poets, priests; heroes and those who had rendered service to mankind.

Hippocrene, The Fountain of (Gr.)--The waters of this fountain on Mt. Helicon in Boetia, Greece, were supposed to impart poetic inspiration.

Ibycus (Gr.)--A poet, beloved of Apollo. He was murdered by robbers at Corinth.

229

Maro (Ro.)--One of the great poets who made notable the age of the Roman emperor, Augustus. Born in Mantua in 70 B.C.

Sappho (Gr.)--A 7th century Greek lyric poetess of Lesbos; called the tenth Muse.

Thamyris (Gr.)--A Thracian bard, who presumed to challenge the Muses to a contest. Conquered, he was deprived of his sight.

POETRY

Apollo (Gr.)--God of the sun, of poetry and music.

Calliope (Gr.)--The Muse of epic poetry and rhetoric.

Daphnis (Gr.)--A Sicilian shepherd; reputed to be the innovator of bucolic poetry.

Erato (Gr.)--The Muse of lyric poetry and music.

Phoebus (Gr.)--Patron of poetry and music.

Phyllis (Gr.)--Served as ideal maiden for pastoral poetry.

Polyhymia (Gr.)--The Muse of sacred poetry.

POISON

Dejanira (Gr.)--She soaked her husband, Hercules' robe in the blood of the centaur Nessus, which poisoned the hero to death.

Hercules (Gr.)-- *See* Dejanira.

Lichas (Gr.)--He carried the poisoned robe from Dejanira to Hercules. After its poison had begun to penetrate his limbs, Hercules hurled Lichas into the sea.

POLITENESS

Graces, The Three (Gr.)--Graceful and beautiful goddess, inspirers of the qualities which give charm. They presided over banquets, the dance and polite accomplishments.

POPPY

Ceres (Ro.); Demeter (Gr.)--Goddess of agriculture; the poppy was sacred to her.

Demeter (Gr.); Ceres (Ro.)--Goddess of the fruitfulness of mankind; she is depicted as holding a torch, ears of corn, wheat and poppies.

Triptolemus (Gr.)--After he had been ill with a fever, Ceres restored him to health with poppy juice mixed with milk.

PORTS

Portumnus (Ro.); Palaemon (Gr.)--The Romans invoked him as god of the jurisdiction of parts and shores.

POWER

Nemesis (Gr.)--An ancient goddess, whose dark, mysterious power over-shadowed even the gods, for evil done brought divine vengeance from which there was no escape.

Neptune (Ro.); Poseidon (Ro.)--His symbol of power was the trident, with which he could shatter rocks, call forth or subdue storms, and shake the shores of earth.

PRAISE

Damocles (Gr.)--King Dionysis rebuked his constant praise of the happiness of kings. *See also* FLATTERER.

PRAYER

Minos II (Gr.)--Boasted of his power to obtain anything he wanted through prayer. After he implored Neptune to send him a bull for sacrifice, there were complications. *See also* Creatan Bull, *under* BULL.

PREDICTION

Cassandra (Gr.)--Loved by Apollo, she was given the gift of prophecy, but later, when she offended him, he made the gift ineffective by ordaining that her predictions should never be believed.

PRIDE

Bellerophon (Gr.)--Minerva gave him the winged steed, Pegasus. When by his pride, Bellerophon drew the anger of the gods, Jupiter sent a gadfly to sting Pegasus, to make him throw his rider.

PRIEST

Chryses (Gr.)--Priest of Apollo, who bore the sacred emblems of his office.

Epimenides (Gr.)--A Cretan herdsman, who awoke from a sleep of fifty-seven years to find himself endowed with the gifts of prophecy and priestcraft.

Laocoön (Gr.)--A priest of Apollo, who warned the Trojans of the treachery of the wooden horse.

Oracles (Gr. and Ro.)--The responses of the oracles were sometimes given by the rustling of oak trees in the wind, interpreted by the priests.

Penates (Ro.)--Gods of the household. Every master of a family was priest to the Penates of his own house.

PRIESTESS

Apollo (Gr.)--At his oracle in Delphi, men tried to seek help from him through his priestess, Pythia, who spoke for him to mortals.

Auge (Gr.)--An Arcadian princess; priestess of Athena.

Cydippe (Gr.)--An ancient priestess in one of Juno's shrines.

Hero (Gr.)--A priestess of Aphrodite at Sestos on the Hellespont.

Iphigenia (Gr.)--Offered by her father as a sacrifice to Artemis; but the goddess snatched Iphigenia from the altar, and carried her to Taurus, where she made her a priestess.

Orestes (Gr.)--At a temple of the Tauri in Scythia, he found that the priestess of Diana was no other than his sister, Iphigenia. They made their escape, and returned to Mycenae.

Pythia (Gr.)--Priestess of Apollo at the oracle of Delphi.

Vesta (Ro.); Hestia (Gr.)--Her temple was the oldest in Rome. Here a sacred fire was kept religiously alive by six virgin priestesses called Vestals.

PRINCE *See also* KING

Aeneas (Gr.)--A Trojan prince who fought to save Troy.

Helenus (Gr.)--A Trojan prince; son of Priam.

Icarius (Gr.)--A Spartan prince; father of Penelope.

Itylus (Gr.)--A Thracian prince; son of Tereus, King of Thebes.

PRINCESS *See also* QUEEN

Aethra (Gr.)--Daughter of King Pittheus, of Troezen.

Arachne (Gr.)--A Lydian princess who challenged Minerva to a weaving contest. The goddess tranformed her into a spider.

Ariadne (Gr.)--Daughter of Pasiphae and King Minos II of Crete. She led Theseus out of the labyrinth of Daedalus by a thread.

Arne (Gr.)--Daughter of King Aelus; a shepherdess loved by Neptune. By her he became the forefather of the Boetians.

Arsinoë (Gr.)--A Messenian name for the Thessalian Princess Coronis. She was the mother of Aesculapias by Apollo.

Auge (Gr.)--An Arcadian pricess; priestess of Athens.

Coronis (Gr.)-- See Arsinoë.

Creusa (Gr.)--A princess of Corinth.

Europa (Gr.)--Daughter of Agenor, King of Phoenicia. She was carried off by Jupiter in the form of a white bull.

Evadne (Gr.)--Daughter of Iphis, an Argive king.

Hesione (Gr.)--Daughter of Laomedon of Troy. Rescued by Hercules.

Hippodamia (Gr.)--Daughter of King Oenomaus, of Elis. She was won by Pelops in a chariot race.

Merope (Gr.)--(a) Daughter of King Cypselus of Arcadia.

Merope (Gr.)--(b) Daughter of Oenopion, King of Chios.

Phyllis (Gr.)--A Thracian princess, betrothed to Acamus, son of Theseus.

Polyxena (Gr.)--Daughter of Hecuba and King Priam of Troy; sacrificed on the tomb of her father.

Tyro (Gr.)--A princess wooed by Neptune in the form of her lover Enipeus.

PRISON

Daedalus (Gr.)--Imprisoned by King Minos, he constructed wings of

Daedalus (cont.)--feathers to fly out.

Danaë (Gr.)--She was shut in an underground chamber by her father, in order that no man might love or wed her. Jupiter distilled himself into a shower of gold to enter the girl's prison, where he wooed and won her.

Icarus (Gr.)--Son of Daedalus, the artificer, and in prison with him. When he flew out he came too near the sun, which melted the wax holding his feather wings, and he fell into the sea. Hercules discovered his body and buried it.

PROPHECY *See also* ORACLE

Acrisius (Gr.)--His death fulfilled a prophecy that he would be killed by his grandson. Perseus accidently hit him with a discus.

Carmenta (Ro.)--A water or spring goddess. Also goddess of healing and prophecy.

Cassandra (Gr.)--She was given the gift of prophecy by Apollo. *See same under* PREDICTION.

Colchas (Gr.)--A prophet who foretold the triumph of the Trojans with the wooden horse.

Egeria (Ro.)--Assoicated with Carmenta, leader of the fountain nymphs, goddesses of healing and prophecy, later identified as the Muses, who sang both the future and the past.

Epimenides (Gr.)--He awoke from a sleep of 57 years to find himself with the gift of prophecy.

Faunus (Ro.); Pan (Gr.)--A rural deity, worshiped as a god of fruitfulness and prophecy.

Helenus (Gr.)--A Trojan prince; gifted with prophecy. Son of Hecuba and Priam.

Laïus (Gr.)--His father, Oedipus, had been warned by an oracle that his

Laïus (cont.)--son, Laïus, would kill him, and he sent the new-born boy off to the mountains with a herdsman. Later, in a chariot mix-up in a narrow pass, the angry Laïus killed the offender, not knowing he was his parent.

PROPHET

Calchas (Gr.)-- *See* Colchas *under* PROPHECY. This soothsayer and prophet accompanied the Greeks during the Trojan War.

Melampus (Gr.)--He was the first Greek to be endowed with prophetic powers. He came to understand the language of birds and creeping things. Some woodworms told him the timbers of a house were eaten and the house was about to fall. He told the occupants and saved their lives.

Neptune (Ro.); Poseidon (Gr.)--During the Trojan War, he appeared in the form of Calchas, the prophet, and raised the ardor of the warriors to such a pitch they forced the Trojans to give way.

Nereus (Gr.)--A genial old man of the sea, distinguished for his prophetic gifts.

Ocyrrhoe (Gr.)--Daughter of the centaur, Chiron. She foretold the glory that would be achieved by Aesculapius.

Proteus (Gr.)--A prophetic sea-god in the service of Neptune. When seized, he could assume different shapes to escape.

Tiresias (Gr.)--A soothsayer, who obtained knowledge of future events from Minerva. He became a prophet in the Under World.

Vulcan (Ro.); Hephaestus (Gr.)--On occasion, he was a god of healing and of prophecy.

Zeus (Gr.); Jupiter (Ro.)--The chosen Sovereign of the World. Justice was his, as well as prophecy.

PROSTITUTE *See* LOVE

PROTECTION

Ceres (Ro.); Demeter (Gr.)--The special protectress of plebeians.

Genius (Ro.)--A Roman guardian spirit, who had given men being and was a protector through life.

Priapus (Ro.)--The male generative power personified as a god, regarded as a protector of the life of gardens, herds, bees and fish.

PROUD

Nemesis (Gr.)--An ancient goddess, personifying the vengeance of the gods, particularly toward the proud, the insolent and the breakers of the law.

PUNISHMENT *See also* TORMENT

Apollo (Gr.)--God of the sun; not only was he revengeful at times, but he punished with severity.

Dirae (Ro.); Erinnyes (Gr.)--The Three Furies, Alecto, Tisiphone, and Megaera; attendants of Proserpina, who punished with frenzy those who escaped from or who deified public justice.

Erysichthon (Gr.)--The Dryads invoked punishment upon him by giving him a hunger that he could never satisfy.

Furies, The Three (Gr.)-- *See* Dirae.

Iasion (Gr.)--A mortal who united with the god, Demeter, and was punished for his presumption by Zeus.

Marsyas (Gr.)--He found a flute and blew such ravishing sounds on it that he challenged Apollo to a music contest. The god won, of course, and punished Marsyas by flaying him alive.

Niobe (Gr.)--When she boasted of her superiority in having fourteen children, over the goddess Latona's two children, Apollo and Artemis punished Niobe by slaying thirteen of her offspring. Niobe, herself, was changed into stone by Zeus.

237

Orthia (Gr.); Diana (Ro.); Artemis (Gr.)--She assisted her brother, Apollo, in punishing Niobe.

Oedipus (Gr.)--When he discovered he had inadvertently married his own mother, he punished himself by tearing out his eyes.

Penelope (Gr.)--Although she remained faithful to her husband, Ulysses, she had many suitors whom he sought out when he returned. He killed all but two.

Poena (Ro.)--The goddess of punishment.

Pirithoüs (Gr.)--With his friend, Theseus, they aspired to espouse the daughter of Jupiter. Pirithoüs wanted Persephone, the wife of Pluto. Theseus accompanied him to the Under World, where they were seized by Pluto, himself, and chained to an enchanted rock. They remained here until Hercules arrived. Theseus was liberated, but Pirithoüs was left to his fate.

Prometheus (Gr.)--Because he devoted himself to the cause of humanity, he drew the anger of Jove, who ordered him chained to a rock on Mt. Caucasus, and exposed to the attack of a vulture, which for ages preyed on his liver, yet did not succeed in consuming it. Hercules finally released him.

Tityus (Gr.)--For insulting the goddess, Latona, he had to lie eternally stretched in a field while a vulture preyed on his liver, which grew back as fast as it was devoured.

PURIFICATION

Epimenides (Gr.)--After a long sleep he awoke to find himself with gifts of prophecy, purification and priestcraft.

PURITY

Astraea (Gr.)--The goddess of innocence and purity. She was placed among the stars as Virgo, the virgin.

PURSUIT

Arethusa (Gr.)-- *See same under* NYMPHS.

Daphne (Gr.)--She repelled advances, and ran when Apollo pursued her. Apealling for help she was changed by a woodland divinity into a laurel tree.

Pan (Gr.)--The nymph, Syrinx, ran when he tried to woo her. The water-nymphs changed her into a tuft of reeds.

Q

QUARREL See *also* USURPER

Eteocles (Gr.)--When he would not share the throne with his brother, Polynices, there began a quarrel which led to the expedition of the Seven against Thebes. Later, in single combat, the two fought and felled each other.

QUEEN

Aëdon (Gr.)--Queen of Thebes.

Aerope (Gr.)--Wife of King Atreus of Mycenae.

Aethra (Gr.)--Wife of Aegeus, of Athens; mother of Theseus.

Alcestis (Gr.)--Wife of Admetus of Thessaly. She died to prolong his life.

Althaea (Gr.)--Wife of Oeneus of Calydon.

Amata (Gr.)--Queen of the Trojans. Opposed the alliance of the Trojans with the Latins.

Andromache (Gr.)--Married to Hector, after whose death she married Neoptolemus; when he cast her aside, she married Hector's brother, Helenus. Still later, she returned to Asia Minor.

Antiope (Gr.)--Queen of the Amazons; later the wife of Theseus, of

Antiope (cont.)--Athens.

Aphrodite (Gr.)--Of Paphos; of Amathus.

Clytemnestra (Gr.)--Wife of Agamemnon of Mycenae.

Dido (Gr.)--After the death of her husband, Sichaeus, she left Tyre with some followers, founded the city of Carthage, and became its queen.

Dirce (Gr.)--The second wife of Lycus of Thebes.

Halycyone (Gr.)--Wife of Ceyx, King of Trachis in Thessaly.

Harmonia (Gr.)--She left Thebes with her husband, Cadmus, and went to the country of the Enchelians, who made them their rulers.

Hecuba (Gr.)--Wife of King Priam of Troy.

Helen (Gr.)--The immediate cause of the Trojan War, she became the wife of Menelaüs, who, with her, obtained the kingdom of Sparta.

Hesione (Gr.)--Wife of Telamon, King of Aegina.

Hippodamia (Gr.)--Wife of Pelops.

Hippolyta (Gr.)--Queen of the Amazons; same as Antiope.

Jocasta (Gr.)--Wife of Laïus, King of Thebes. Mother of Oedipus, and ruled with him as Queen of Thebes.

Lavinia (Ro.)--Wife of Aeneas, who left Troy as it burned, and embarked for Italy, where he founded the Roman race. Lavinia was his second wife.

Leda (Gr.)--Wife of Tyndareus, King of Sparta.

Medea (Gr.)--Second wife of Aegeus, King of Athens.

Merope (Gr.)--Wife of Cresphontes, King of Messenia; after his death, wife of Polyphontes of Messenia.

QUEEN (cont.)

Niobe (Gr.)--Wife of Amphion, King of Thebes.

Omphale (Gr.)--Queen of Lydia.

Pasiphaë (Gr.)--Wife of Minos II, of Crete. Neptune had driven her into a passion for the Cretan bull.

Persephone (Gr.)--Queen of Hades; wife of Pluto.

Phaedra (Gr.)--After the death of Antiope, Phaedra became the second wife of Theseus, King of Athens.

Philomela (Gr.)--Wife of Tereus, King of Thrace, who plucked out her tongue to insure her silence, and to marry her sister, Procne.

Semiramis (Gr.)--Queen of Babylonia, and ruler after the death of her husband, Ninus.

R

RACE

Hellen (Gr.)--He became the founder of the Hellenic race. His son, Aeolus became an ancestor of the Aeolians, and his son, Dorus, the first of the Dorians.

Iasius (Gr.)--Of the race of Callisto.

Neptune (Ro.)--He and Jupiter being dissatified with conditions in the world, swept away the race of men by a deluge.

Pyrrha (Gr.)--She and her husband, Deucalion, were the only survivors in a great flood sent by Neptune. Concluding that earth was the parent of all, and stones were her bones, they scattered these. The stone grew soft, assumed shapes, and became a hardy race, well adapted to labor.

RACES *See also* CONTEST

Atalanta (Gr.)--A heroine widely famed for her running. She challenged all her suitors to a race, their death being the penalty of defeat; her hand the prize. Hippomenes won.

Gemini (Gr.)--The twins, Castor and Pollux; horsemen and patrons of games and chariot races.

Hippodamia (Gr.)--Her father, King Oenomaüs, offered her to the suitor who could defeat his horses in a chariot race. Pelops won, and married her.

Hippomenes (Gr.)--By throwing three golden apples in her path, which Atalanta stopped to pick up, he won a running race with her.

Myrtilus (Gr.)--The charioteer of King Oenomaüs, who was bribed by Hippodamia to remove a bolt from her father's chariot wheel, to enable Pelops to win the race.

Neptune (Ro.)--He created the horse and was patron of horse races. Once he engaged in a peaceful contest with Minerva for the city of Athens, and lost to her.

Oenomaüs (Gr.)-- *See* Hippodamia.

Pelops (Gr.)--Neptune helped him win the race for Hippodamia, by training him to drive horses, and by supplying him winged steeds for the event.

RAFT

Leucothea (Gr.)--She was Ino who was made a goddess of the sea under the name of Leucothea. In the form of a cormorant, she lit on the raft of Ulysses and gave him a life-belt for emergencies.

RAGE *See also* MADNESS

Hercules (Ro.)--In a rage he struck and killed his music teacher with a lute. Later, he killed his own children, and would have slain his mortal father, Amphitryon, had not Minerva intervened.

RAGE (cont.)

Oedipus (Gr.)--In a narrow pass where another chariot blocked his way, a quarrel ensued during which Oedipus killed the charioteer, and the offender, Laïus, who turned out to be his real father.

RAINBOW

Iris (Gr.)--Goddess of the rainbow; a symbol of the connection between heaven and earth.

RAM *See also* SHEEP

Golden Fleece (Gr.)--Fleece taken from the ram that bore Phrixus through the air to Colchis. It was placed in a sacred grove, by Aeëtes, the king of Colchis, and guarded by a sleepless dragon, until it was won stealthily by Jason.

Helle (Gr.)--She fell off the ram while vaulting trough the air with her brother, Phrixus. The strait she fell into was named the Hellespont, now the Dardanelles.

Nephele (Gr.)--Mother of Helle and Phrixus, who sent them off on the back of the ram to protect them from her ex-husband, Athamas's second wife, Ino.

Phrixus (Gr.)-- *See* Golden Fleece.

Polyphemus (Gr.)--Caught in the cave of the Cyclops Polyphemus, Ulysses and his men put out the giant's one eye with a burning coal. Then to escape from him when the Cyclops rolled away the stone from the entrance, Ulysses and his men harnessed three rams together, to enable each man to suspend himself from the middle ram, to escape the touch of Cyclops as he counted them on the way out.

RANSOM

Chryseïs (Gr.)--Captured by the Greeks for Agamemnon. When the King refused to return her to her father, Chryses, for ransom, he offended Apollo, who sent a pestilence upon the Greeks as punishment.

RAVEN

Coronis (Gr.)--The Thessalian princess who bore the child Aesculapias to Apollo. When a raven told the god that Coronis was unfaithful to him, he became so angry he changed the color of the raven from white to black.

REAPING

Ceres (Ro.); Demeter (Gr.)--The goddess of sowing and reaping.

Daphnis (Gr.)--Pursuing his kidnapped, loved Piplea, he found her in the power of King Lityerses of Phrygia. The king suggested a reaping contest, the winner to have the girl, the loser to be beheaded. As Daphnis was about to lose, Hercules appeared and cut off the head of the king.

Lityerses (Gr.)-- *See* Daphnis.

REBELLIOUS *See also* SLAIN

Cresphontes (Gr.)--King of Messenia, who had been slain by rebellious noblemen.

REEDS

Midas (Gr.)--Serving as a judge in a music contest between Pan and Apollo, he chose Pan, whereupon the god of music changed his ears into those of an ass. His hairdresser tried to keep the secret, but finally dug a hole in the ground, whispered the story into it, and covered it up. But a thick bed of reeds springing up in the field began to whisper about it, and they continue to do so, every time a breeze passes over the place.

Syrinx (Gr.); Faunus (Ro.)--When Pan began to woo her, she ran away until he overtook her at a river bank. Calling for help, she was changed by her friends, the water-nymphs, into a tuft of reeds. Finding that he was embracing only these, he breathed a sigh, and the air over the reeds made a plaintive sound. He placed reeds of unequal length side by side, making an instrument which he named the

REEDS (cont.)

Syrinx (cont.)--Syrinx, in her honor.

REGENT

Creon (Gr.)--He was made a regent for Eteocles and Polynices, who had thrust their father, Oedipus, into exile.

RELIGION *See also* TEMPLE

Bachantes (Gr.)--Women worshippers of Bacchus who were filled with religious frenzy, followed in his train and indulged in wild orgies.

RENEGE

Eteocles (Gr.)--He reneged on his promise to share the throne of Thebes with his brother, Polynices.

Laomedon (Gr.)--Founder and King of Troy. After Hercules had rescued the king's daugther, Hesione, from a sea-monster, Laomedon reneged on his promise to reward him with the horses of Neptune. This prompted Hercules to sail with eighteen ships against Troy, to kill Laomedon, and to place Priam on the throne.

REPENTANCE

Oenone (Gr.)--After she refused to heal the wound of Paris, he returned to Troy and died. The repentant nymph hastened after him with remedies, but arrived too late. In remorse she hanged herself.

REPRESENTATION *See also* SYMBOL

Portumnus (Ro.); Palaemon (Gr.)--He was represented as riding on a dolphin.

RESIDENCE

Helicon (Gr.)--A mountain in Greece, supposed to be the residence of Apollo and the Muses.

Olympus (Gr.)--The heaven of the Greek gods was the summit of an ideal mountain called Olympus.

RETRIBUTION *See also* AVENGE; VENGEANCE

Erinnyes (Gr.)--They (The Furies) brought retribution on those who violated the laws of piety, hospitality, etc., or who were guilty of perjury or homicide.

Nemesis (Gr.)--An ancient goddess who personified retributive justice, representing the righteous anger and vengeance of the gods, toward the proud, the insolent and the breakers of the law.

REVELRIES *See also* ORGIES

Agave (Gr.)--Daughter of Harmonia and Cadmus; mother of Pentheus, whom she killed mistaking him for a wild boar, during Bacchanalian revelries.

Cybele (Ro.); Rhea (Gr.)--She was accompanied by wild attendants, who celebrated with orgiastic rites and revelries in honor of her and her god lover, Attis.

REVENGE *See also* AVENGE

Apollo (Gr.)--He was revengeful, and punished with severity. In revenge, he shot arrows at the Cyclopes.

Eriphyle (Gr.)--She was killed by her son, Alcmaeon, in revenge for her causing the death of his father, Amphiaraüs.

Medea (Gr.)--She made her sorcery an instrument of revenge by persuading the daughters of Pelias, that by cutting him up and boiling the pieces, he could be restored to youth.

Pandora (Gr.)--When she opened the box Jupiter had given her, and forbade her to open, there escaped among a multitude of plagues, envy, spite and revenge.

Procne (Gr.)--After her sister, Philomela, had had her tongue plucked out by her husband, Tereus, she married him, also; had a son, Itylus, by him, and served the child as food in revenge, to his father.

REVOLT

Polyphontes (Gr.)--He was the leader of a revolt against Cresphontes, King of Messenia. He assumed the throne, and took Merope, the queen, for his wife.

RHETORIC

Calliope (Gr.)--The Muse of epic poetry and rhetoric; loved by Apollo, and by him the mother of Orpheus.

RHYTHM

Dactyls (Gr.)--Attendants of Cybele, credited with the introduction of rhythm into Greece.

RICH *See also* WEALTH

Erichthonius (Gr.)--He became the world's richest man; the owner of 3,000 horses.

Geryon (Gr.)--A rich monster; owner of thousands of oxen. *See same under* OXEN.

Gyges (Gr.)--First King of Lydia; famous for his riches.

Minyas (Gr.)--Father of Clymene; first man to build a treasury, a structure as remarkable as the pyramids.

RIDDLE

Oedipus (Gr.)--When he returned to Thebes, he found the city scourged by a monster called the Sphinx, who arrested all travelers and asked them a riddle. Oedipus guessed it and so mortified the Sphinx that she cast herself from a rock and perished.

Sphinx (Gr.)--She had the body of a lion and the upper torso of a woman. The riddle she asked all travelers was: "What animal goes on four feet in the morning, on two at noon, and on three in the evening?" Oedipus guessed that it was man, who creeps on hands and knees in childhood, walks erect in manhood, and goes with the aid of a staff in old age. *See* Oedipus.

RIDICULE

Momus (Gr.)--The god of ridicule, blame and mockery.

Tantalus (Gr.)--He ridiculed the omniscience of the gods.

Thersites (Gr.)--He was a member of the council of Greeks called by Agamemnon. Thersites was always striving against the chieftains, and trying to turn their authority into ridicule.

RIVER

Acheloüs (Gr.)--A river-god who could change form.

Acheron (Gr.)--One of the rivers protecting Hades.

Aesepus (Gr.)--A river in Mysia on the banks of which Memnon was buried.

Alpheüs (Gr.)--God of the river. It was his river, Forone, whose course Hercules changed to clean out the stables of King Augeas.

Amasenus (Gr.)--The river across which Metabus threw his baby tied to a javelin.

Amphrysus (Gr.)--Apollo pastured flocks for King Laomedon on the banks of this river.

248

Asopus (Gr.)--A river-god.

Calcus (Gr.)--A river.

Caÿster (Gr.)--A river where the swans resorted.

Cephissus (Gr.)--A river-god; father of Narcissus.

Charon (Gr.)--The grim boatman who ferried the dead across the River of Woe.

Cyane (Gr.)--A Sicilian nymph who found Proserpina's girdle floating on the Anapus River.

Elysian Fields (Gr.)--Past these fields flowed the River Lethe from which the souls of the earth drank oblivion of their former lives.

Hades, The Realm of (Gr.)--This Under World was isolated by four rivers: Acheron, the River of Woe; Cocytus, the River of Wailing; Phlegethon, the River of Fire; and the Styx, River of Hate, across which Charon conducted souls which had been buried with due rites.

Hercules (Ro.)--He changed the courses of both the River Alpheüs and the River Peneüs, to purify the stables of King Augeas in one day.

Inachus (Gr.)--A river-god.

Lethe (Gr.)-- *See* Elysian Fields.

Maeander (Gr.)--Hercules punished him for challenging the god to a music contest. Apollo won, and punished Marsyas by flaying him alive, forming the River Marsyas from his blood.

Memnon (Gr.)-- *See* Aesepus.

Midas (Gr.)--He washed away his gold-creating power into the River Pactolus, and the river sands are mixed with gold to this day.

Naiads (Gr. and Ro.)--These were nymphs who gave life and perpetuity to rivers, as well as to streams, lakes and fountains.

Oceanus (Gr.)--Oldest of the Titans, he married Tethys, and their child-ren were the Oceanides and rivers of the earth.

Orithyia (Gr.)--Boreas swept her from the banks of the River Ilissus.

Pactolus (Gr.)-- *See* Midas.

Peneüs (Gr.)-- *See* Hercules.

Phaëton (Gr.)--After a wild ride in Apollo's chariot, Jupiter stopped him with a bolt of lightning, and he fell like a shooting star into the River Eridanus.

Pluto (Class.)--At the bank of the River Cyane, he struck the earth with his trident to give him passage back to Hades.

River Ocean (Gr.)--This was a deep and mighty flood which encircled land and sea like a serpent with its tail in its mouth; the source of all.

Romulus (Ro.)--He and his twin brother, Remus, had been thrown as in-fants into the Tiber River, from which they were rescued and suck-led by a she-wolf.

Scamander (Gr.)--A river-God. A river named after him runs into the Hellespont.

Styx (Gr.)--*See* Hades.

Tagus (Gr.)--Called the river of the golden sands.

Tanaïs (Gr.)--An ancient name for the Don River.

Thetis (Gr.)--It was she who tried to make her son, Achilles, invulnerable to the weapons of war, by dipping him, holding the infant by the heels, in the River Styx.

ROADS

Hecate (Gr.)--A three-headed goddess of the cross-roads.

ROADS (cont.)

Hercules (Ro.)-- *See same under* CROSS-ROADS.

Mercury (Ro.); Hermes (Gr.)--He was the guardian of roads and their commerce, as well as guardian of boundaries.

ROBBERS

Ibycus (Gr.)--A poet who was attacked and killed by two robbers in a grove of Neptune. A flock of cranes flying overhead were witnesses and gave information that caused the murderers to confess.

Hercules (Ro.)--His most difficult labor was the robbery of the golden apples of the nymphs, the Hesperides.

Mercury (Ro.)--He robbed Apollo of some of his cattle.

Piplea (Gr.)--She was loved by Daphnis, but borne away to Phrygia by robbers.

ROBE

Dejanira (Gr.)--Wife of Hercules; she soaked his robe in the blood of Nessus.

Laërtes (Gr.)--Father-in-law of Penelope, who wove a robe for him while her husband, Ulysses, was away.

Lichas (Gr.)--He carried the blood—soaked robe from Dejanira to Hercules.

Medea (Gr.)--After Jason tired of his wife, Medea, and wanted to marry Creusa, the sorceress became enraged, sent a poisoned robe to the bride; killed her own children, set fire to the palace and fled to Athens.

Nessus (Gr.)--A centaur who tried to kidnap Dejanira. Hercules shot him in the heart. Before he died he misled Dejanira into believing that a portion of his blood could be used to perserve the love of her husband.

ROCK See *also* STONE

Acis (Gr.)--The jealous Cyclops Polyphemous threw a rock at Acis and destroyed him, for his attention to Galatea.

Andromeda (Gr.)--Perseus found her chained to a rock, released her and claimed her for his wife.

Giants, The (Gr.)--These novel creatures clothed themselves in skins of beasts, and armed with rocks and trunks of trees.

Perseus (Gr.)-- See Andromeda.

Phantasus (Gr.)--Assumed forms of rocks, streams, and other inanimate things.

Pirithoüs (Gr.)--He and his friend, Theseus, went to the Under World to kidnap the queen, Persephone. Pluto seized them and set them on an enchanted rock at his palace gate. They remained fixed there, until Hercules arrived, rescued Theseus, and left Pirithoüs to his fate.

Polyphemus (Gr.)-- *See* Acis.

Poseidon (Gr.); Neptune (Ro.)--After Ulysses' wanderings, his shipwreck and rescue by the Phaecians, Neptune was so displeased that he had been saved from him that at the port of Ithaca, he transformed the ship into a rock, which still stands at the mouth of the harbor.

Prometheus (Gr.)--For his devotion to humanity, he drew the anger of Jove, who ordered him chained to a rock on Mt. Caucasus. He was rescued by Hercules.

Sphinx, The (Gr.)--She lay crouched on a rock, and arrested all travelers to ask them a riddle.

Talus (Gr.)--The giant made of living brass threw rocks at the ships of the Argonauts to repel them from the bay.

ROME See *also* ITALY

Ascanius (Gr.); Iulus (Ro.)--Founded the city of Alba Longa, which be-came the birthplace of Romulus and Remus, and the cradle of

ROME (cont.)

Ascanius (cont.)--Rome.

Genius (Ro.)--A Roman guardian spirit.

Iulus (Ro.)-- *See* Ascanius.

Ianus (Ro.); (Consivius)--An ancient and most important of Roman deities.

Lemures (Ro.)--Spirits to whom the Romans addressed their prayers.

Maia (Ro.); (Majesta)--An ancient goddess in Roman religion. Often confused with the Greek Maia.

Manes (Ro.)--Shades that hovered over the place of burial, to whom Roman family prayers were addressed.

Maro (Ro.)--The surname of Virgil, whose poem, the Aeneid told the story of Aeneas. He was one of the great poets who made the age of the Roman Emperor, Augustus, celebrated. He was born in 70 B.C.

Mars (Ro.); Ares (Gr.)--The patron god of the Romans.

Ops (Ro.)--An ancient Italian god of sowing and the harvest.

Orcus (Ro.); Hades (Gr.)--Known among the Romans also as Dis and Tartarus; god of Death; ruler of the Under World, rather than of the shades.

Poena (Ro.)--The goddess of punishment.

Pollux (Gr.)--He and his half-brother, Castor, were honored with a temple in the Forum and made the patrons of Knighthood.

Portumnus (Ro.); Palaemon (Gr.)--The Romans invoked him as god of the jurisdiction of ports and shores.

Priapus (Ro.)--The male generative power personified as a god.

Quirinus (Ro.)--An ancient god of war. He, Jupiter and Mars formed the dominant triad of the Roman state.

Trivia (Ro.)--In Roman religion she was Diana of the three-faced goddess, Hecate.

RULER *See also* KING

Priam (Gr.)--A wise ruler. He had good government at home and powerful alliances with his neighboring states.

RUNNER

Atalanta (Gr.)--She was widely famed for her beauty and swiftness in running.

RURAL

Faunus (Ro.); Pan (Gr.)--A rural deity, worshipped as a god of animal life, fields, fruitfulness and shepherds.

Silvanus (Ro.)--A rural deity; genius of the woods, fields, flocks and homes of herdsmen; guardian of rural boundaries and country villas.

RUTULI

Turnus (Gr.)--Chief of this Italian tribe. During the Trojan War he protected Mezentius, who had been cast out of Etruria.

Volscens (Gr.)--A Rutulian soldier. In a sword fight, he killed Euralus and Nisus, and was himself slain.

S

SACRIFICE

Alcestis (Gr.)--She died to prolong the life of her husband, Admetus.

Artemis (Gr.); Diana (Ro.)--She was worshipped among the Taurians with human sacrifices.

Busiris (Ro.)--A mythical Egyptian king who tried to sacrifice Hercules at the altar and was killed by him.

Cassiopeia (Gr.)--She was offered as a sacrifice by her father, Cepheus, to appease a monster who had been ravaging the land.

Daphnis (Gr.)--A Sicilian shepherd, after whose death the Sicilians offered yearly sacrifices in his honor.

Erechtheus (Gr.)--In obedience to an oracle he sacrificed his youngest daughter to save Athens from the enemy.

Iphigenia (Gr.)--She was offered by her father, Agamemnon, as a sacrifice to Artemis, to appease the goddess.

Minos II (Gr.)--He refused to sacrifice a bull sent him by Neptune.

Minotaur, The (Gr.)--Each year as a penalty the Athenians were required to sacrifice seven maidens and seven young men to feed this monster in Crete.

Neptune (Ro.); Poseidon (Gr.)--Black and white bulls, white boars, and rams were sacrificed in his honor.

Oeneus (Gr.)--In offering sacrifices, he forgot to pay due honor to Diana, wherefore she became so indignant she sent an enormous boar to lay waste the fields of Calydon.

Polyxena (Gr.)--Sacrificed on the tomb of her father, King Priam.

Protesilaüs (Gr.)--Before the seige of Troy an oracle had predicted that the first person to step on land would be killed and it was Protesilaüs alone who dared sacrifice himself.

Pylades (Gr.)--In a temple of the Tauri in Scythia, he and his friend, Orestes, found a barbarous people that sacrificed all strangers to the goddess Diana. He and Orestes were bound and carried to the altar, only to find that the priestess of Diana was no other than Iphigenia, sister

Pylades (cont.)--of Orestes. They made their escape with the statue of Diana.

SAILOR

Argonauts (Gr.)--These were the sailor companions of Jason, who left Thessaly to sail to Mysia and Thrace, to land finally in Colchis, in search of the Golden Fleece.

Dioscuri (Gr.)--They were Castor and Pollux, known among the constellations as Gemini; patrons of sailors, to whom they appear as balls of fire (St. Elmo's fire), on masts, giving promise of clear weather after a storm.

Leucothea (Gr.)--She was Ino, made a goddess of the sea; invoked by sailors who thought she had the power to prevent shipwrecks.

Palaemon (Gr.); Portumnus (Ro.)--A sea-name for Melicertes, whose mother, Ino, had jumped with him into the sea. He was also made a sea-god.

Portumnus (Gr.)-- *Same as* Palaemon. Invoked as god of jurisdiction of ports and shores.

SALVE

Phaon (Gr.)--A ferryman between Lesbos and Chios. One day during a passage Aphrodite gave him a salve possessing magical qualities. As a consequence of his using it, the women of Lesbos went wild for love of him.

SATYR

Amymone (Gr.)--A Danaïd, who cried out when she was pursued by a satyr. Neptune heard her, dispatched the satyr and made love to the maiden himself.

Bacchus (Gr.); Dionysus (Gr.)--God of wine; attended by Satyrs; other

SATYR (cont.)

Bacchus (cont.)--woodland deities, the Sileni, and women attendants called the Maenades.

Echo (Gr.)--A beautiful, talkative Oread, who fell in love with the satyr, Narcissus.

Iacchus (Gr.)-- *Same as* Bacchus. One of his guardians and tutors was the jovial Silenus, oldest of the Satyrs.

Narcissus (Gr.)--A handsome satyr for whose unrequited love Echo faded away. Nemesis punished his indifference by causing him to fall in love with his own reflection.

Satyrs (Gr.)--Deities of the woods and fields, they were depicted early as bearded creatures with snub noses, goat's ears and horse's tails. Later, they resembled youths, sometimes with sprouting horns. The goat-legged satyr is found in Roman poetry. They were usually restricted to a single wooded area.

Silenus (Gr.)--Oldest of the Satrys, he was generally tipsy, and would have broken his neck had not the Satyrs held him upright as he reeled along on his ass's back.

SAVAGE *See* Periphetes *under* TRAVELERS

SAW

Perdix (Gr.)--An inventor. He imitated in iron the spine of a fish, and came out with the saw.

SCALDED

Minos II (Gr.)--While he was bathing one of the daughters of King Cocalis (of Sicily) scalded him to death.

SCALES

Astraea (Gr.), (Virgo)–She held aloft a pair of scales, in which she weighed conflicting claims of others.

SCAR

Euryclea (Gr.)--She was the old nurse of Ulysses, who recognized him by a scar left long before by a boar, when he returned in disguise.

SCHOLAR

Perdix (Gr.)--He was an apt scholar and showed ingenuity. *See also* SAW.

SCIENCE

Hermes (Gr.); Mercury (Ro.)--He was a god of science, of luck, treasure trove, cunning and gymnastic exercises, etc.

SCORNED *See also* LOVE UNREQUITED·

Lyde (Gr.)-- *See same under* LOVE.

SCORPION

Tisiphone (Gr.)--One of the three Furies. She used a whip of scorpions on her victims, and passed them along to her sisters, Alecto and Megaera.

SCULPTURE *See also* STATUE

Pygmalion (Gr.)--A woman hater, but he sculpted a state of ivory so beautiful no woman could compare with it. It was life-like, he fell in love with it.

Acrisius (Gr.)--Because he had been told that he would be killed by his grandson, he enclosed his daughter, Danäe, and her new infant in a great chest and set it adrift at sea.

Aphrodite (Gr.); Venus (Ro.)--According to Hesiod, she arose from the foam of the sea.

Eurynome (Gr.)--A sea goddess. She and Thetis, another sea goddess, took care of Vulcan for nine years until he could learn his trade.

Galatea (Gr.)--A sea-nymph; one of the fifty mermaid daughters of Doris and Nereus.

Glaucus (Gr.)--A lesser power of the Ocean; guardian of fishes and divers, and of those who go to sea in ships.

Graeae, The (Gr.)--The three daughters of Phorcys, a sea-deity.

Hecatonchires (Gr.)--Three 100-handed monsters, Briareus, Cottus and Gyges. Probably the Greeks imaged in them the sea with its multitudinous waves, its roar and breakers that shake the earth.

Hesione (Gr.)--Her father, Laomedon, offered her to appease a sea monster who had ravaged the land.

Iaachus (Gr.)--He was the only one who could persuade Vulcan to free his mother, Juno, who had been chained to a throne in the depths of the sea.

Icarus (Gr.)--When the wax melted which had enabled him to attach wings and fly out of prison, he was dumped into the sea, now named Icarian.

Ino (Gr.)--She was made a sea-goddess under the name of Leucothea.

Juno (Ro.); Hera (Gr.)--Although she was the daughter of Rhea and Cronus, she was brought up by Tethys and Oceanus in their home in the remote west beyond the sea.

Leander (Gr.)--Each night he swam the Hellespont to meet his beloved Hero, until he was caught in a tempest and drowned.

Lichas (Gr.)--After he had delivered a poisoned robe to Hercules, the hero, in a frenzy, seized him and hurled him into the sea.

Melicertes (Gr.)--Son of Ino. He became the sea-god Palaemon.

Myrtilus (Gr.)--A charioteer who had been bribed to lose a race with Pelops. Pelops threw him into the sea, where he drowned.

Neptune (Ro.); Poseidon (Gr.)--God of the sea and of all waters. His palace was in the depths of the sea in Euboea, near the Greek coast, but he lived in Olympus when he chose.

Nereus (Gr.)--A genial old man of the sea.

Oceanus (Gr.)--He was the Neptune of the older dynasty of gods. See also Juno.

Oenopion (Gr.)--When he tried to force his marriage to Oenopion's daughter, Merope, Orion was blinded and cast out on the seashore.

Parthenope (Gr.)--A siren who was so discouraged at not being able to charm Ulysses that she cast herself into the sea and drowned.

Pelagia (Gr.)--Aphrodite of the sea.

Pelops (Gr.)-- See Myrtilus.

Phorcys (Gr.)--Offspring of Pontus, who rejoiced in the horrors of the sea.

Polydectes (Gr.)--King of Seriphus, who took in Danaë and her son, Perseus, after they had been set adrift at sea.

Pontus (Gr.)--God of the deep sea or the waterways.

Poseidon (Gr.); Neptune (Ro.)--God of the kingdom of the sea.

Proteus (Gr.)--A prophetic sea-god in the service of Neptune.

Sciron (Gr.)--A giant who kept watch on a pass where cliffs fell abruptly into the sea. He kicked travelers into the waters below.

SEA (cont.)

Tethys (Gr.)–A Titan who lived with Oceanus in their home in the remote west beyond the sea.

Venus (Ro.); Aphrodite (Gr.)--One theory is that she arose from the foam of the sea.

Vulcan (Ro.); Hephaestus (Gr.)--When he was cast out of Heaven by his mother, Juno, on account of his lameness, the two sea-goddesses, Eurynome and Thetis, took him in and cared for him nine years.

SEA ANIMALS AND MAMMALS

Andromeda (Gr.)--An Ethiopian young woman whom Perseus rescued from a horrible sea-monster.

Aphrodite (Gr.); Venus (Ro.)–Dolphins were sacred to her.

SEAFARERS *See also* SAILOR

Dictynna (Gr.)--Protectress of seafarers and hunters.

Sirens (Gr.)--The sweet singing of these muses of the sea enticed seafarers to their destruction.

SEA NYMPHS *See also* NYMPHS

Calypso (Gr.)--A sea nymph who received Ulysses on her island, Oxygia.

Nereids (Gr.)--The fifty mermaid daughters of Doris and Nereus.

SEARCH

Cilix (Gr.)--When their sister, Europa, was carried off by Jupiter, Cilix and Cadmus conducted a world search for her.

SEASONS

Horae (Gr.)--Three goddesses of the seasons and hours who took charge of the gate of clouds at Olympus.

Themis (Gr.)--She was the mother of the Horae, by Jupiter.

Vertumnus (Gr.)--A deity of gardens and the changing seasons.

SECRET

Battus (Gr.)--He promised Mercury secrecy, then told the whole story. For this Mercury petrified him.

Midas (Gr.)--His hairdresser found the secret of his having the ears of an ass too great to keep, and whispered it into a hole in the ground.

SEDUCED *See also* CARRIED OFF

Aërope (Gr.)--She was seduced by Thyestes.

SEER

Polyidus (Gr.)--An Argive seer.

SENTINEL

Graeae, The (Gr.)--Hoary witches who served as sentinels for the habitation of the Gorgons.

SERPENT *See also* SNAKES

Acheloüs (Gr.)--A river-god who could change form; in wrestling with Hercules he tried to glide away in the form of a serpent.

Aloadae (Gr.)--Otus and Ephilaltes who tried to dethrone the immortals. For this, Jupiter killed them with his lightning, and they atoned in Hades by being bound to a pillar with serpents.

262

SERPENT (cont.)

Apollo (Gr.)-- *See* Phoebus.

Cadmus (Gr.)-- *See same under* WISH.

Caduceus (Gr.)--The magic wand of health, happiness and dreams given to Mercury by Apollo. It was originally adorned with garlands, but later with two serpents coiled around it and two wings at the top.

Cerberus (Gr.)-- *See same under* SNAKES.

Echidna (Gr.)--A monster, half serpent, half woman; mother of the Sphinx, the Chimaera and other monsters.

Erechtheus (Gr.)--He took the form of a serpent reputedly the builder of the temple Erechtheum.

Eurydice (Gr.)--In fleeing from Aristaeus, she stepped on a snake which bit and killed her.

Furies, The (Gr.)--Goddesses of vengeance, with serpents curling around their brows.

Gorgons (Gr.)--Three monster sisters, who had claws of bronze, serpents for hands, and snaky hair.

Harmonia (Gr.)--Her husband Cadmus, remarked that if the serpent is so highly regarded by the gods he wished he were one himself. As if in answer, he began to change form. Harmonia petitioned the gods to let her share his fate, and they both became serpents.

Hercules (Ro.); Alcides (Gr.)--He strangled two serpents which Hera had put into his cradle to destroy him. For his second Labor, he destroyed the water serpent, Hydra.

Hydra (Gr.)--A water serpent that lived in the marsh of Lerna in Argos. It had nine heads, any one of which would grow two more when cut off.

Icelus (Gr.)--He personated serpents, birds and beasts.

Ladon (Gr.)--The serpent that guarded the golden apples of the Hesper-

Ladon (cont.)--ides.

Laocoön (Gr.)--Athena caused two immense sea serpents to emerge from the ocean to coil around the bodies of Laocoön and his two sons to strangle them to death.

Medea (Gr.)--A sorceress, whose chariot was drawn by serpents.

Medusa (Gr.)--The most terrifying of the three Gorgon sisters. She had not only serpents for hands but Minerva had changed her beautiful hair into hissing serpents.

Megaera (Gr.)--One of the three Furies, with her head wreathed with serpents.

Melampus (Gr.)--One day when he was asleep, some young serpents licked his ears, enabling him to understand the language of creeping things and birds.

Phoebus (Gr.) (Apollo)--After fearful combat he shot and killed the serpent, Python, with arrows from his silver bow.

Python (Gr.)--This enormous serpent crept 'out from the slime which covered the earth after the great flood, and lurked in the caves of Mt. Parnassus, terrifying the people.

Scylla (Gr.)--Circe transformed her into a monster made of serpents with sharp teeth and the yelp of a dog.

SERVICE

Elysian Fields (Gr.)--Spirits here were those who had rendered a service to mankind, such as priests, poets, and heroes, etc.

Gemini (Gr.)--Castor and Pollux, brothers who rendered noteworthy service to the Argonauts returning from Colchis.

Perseus (Gr.)--One of the Older Heroes, endowed with god-like qualities, which they devoted to the service of mankind.

264

SEVEN AGAINST THEBES

Adrastus (Gr.)--A leader of the expedition of the Seven against Thebes, and its sole survivor.

Eteocles (Gr.)--When he refused to share the throne of Thebes with his brother, Polynices went to King Adrastus of Argos, who gave him an army to enforce his claim. This led to the expedition of the Seven Against Thebes.

Menoeceus (Gr.)--A heroic youth who threw his life away in the first encounter of the expedition.

Parthcnopaeus (Gr.)--He was one of the allies of Polynices in the enterprise against Thebes.

Polynices (Gr.)-- *See* Eteocles.

SEVEN AGAINST THEBES (Gr.)--The expedition of seven heroes: Adrastus, Amphiaraüs, Capaneus, Hippomedon (of Argos), Polynices, Parthenopaeus and Tydeus, against Eteocles in Thebes.

SHADES *See also* SOULS

Manes (Ro.)--Shades that hovered over the place of burial, to whom the Roman family prayers were addressed.

Orcus (Ro.)--The god of death; ruler of the Under World, rather than of the shades.

Orpheus (Gr.)--His shade went for a second time to Hades, where he rejoined his wife, Eurydice.

SHEEP

Cyclops Polyphemus (Gr.)--He kept his sheep in a cave. To escape from the Cyclops, Ulysses had to harness three rams together, to suspend a man under the middle one to be carried out unnoticed.

Cynthia (Gr.); Diana (Ro.)--Goddess of the moon, in love with Endymion, who fed his flock on Mt. Cynthus.

265

SHEEP (cont.)

Hades (Gr.); Pluto (Class.)--Mortals sacrificed black sheep to him.

SHELLS

Epimetheus (Gr.)--He gave to man and animals faculties necessary to preserve themselves: courage, strenth, swiftness, sagacity, claws to one, wings and shells to others.

SHEPHERD

Adonis (Gr.)--A handsome, young shepherd, with whom Aphrodite fell in love. He was killed by a wild boar.

Antiope (Gr.); Hippolyta (Gr.)--Wooed by Jupiter, she bore him two sons, Amphion and Zethus, who were brought up by shepherds on Mt. Cithaeron, not knowing their parentage.

Apollo (Gr.)--He spent many of his younger years as a herdsman for mortal masters in Arcadia, Laonis and Thessaly.

Arne (Gr.)--A shepherdess loved by Neptune; daughter of King Aelus.

Daphnis (Gr.)--The ideal Sicilian shepherd; the innovator of bucolic poetry.

Drydas (Gr.)--Wood-nymphs who at times assumed the forms of shepherdesses or peasant girls.

Faunus (Ro.); Pan (Gr.)--A rural deity, worshipped as a god of animal life, sheperds, etc.

Oedipus (Gr.)--As an infant, sent off to die, he was saved by a herdsman.

Paris (Gr.)--He was sent to be raised by shepherds on Mt. Ida.

Polyphemous (Gr.)--One of the Cyclops, who lived as shepherds on what their flocks yielded, plus wild fruits.

Zethus (Gr.)--Brother of Amphion; both were brought up by shepherds

266

SHEPHERD (cont.)

Zethus (cont.)--on Mount Cithaeron.

SHIELD

Jupiter (Ro.); Zeus (Gr.)--According to the Greek conception, Jupiter wore a shield of storm-cloud, and lashed his enemies with lightning.

Medusa (Gr.)--With the aid of Minerva's shield and Mercury's knife, Perseus was able to approach Medusa and cut off her head.

Mezentius (Gr.)--In a personal encounter, Aeneas hurled his lance which pierced the shield of Mezentius and wounded him in the thigh.

Perseus (Gr.)--He was able to approach the Gorgon Medusa safely by looking at her reflection in his bright shield. After cutting off her head, he flew far and wide with it, turning to stone all who glanced at it. Later he bestowed the head on Athena, who bore it on her *aegis* or shield.

SHINING

Diana (Ro.); Artemis (Gr.)--Goddess of the moon; also known as Phoebe, the Shining One.

SHIP

Aeneas (Gr.)--After Troy burned he built several ships and embarked for Italy, where he founded the Roman race.

Alcinoüs (Gr.)--Beloved king of the Phaeacians who befriended Ulysses by furnishing a ship for his return to his own land of Ithaca.

Argonauts (Gr.)--The sailed on the ship *Argo* for the kingdom of Colchis, in search of the Golden Fleece.

Argus (Gr.)--He was the builder of the ship *Argo*.

Eurylochus (Gr.)--Companion of Ulysses on board his ship.

Glaucus (Gr.)--Once a fisherman; later the helmsman of the ship *Argo*.

Hercules (Ro.)--Sailed with a fleet of eighteen ships against Troy.

Iphigenia (Gr.)--She had been offered as a sacrifice to Artemis, who had been angered by the killing of a sacred hind, and had becalmed the fleet at Aulis.

Jason (Gr.)--He organized the Argonautic expedition, engaged the ship-builder, Argus, and with other famous heroes, sailed from Thessaly to Mysia, Thrace, and finally to Colchis, to find the Golden Fleece. Upon reaching him, they dedicated the ship to Neptune.

Leucothea (Gr.)--She was Ino, made a goddess of the sea. She and her son, Portumnus, were invoked by sailors and considered powerful in preventing shipwrecks.

Lotus-Eaters (Gr.)--They gave Ulysses' men the lotus plant to eat, which made the sailors lose all thought of home. Ulysses had to drag the men to his ship and tie them under benches to get them home.

Minerva (Ro.); Athena (Gr.)--Goddess of storms and the thunderbolt, she was a protectress of warships.

Minos II (Gr.)--After the artificer, Daedalus, had lost favor with him and flown to Sicily, Minos followed him there with a great fleet. After he had conquered Megara, he took Scylla, daughter of King Nisus there, and tied her to the rudder of his ship, thus dragging her through the waves to Crete.

Palinurus (Gr.)--He was pilot of the ship of Aeneas who encountered many adventures on the way to Italy. When Venus asked Neptune to stop imperilling her son, Aeneas, he demanded one life as ransom. Palinurus was the victim. He was pushed overboard.

Portumnus (Ro.)-- *See* Leucothea.

Poseidon (Gr.); Neptune (Ro.)--After Ulysses' ship returned to the port of Ithaca, this god of the sea transformed it into a rock, which still stands opposite the mouth of the harbor.

SHIP (cont.)

Protesilaüs (Gr.)--When the Greeks tried to land along the coast of Troy, he was the first to step off the ship, and was killed by Hector.

Scylla (Gr.)-- *See* Minos II.

Talus (Gr.)--A giant who threw rocks at the ships of the Argonauts to repel them from a bay along the coast of Crete.

Thalassios (Gr.)--(Hymen) He brought a shipload of kidnapped Athenian maidens across the sea to their home.

Triton (Gr.)--When Juno upset the ships of Aeneas, Neptune soothed the waves, and pried some of the ships loose from the rocks with his trident, while Triton, the trumpeter of Ocean, put his shoulders under the others to set them afloat again.

Typhon (Gr.)--He helped Aeolus and Boreas, sons of Juno, to toss the ocean and to upset the ships of Aeneas.

Ulysses (Gr.)--Began his ten years of wanderings between Troy and his own kingdom, Ithaca, with twelve ships.

SHIPWRECK

Ceyx (Gr.)--King of Trachis in Thessaly; died in a shipwreck.

Ino (Gr.)--The gods made her a goddess of the sea. *See* Leucothea.

Halcyone (Gr.)--She was informed by Morpheus in the form of Ceyx, that her husband had been drowned in a shipwreck.

Juno (Ro.); Hera (Gr.)--Due to her discontent at Paris's having selected Helen as the fairest in the land instead of her, Juno nearly shipwrecked the Trojans.

Leucothea (Gr.)--She had the power to prevent shipwrecks.

Nausicaä (Gr.)--She found Ulysses on the shore where he had been shipwrecked, and led him to her father, King Alcinoüs, of the Phaeacians on the isle of Scheria.

SHIPWRECK (cont.)

Portumnus (Gr.)-- *See* Leucothea, *under* SHIP.

SHOES

Hermes (Gr.); Mercury (Ro.)--A messenger of the gods, represented as a beardless youth with winged shoes (talaria), fastened to his ankles, a winged cap (petasos) on his head, and carrying a caduceus.

Mercury (Ro.)-- *See* Hermes *above.*

SHORES

Portumnus (Ro.)--The Romans invoked him as god of the jurisdiction of ports and shores.

SHRINE

Ajax the Less (Gr.)--Violated the shrine of Athena by tearing away Cassandra, and making her a captive in Greece.

Quirinus (Ro.)--An ancient god of war, who with Jupiter and Mars, formed the dominant triad of the Roman state. His chief shrine was on the Quirinal.

SICILY

Acestes (Gr.)--He was the King of Sicily who gave Aeneas a hospitable reception.

Cocalis (Gr.)--King of Sicily.

Daphnis (Gr.)--The ideal Sicilian shepherd.

SIGH *See* Syrinx *under* MUSIC

SIGHT *See also* BLINDNESS

Phineus (Gr.)--Because he had been a cruel King (of Thrace), Jupiter deprived him of his sight.

Polyphemus (Gr.)--Ulysses poked out this Cyclops' one eye with a burning stake.

SILENCE

Tereus (Gr.)--The cruel husband of Procne, who tired of her, plucked out her tongue to insure her silence, then married her sister, Philomela.

SILENI

Sileni (Gr.)--Attendants of Bacchus, deriving their name from the satyr, Silenus, the jovial tutor of Bacchus.

SINGING *See* SIRENS

SIRENS

Orpheus (Gr.)--He vanquished even the seductive strains of the sea-muses with his own more persuasive song, and he could charm wild beasts with his music.

Parthenope (Gr.)--A siren who was discouraged because she could not charm Ulysses.

Sirens (Gr.)--Muses of the sea and of death, who by their sweet singing enticed seafarers to their destruction.

SISTERS

Charites (Gr.)--The Graces, daughters of Eurynome and Jupiter.

Danaides (Gr.)--The fifty daughters of Danaüs, who married the fifty sons of Aegyptus.

271

SISTERS (cont.)

Fates, The (Gr.)--The three daughters of Night, who determined the course of human life. The Destinies.

Furies, The (Gr.)--The three goddesses of vengeance, Alecto, Megaera and Tisiphone.

Graces, The (Gr.)--Three beautiful goddesses: Aglaia, Euphrosyne and Thalia, who presided over polite accomplishments.

Gorgons (Gr.)--Three monster sisters, Euryale, Medusa and Stheno, who had claws of bronze, serpents for hands, and snaky hair.

Graeae, The (Gr.)--Three daughters of Phorcys, a sea deity, and Ceto; hoary witches who served as sentinels for the Gorgons.

Harpies (Gr.)--Disgustingly foul creatures with heads and bosoms of maidens, and wings, tail, legs and claws of birds. Goddesses of storm and death, they were Aëllo, Ocypete and Celaeno.

Heliades (Gr.)--Daughters of Helios, who were changed into popular trees.

Hesperides (Gr.)--Four nymph daughters of Atlas: Aegle, Arethusa, Erytheia and Hestia. They guarded the golden apples.

Nereids (Gr.)--The fifty mermaid daughters of Doris and Nereus.

Pleiades (Gr.)--The seven daughters of Pleione and Atlas, whom Jupiter turned into pigeons, and then made them a constellation.

SIZE *See also* GIANT

Ajax, the Great (Gr.)--Gigantic in size; next to Achilles in prowess and beauty, but dull of intellect.

SKY

Aether (Gr.)--A personification of the sky.

Hermes (Gr.); Mercury (Ro.)--The god of twilight.

SKY (cont.)

Jove (Ro.); Jupiter (Ro.)--God of the sky.

Juno (Ro.); Hera (Gr.)--A deity of light and of the sky.

SLAIN *See also* MURDER; VENGEANCE

Achilles (Gr.)-- *See same under* MURDER.

Aloadae (Gr.)--For their presumption in trying to emulate the power of the gods, they (Otus and Ephialtes) were struck dead with Jupiter's lightning.

Cresphontes (Gr.)--King of Messenia; slain by rebellious noblemen.

Danaides (Gr.)--The fifty daughters of Danaüs. *See same under* MURDER.

Erysichthon (Gr.)--While he was cutting down a sacred oak tree, to show his contempt of the gods, a bystander told him to desist and was slain by him. They Dryads invoked Famine upon him. *See same under* HUNGER.

Hydra (Gr.)--The water serpent with nine heads was slain by Hercules.

Ladon (Gr.)--The serpent guard of the golden apples, slain by Hercules.

Orestes (Gr.)--He avenged his father's (Agamemnon's) murder by slaying his mother, Clytemnestra and her lover, Aegisthus.

Palamedes (Gr.)--During the Trojan War he was slain by the Greeks.

Paris (Gr.)--He was killed by an arrow from the bow of Philoctetes.

Polyphontes (Gr.)--A leader of the revolt against Cresphontes, whom he killed with two sons. A third son of Cresphontes, Aepytus, avenged his father by slaying Polyphontes and taking possession of the kingdom.

Protesilaüs (Gr.)--One of the most admirable of the Greeks; slain early in the Trojan War by Hector.

Volscens (Gr.)--A Rutulian soldier who slew the young Trojans, Euryalus and Nissus, with his sword.

SLAVE

Hercules (Ro.)--For killing his friend, Iphitus, he was condemned to spend three years as the slave of Queen Omphale, spinning wool.

SLEEP

Argus (Gr.)--A 100-eyed creatured, all of whose eyes were lulled to sleep by Mercury's telling him god's tales.

Death (Gr.); Thanatos (Gr.)--The twin brother of sleep.

Endymion (Gr.)--Jupiter gave him a choice between death in any manner he chose, or perpetual youth united with perpetual sleep. He chose the latter.

Epimenides (Gr.)--A Cretan herdsman, who awoke from a fifty-seven years' sleep to find himself endowed with gifts of prophecy and priestcraft.

Hercules (Ro.)--During one of his fits of madness when he killed his own children, Minerva knocked him over with a stone and plunged him into a deep sleep, from which he awoke in his right mind.

Hypnos (Gr.)--The god of sleep.

Io (Gr.)--To release her from Argus, the 100-eyed monster, Mercury told stories and used his sleep-producing wand, then slew the sleeping monster.

Mercury (Ro.); Hermes (Gr.)--His wand (caduceus) of wood or gold twined with snakes, had magical powers over sleeping, waking and dreams.

Mors (Ro.); Thanatos (Gr.)--The god of Death; brother of Sleep (Hypnos).

SLEEP (cont.)

Nymphs (Gr.)--There were sleepless nymphs: Eunice, Malis and Nycheia, dread goddesses of the country people.

Nyx (Gr.); Nox (Ro.)--Mother of the Fates; Death; Sleep; Dreams, and others.

Palinurus (Gr.)--The pilot of Aeneas's ship, whom Somnus made sleepy by waving over him a branch moistened with Lethaean dew, before pushing him overboard.

Psyche (Gr.)--In Pluto's kingdom she was given a box filled with the beauty of Proserpina, and told not to open it. When her curiosity overcame her, she lifted the lid, and Sleep escaped to make her unconscious.

Sleep (Gr.); Somnus (Gr.)--A son of Night, who brought to mortals solace and fair dreams.

SNAKES *See also* SERPENT

Aristaeus (Gr.)--In love with Eurydice, unrequited, she ran from him and in doing so stepped on a snake which bit her on the foot and killed her.

Cecrops (Gr.)--Half-snake, half-man, who came into Attica, founded Athens and named it Cecropia.

Cerberus (Gr.)--A three-headed dog with a serpent-tail and his necks bristling with snakes, which guarded the gate to the Under World.

Erinnyes (Gr.)--Snaky-haired women, who, as avengers, pursued an offender and inflicted madness.

Giants, The (Gr.)--A race of monsters, whose lower limbs and bodies were snakes.

Herse (Gr.)--Athena gave her and her sister, Aglauros, a box which was to remain closed. Yielding to curiosity, they opened it. Aghast at finding a snake within, they threw themselves from the Acropolis.

275

SNAKES (cont.)

Orpheus (Gr.)--After his beloved Eurydice was killed by a snake-bite, he sang his sorrows in a desert cave for seven months.

SOCIAL PLEASURE

Charites (Gr.)--The Graces, Euphrosyne, Aglaia and Thalia, goddesses who presided over all social pleasures.

SOFTEN

Mulciber (Ro.) A descriptive name for Vulcan, from *mulceo*, meaning to soften.

SOLACE

Hypnos (Gr.)--The god of sleep, who brings to mortals solace and fair dreams.

SOLDIERS *See also* ARMY

Euryalus (Gr.)--A young Trojan soldier, distinguished for grace of person and fine qualities.

Mezentius (Gr.)--In the war between the Trojans and the Etruscans, he was killed by Aeneas. One of his cruelties had been to fasten the living to the dead, face to face, and leave the victims to die in the dreadful embrace.

Myrmidons (Gr.)--The soldiers of Achilles, created by Jupiter for his grandfather, Aeacus.

SONG *See also* MUSIC

Python (Gr.)--After Apollo had slain this enormous serpent with arrows from his silver bow, he organized the Pythian Games, to commemorate his illustrious conquest. Here he sang for the first time, the

SONG (cont.)

Python (cont.)--*Paean*, that song of victory, which is still among all nations synonymous with jubilation, praise and thanksgiving.

Terpsichore (Gr. and Ro.)--The Muse of choral song and dance. Her symbol: the cithara, a form of lyre.

SOOTHSAYERS

Amphiaraüs (Gr.)--He opposed the expedition against Thebes, knowing as a soothsayer, that none of the leaders, except Adrastus, would live to return.

Calchas (Gr.)--A soothsayer and prophet who accompanied the Greeks during the Trojan War.

Menoeceus (Gr.)-- *See* Tiresias.

Mopsus (Gr.)--A soothsayer who attended the Argonauts.

Polyidus (Gr.)--A soothsayer who counseled Bellerophon to procure the winged horse, Pegasus.

Tiresias (Gr.)--In the exploit, Seven against Thebes, he declared that victory would fall to Thebes if the heroic youth, Menoeceus, made himself a voluntary victim. Menoeceus threw away his life in the first encounter.

SORCERESS

Aeson (Gr.)-- *See same under* YOUTH.

Circe (Gr.)--A beautiful sorceress on the island of Aeaea, who feasted her visitors, then turned them by magic into the forms of beasts. When Ulysses visited the island, Mercury met him along a road and gave him a sprig of Moly plant to give him the power to resist her sorceries.

Jason (Gr.)--He married the sorceress, Medea, and when he tired of her, she sent a poisoned robe to her successor, Creusa.

SORCERESS (cont.)

Medea (Gr.)--A sorceress at Colchis, wife of Jason. *See* Aeson, and Jason, *above*. She cast a spell over the giant, Talus, enabling Castor and Pollux to capture him.

Medusa (Gr.)--A Gorgon and sorceress who lay the countryside to waste. Perseus cut off her head as she slept, and used it to change to stone all who glanced at it.

SOULS

Elysian Fields (Gr.)--The souls of the guiltless passed to the Elysian Fields, where each followed the chosen pursuit of his former life.

Erebus (Gr.)--A place of nether darkness through which souls passed on the way to Hades.

Harpies (Gr.)--They snatched up and carried off the souls of the dead.

Mercury (Ro.); Hermes (Gr.)--Herald of the gods, and conductor of souls to the Lower World.

Minos I (Gr.)--A judge of the souls in Hades.

SOVEREIGN

Iapetus (Gr.)--He, with Cronus, opposed the sovereignity of Jupiter.

Jupiter (Ro.); Zeus (Gr.)--In the council of the gods which followed the Titan War, he was chosen Sovereign of the World.

Zeus (Gr.)-- *Same as* Jupiter.

SOWING

Ceres (Ro.)--Goddess of sowing. *See same under* AGRICULTURE.

Janus (Ro.)--Sometimes called Consivius, or the Sower.

278

SOWING (cont.)

Ops (Ro.)--An ancient goddess of sowing and the harvest; wife of Saturn.

Saturn (Ro.); Cronus (Gr.)--An ancient diety of seeds and sowing; the introducer of agriculture.

SPEAR

Arcas (Gr.)-- *See same under* HUNTER.

Athena (Gr.)-- *See same under* HEAD.

Diomede (Gr.)--Struck by an arrow shot by Pandarus, he felled the archer with his spear.

Hector (Gr.)--During the Trojan War he mortally wounded Patroclus with his spear. Achilles in turn struck Hector in the neck with his spear and killed him.

Laocoön (Gr.)--He hurled a spear at the side of the wooden horse, and its hollow sound made him suspicious.

Mars (Ro.); Ares (Gr.)--His emblems were the spear and a burning torch.

Neptune (Ro.); Poseidon (Gr.)--His symbol of power was the trident, or three-pronged spear.

Pandarus (Gr.)-- *See* Diomede.

Patroclus (Gr.)-- *See* Hector.

Pyrrhus (Gr.)--On the night the Greeks took Troy, Priam hurled a spear at Pyrrhus and was immediately slain by him.

Telephus (Gr.)--He was wounded by Achilles, but cured by the rust of the spear.

Toxeus (Gr.)--In defense of Atalanta, Meleager killed his two uncles, Toxeus and Plexippus, with his spear.

SPEED

Atalanta (Gr.)--Famed for her speed in running.

SPELL

Medea (Gr.)--She cast a spell over the giant, Talus, to enable Castor and Pollux to make him captive.

SPHINX: The

Echidna (Gr.)--Mother of the Sphinx; half serpent, half woman.

Oedipus (Gr.)--He guessed the riddle of the Sphinx.

Sphinx, The (Gr.)--A monster, with the body of a lion, and the upper torso of a woman.

SPIDER

Arachne (Gr.)--For challenging Minerva to a weaving contest, she was transformed by the goddess into a spider.

SPINNING

Arachne (Gr.)--Changed into a spider, she was forever spinning the thread by which she was suspended.

Athena (Gr.); Minerva (Ro.)--She presided over the useful and ornamental arts, including spinning, weaving, etc.

Hercules (Ro.)--He was condemned to spend three years as the slave of Queen Omphale, spinning wool.

Omphale (Gr.)-- *See* Hercules.

SPIRITS *See also* DAIMONES

Genius (Ro.)--A Roman spirit who gave man his being and served as his protector through life.

SPIRITS (cont.)

Lares (Ro.)--The deified spirits of ancestors who watched over and protected their descendants.

Lemures (Ro.)–Spirits to whom the Romans addressed their prayers.

SPRING

Proserpina (Gr.)–She was pleasant and dear to mankind as the goddess of
spring.

SPRINGS

Amymone (Gr.)-- *See same under* TRIDENT.

Artemis (Gr.); Diana (Ro.)--A virgin goddess. *See same under* STREAM.

Camenae (Ro.)–The nymphs of springs and fountains in ancient Rome.

Carmenta (Ro.)-- *See same under* FOUNTAIN.

Danaïdes (Gr.)--After slaying their husbands, they were condemned to
Tartarus, where they tried to fill with water a vessel full of holes.
These probably represent the springs of Argolis, whose waters run
away quickly into the dry, porous soil.

Hylas (Gr.)--A young friend of Hercules; pulled by the hand down into
the depths of a spring by the Naiads.

Juturna (Ro.)--A water-nymph; goddess of the springs and brooks, whose
pool in the Forum was sacred.

SPRINGTIME

Adonis (Gr.)–A handsome young shepherd, who personified springtime.

Hyacinthus (Gr.)–The personification of the blooming vegetation of
spring which withers under the heat of summer.

Persephone (Gr.)--The goddess of spring, revisiting the earth in duly recurring seasons.

Phoebus (Gr.)--The golden god, who brought warm spring and summer.

Proserpina (Gr.)--Sometimes she visited companions in the vale of Enna where spring reigned perpetually.

SPURNED *See* LOVE UNREQUITED

SPYING

Cephalus (Gr.)--A young hunter. *See same under* MISTAKEN IDENTITY.

STABLES

Augeas (Gr.)--King of Elis, who owned a herd of 3,000 oxen, whose stables had not been cleaned out in thirty years.

Hercules (Ro.)–It was his sixth labor to clean the Augean stables.

STAFF *See also* CADUCEUS; WAND

Maenades (Gr.)--As they danced and sang, these women attendants of Bacchus waved in the air a staff (the *thyrus*), entwined with ivy and surmounted by a pine cone.

STAG

Actaeon (Gr.)-- *See same under* HUNTER.

Cyparissus (Gr.)--A boy who killed his pet stag accidentally. He begged Apollo to allow him to mourn forever, and the god changed him into a cypress tree, which, with its dark foliage, is still associated with mourning.

STAG (cont.)

Iulus (Ro.)--His killing a tame stag of Silvia, started the war between the Trojans and the Latins.

Orthia (Gr.); Diana (Ro.)--She punished Agamemnon for killing a stag sacred to her.

Silvia (Gr.)--Daughter of Tyrrheus, the king's herdsman. *See also* Iulus.

STARS *See also* CONSTELLATION

Ariadne (Gr.)--When she married Bacchus, he gave her as a wedding gift a crown studded with stars. When she died, he threw the crown into the heavens, where it can still be seen as Corona, or Ariadne's crown.

Asteria (Gr.)--The starry heavens.

Astraea (Gr.)--Goddess of innocence. She was placed among the stars as Virgo, the virgin.

Atlantides (Gr.)--These were the seven stars, called the Pleides.

Aurora (Ro.); Eos (Gr.)--Goddess of the Morn; mother of the stars.

Cassiopeia (Gr.)--Wife of Cepheus; mother of Andromeda. In the heavens, she is a northern constellation between Cepheus and Andromeda.

Castor (Gr.)--During a voyage to Colchis, he and his brother, Pollux, survived a storm, and when stars appeared on their heads, they were honored as the patrons of voyagers. After their deaths, Jupiter rewarded the attachment of the brothers by placing them among the stars as Gemini, the Twins.

Dioscuri (Gr.)-- *See* Castor *above.*

Eos (Gr.)– *See* Aurora.

Gemini (Gr.)– *See* Castor.

Hesper (Gr.)--The evening star.

Hyades (Gr.)--Nymph daughters of Atlas; placed in the heavens by Zeus.

Lucifer (Gr.)--The morning star; son of Aurora and Cephalus.

Phaëton (Gr.)--He drove Apollo's chariot across the heavens until Jupiter brandished a lightning bolt, and Phaëton fell headlong like a shooting star into the river Eridanus.

Phosphor (Gr.)--Son of Aurora and the hunter, Cephalus, he was the morning star, or the star of Venus.

Sirius (Gr.)--The dog of Orion, transformed into a star.

Vesper (Gr.)--Hesper, or the evening star, Venus. Sometimes identified with Phosphor.

STATUE *See also* SCULPTURE

Aphrodite (Gr.)--It was she who made the artist Pygmalion's statue, Galatea, come to life.

Galatea (Gr.)–An ivory statue created by the king and sculptor, Pygmalion, who fell in love with it.

Icarius (Gr.)--Father of Penelope. When she married Ulysses and went to Ithaca, Icarius erected a statue to Modesty on the spot where they had parted.

Iphigenia (Gr.)--She left with the statue of Diana from the temple in Tauris, and carried it to Mycenae.

Palladium, The (Gr.)–It was a celebrated statue of Minerva in Troy. It was believed that the city could not be taken as long as this statue remained in it. Ulysses and Diomede entered the city in disguise, and carried it to the Grecian camp.

Pygmalion (Gr.)–He made a statue of ivory so beautiful that no woman could compare with it. *See* Galatea.

Terminus (Ro.)--The god of landmarks. His statue was a crude stone or

STATUE (cont.)

Terminus (cont.)--post set in the ground to mark the boundaries of men's fields.

STATURE *See also* GIANT; SIZE

Aloadae (Gr.)--These monsters reprsent the unregulated forces of vegetation, since they were renowned for their courage, strength and stature, growing at the rate of three cubits in height and one in breadth each year.

STEALING See also ROBBERY

Cacus (Gr.)--A giant who stole some of Hercules' cattle, and dragged them by the tail backwards into his cave, to make the tracks misleading.

Phaeton (Gr.)--He stole his father's chariot, and the horses dashed him across the heavens.

STONE *See also* PETRIFIED; ROCK

Aegeus (Gr.)--He placed a sword and shoes under a large stone and directed his wife, Aethra, to send his son to him if he should prove strong enough to roll away the stone. His son proved to be the Attic hero, Theseus.

Amphion (Gr.)-- *See same under* LYRE.

Anaxerete (Gr.)--A Cyprian maiden who spurned Iphis, causing him to hang himself to her gatepost. Aphrodite then turned the hard-hearted virgin to stone as she attended her lover's funeral.

Athena (Gr.)--Goddess of the thundercloud, who carried a tasseled breatplate with its aegis, the head of Medusa, that turned all beholders to stone.

Atlas (Gr.)--Perseus came for some apples which Atlas was guarding. He bore with him the head of Medusa, and when Atlas tried to push him

Atlas (cont.)--out, he held up the head which changed the giant to stone.

Cronus (Gr.)--To assure his not losing this throne to an heir, he swallowed his first five children as soon as they were born. His wife, Rhea, saved the sixth, Jupiter, by wrapping a stone in the infant's clothing and having Cronus swallow that.

Deucalion (Gr.)--Believing that the earth's stones were her bones, he cast them behind him. The stones began to grow soft, and to assume human shape. Those thrown by Deucalion became men; those by his wife, Pyrrha, women. A hardy race sprang up.

Diomede (Gr.)--He crushed Aeneas with a stone.

Gorgons (Gr.)--The three monster sisters, whom no living thing could behold without turning to stone.

Hector (Gr.)--During the Trojan War, he was struck by a huge stone thrown by Ajax. But he recovered and returned to the combat.

Hercules (Ro.)--When he was driven insane by Juno, Minerva knocked him over with a stone. This plunged him into a deep sleep, from which he awoke in his right mind.

Medea (Gr.)--She saved Jason from a company of armed men by throwing a stone in their midst and turning their arms against each other, while he escaped.

Medusa (Gr.)--A Gorgon who lived in a cavern surrounded by stone figures of men and animals that had been petrified at the sight of her.

Niobe (Gr.)--As punishment for her boasting superiority over Latona, she was changed by Zeus into stone. Her tears continued to flow, and she remains a mass of rock from which a tricklying stream flows, a tribute to her never-ending grief.

Perseus (Gr.)--He conquered Medusa, the Gorgon, and flew far and near with her head, to change to stone all enemies. He left Polydectes and his court in merited petrifaction.

Phineas (Gr.)--A suitor of Andromeda, turned to stone by Perseus and

STONE (cont.)

Phineas (cont.)--the Gorgon head.

Polydectes (Gr.)-- *See* Perseus.

Procris (Gr.)--She had a dog, a gift from Diana, which she gave to her huntsman husband Cephalus. When the dog was about to overtake the swiftest fox in the country, the goddess changed him and his victim into stone.

Pyrrha (Gr.)-- *See* Deucalion.

Sisyphus (Gr.)--For disclosing the intrigue of Jupiter with Aegina, he was condemned to Hades, there to roll a huge stone to the top of a hill, only to have it go headlong down to the plain, from where he had to roll it up again endlessly.

Stheno (Gr.)--One of the three Gorgons, who turned all beholders to stone.

Terminus (Gr.)--The god of landmarks; his statue a crude stone or post.

Venus (Ro.); Aphrodite (Gr.)--She heaped her vengeance upon those who dishonored her rites. Among others, she transformed Arsinoë into a stone.

STOPPER

Talus (Gr.)--A giant of living brass, who had but one vein in his body, and that plugged on the crown of his head with a nail. Medea pulled out the stopper.

STOREHOUSE

Penates (Ro.)--Gods of the household. Their name derived from Penus, the storehouse or inner chamber, which was sacred to them.

STORES

Consus (Ro.)--An early Italian god of the earth; keeper of the stores; god of the stored-up harvest. It is said his altar was discovered underground by Romulus.

STORM *See also* LIGHTNING; THUNDER

Alcyoneus (Gr.)--An earth-born Giant, of the winter storms and icebergs.

Athena (Gr.); Minerva (Ro.)--Goddess of the thundercloud and storms.

Castor (Gr.)--During a voyage to Colchis, he and his half-brother, Pollux, survived a storm, and when stars appeared on their heads, they came to be honored as the patrons of voyagers.

Harpies (Gr.)--Goddesses of storm and death; personifications of devasting winds.

Jupiter (Ro.); Zeus (Gr.)--The Greeks conceived him as riding in his thunder-car, and wearing a breast-plate or shield of storm-cloud.

Minerva (Ro.)--See Athena.

STORIES

Mercury (Ro.)--He told stories to put all 100 eyes of Argus to sleep.

Midas (Gr.)--His hairdresser whispered the story of his having ass's ears to a hole in the ground.

STRANGLED

Antaeus (Gr.)--A giant wrestler whose strength was invincible as long as he remained in contact with his mother Earth. Hercules lifted him away from the earth and strangled him in the air.

Hercules (Ro.)--He strangled two serpents sent by Juno to destroy him as he lay in his cradle. Later, for his first Labor, he strangled the Nemean lion with his hands.

STRANGLED (cont.)

Laocoön (Gr.)--Athena caused two sea serpents to emerge, wind their coils around Laocoön and his two sons and strangle them to death.

STREAM *See also* BROOK

Acis (Gr.)--He was killed by a rock thrown at him by the Cyclops Polyphemous. Blood spurting from beneath the stone became a stream which still bears his name.

Arethusa (Gr.)-- *See same under* NYMPHS.

Artemis (Gr.); Diana (Ro.)--She favored springs and woodland brooks, in which she bathed.

Niobe (Gr.)--Her tears over the death of her children became a trickling stream, a tribute to her never-ending grief.

Oracles (Gr. and Ro.)--Often these mediums situated themselves in deep and melancholy streams.

Phantasus (Gr.)--He assumed the forms of streams, rocks, etc.

STRENGTH

Aloadae (Gr.)--Giants renowned for their stature, strength and courage.

Antaeus (Gr.)-- *See same under* STRANGLED.

Bacchus (Gr.); Dionysus (Ro.)--The god of wine, who represented the vital strength of everything that grows, and the joyful life.

Briareus (Gr.)--Called the "Strong." He was one of the Hecatonchires, assigned to guard the descent to Hades.

Hercules (Ro.); Alcides (Gr.)--Celebrated for his strength.

Mercury (Ro.); Hermes (Gr.)--His agility and strength made him easily prince in athletic pursuits.

STRENGTH (cont.)

Theseus (Gr.)--A second Hercules, who joined every expedition and hunt, exhibiting great strength.

Zeus (Gr.); Jupiter (Ro.)--Sovereign of the World; bodily strength and valor were dear to him.

STRETCHER

Procrustes (Gr.)--Son of Neptune. He made all travelers fit his bed. *See same under* BED.

STRIFE

Arimasp (Gr. and Ro.)--One of a race of one-eyed men, in constant strife with the gryphons for the gold they were guarding.

Ate (Gr.)--Daughter of Eris, (Strife).

Discord (Gr.)-- *See* Eris.

Eris (Gr.)--Goddess of discord or strife; sister of Mars. It was she who threw a golden apple into an assembly of gods to cause contention.

Titans, The (Gr.)--Instigators of hatred and strife.

STRIKER

Cottus (Gr.)--One of the three 100-handed monsters, the Hecatonchires; called "The Striker."

STYGIAN REALM *See* HADES

SUICIDE

Ajax, the Great (Gr.)--First cousin of Achilles; a valiant warrior. He killed himself because the armor of Achilles was awarded to Ulysses in-

290

Ajax, (cont.)--stead of to him.

Alcestis (Gr.)--Although she died to prolong the life of her husband, Admetis, she was restored to the Upper World by Hercules.

Althaea (Gr.)--When she threw a burning brand, representing the life of her son, Meleager, in the fire, she extinguished him, then committed suicide.

Amphion (Gr.)--Distressed by the death of his many children, slain by Apollo and Artemis, he destroyed himself.

Arachne (Gr.)--After she lost in a weaving contest with Minerva, she was so humiliated she hung herself. Minerva transformed her into a spider.

Dejanira (Gr.)--Because she had unwittingly killed her husband, Hercules, with a poisoned robe, she hanged herself.

Dido (Gr.)--Queen of Carthage, in love with Aeneas. When he left her, the blow to her pride was so severe that she mounted a funeral pile, stabbed herself and died in the flames.

Erechtheus (Gr.)--He took the form of a serpent. When the three daughters of Cecrops carried a basket containing Erechtheus from Athens, they discovered with such fright that he was a serpent that they jumped off the rock of the Acropolis.

Erigone (Gr.)--In grief over the murder of her father, Icarus, she hanged herself.

Evadne (Gr.)--After her husband, Capaneus, had been slain by one of Jupiter's thunderbolts, she cast herself on his funeral pyre.

Haemon (Gr.)--He committed suicide after his loved Antigone was buried alive.

Halcyone (Gr.)--After her husband, Ceyx, was drowned in a shipwreck, she threw herself into the sea. The gods, out of compassion, changed her and her husband into kingfishers.

Hero (Gr.)--After a tempest caused the death of her lover, Leander, while he was trying to swim the Hellespont to reach her, she cast herself into the sea and perished.

Herse (Gr.)--Yielding to curiosity over a box Athena had given her, she was so aghast at finding a snake within that she and two sisters who were with her, threw themselves from the Acropolis. *See also* Erechtheus.

Ino (Gr.)--She was so persecuted by her mad husband, Athamas, that she took her son, Melicertes in her arms and jumped with him from a cliff into the sea.

Iphis (Gr.)--Because he was spurned by Anaxerete, he hanged himself to her gatepost.

Jocasta (Gr.)--Wife of Laïus. After many years, she was so horror-stricken to learn that she had married her own son, Oedipus, that she hanged herself.

Oenone (Gr.)--Repentant that she had refused to heal the wound of Paris, she hanged herself.

Phaedra (Gr.)--As Theseus' second wife, she became enamored of his son, Hippolytus. Repulsed, she hanged herself.

Phaon (Gr.)--A ferryman. Sappho's love for him, unrequited, caused her to leap from the Leucadian rock.

Phyllis (Gr.)--When her betrothed, Acamus, failed to return at the time set, she thought she had been deserted and hanged herself.

Pyramus (Gr.)--When he thought his loved Thisbe had been killed by a lion, he threw himself on his sword.

Sappho (Gr.)-- *See* Phaon.

Sphinx (Gr.)--When Oedipus came by and guessed the riddle she had been asking all travelers, she cast herself from a rock.

Thisbe (Gr.)--Committed suicide after finding Pyramus dying.

SUITORS

Atalanta (Gr.)–In Boeotian legend, she challenged her suitors to a running race; death was the penalty of defeat; her hand the prize.

Pelias (Gr.)--Father of Alcestis, whose hand he had promised to the suitor who came for her in a chariot drawn by lions and boars.

Pelops (Gr.)--He was Hippodamia, whose father, Oenomaüs, had demanded that no suitor could win his daughter without first besting him in a chariot race.

Penelope (Gr.)--Wife of Ulysses, who put off her many suitors for twenty years while her husband was off adventuring between Troy and his own kingdom of Ithaca.

Phineus (Gr.)--A rival for the hand of Andromeda, showing up only after Perseus had rescued her from being chained to a rock, and had married her. When Phineus attacked the wedding party, Perseus held up the Gorgon's head and changed him to stone.

Telemachus (Gr.)--Son of Penelope and Ulysses. When his father returned, Telemachus helped him dispatch with bow and arrow Penelope's many suitors.

SUN

Apollo (Gr.)--God of the sun, and of poetry and music.

Elysian Fields (Gr.)--A land of sunlight where the happy lived. The region had a sun and stars of its own.

Helios (Gr.)--An ancient sun-god.

Hyperion (Gr.)--A Titan; father of Helios, the sun-god. In later myth, he is identified with Apollo, god of manly beauty.

Orion (Gr.)--Son of Neptune. When he tried to gain possession of Merope by force, her father, Oenopion, deprived him of his sight. Apollo restored his eyesight with a sun-beam.

Phaëton (Gr.)--Son of Apollo. He drove the chariot of the sun wildly

293

SUN (cont.)

Phaëton (cont.)--around the earth until it caught fire.

Phoebus (Gr.); Apollo (Gr.)--His name signifies the radiant nature of sunlight. The golden god chose to spend most of his time where there is sunshine.

SUPERIORITY

Niobe (Gr.)--She boasted of her superiority over Latona. *See* BOASTING

SURGEON *See also* MEDICINE

Machaon (Gr.)--Son of Aesculapius. He proved of high value to the Greeks as a surgeon.

SWALLOWED

Cronus (Gr.); Saturn (Ro.)--To assure his not losing his throne to an heir, he swallowed the first five as soon as they were born. His wife, Rhea, saved the sixth, Jupiter, by giving Cronus a stone wrapped in the infant's clothing to swallow.

Metis (Gr.)--She was the first love of Jupiter. Warned that if she bore him a child, it would be greater than he, he swallowed Metis. In time there sprang from his head the goddess Athena.

SWAMP

Hydra (Gr.)--The water serpent that ravaged the country of Argos, and dwelt in the marsh of Lerna.

Lernaean Swamp (Gr.)--In this swamp near Argos, Hercules killed the serpent Hydra.

SWAN

Cycnus (Gr.)--Grieved over the death of his friend, Phaëton, and dying,

SWAN (cont.)

Cycnus (cont.)--he was changed by kindly gods into a swan. Remembering how his friend had been brought down from the sky, he did not trust himself to fly.

Leda (Gr.)--Wooed by Jupiter in the guise of a swan, she bore him Pollux and Helen.

SWIFTNESS *See also* SPEED

Hermes (Gr.); Mercury (Ro.)--Famed for his swiftness of foot, he was herald and messenger of the gods.

SWIMMING *See also* SEA

Leander (Gr.)--He swam the Hellespont each night to meet Hero.

SWINE

Ulysses (Gr.)--On the Aeaean Isle, his men were touched one by one by the hand of Circe and transformed into swine. They were enclosed in a stye and supplied with acrons.

SWINEHERD

Eumaeus (Gr.)--He was the faithful swineherd of Ulysses.

SWORD

Aeneas (Gr.)--To avenge Pallas, who had been lanced by Turnus, he thrust his sword through Turnus.

Pallas (Gr.)-- *See* Aeneas.

Damocles (Gr.)--To rebuke his praise of the ahppiness of kings, he was seated by Dionysus I at a royal banquet with a sword hung over his head by a single hair.

SYLVAN

Zephyrus (Gr.)--He was the most mild and gentle of all the sylvan deities.

SYMBOLS *See also* SHIELD

Aegis (Gr.)--A sacred breastplate or shield.

Anteros (Gr.)--He was a symbol of reciprocal affection.

Apollo (Gr.)--His symbol, the lyre.

Artemis (Gr.); Diana (Ro.)--Her symbols: the bow and arrow.

Astraea (Gr.)--Goddess of innocence and purity. She was placed among the stars as Virgo, the virgin.

Athena (Gr.); Minerva (Ro.)--Her symbol: the tasseled breastplace of goatskin, with its *aegis* the head of the gorgon Medusa that turned all beholders to stone.

Bacchus (Gr.)--Had a crown of ivy.

Caduceus (Gr.)--The magic wand given Mercury by Apollo, originally adorned with garlands, but later with two serpents coiled around it and two wings at the top.

Calliope (Gr.)-- *See same under* MUSES.

Clio (Gr.)--The Muse of History; she holds a roll of papyrus unfolded on-to her lap. *See same also under* MUSES.

Clotho (Gr.)--Depicted winding wool around a spindle.

Corona (Gr.)--Adriane's crown.

Cupid (Ro.); Eros (Gr.)--He always carried a bow and quiver of arrows.

Demeter (Gr.); Ceres (Ro.)--Worshiped by harvesters. She is depicted as holding a torch, ears of corn, wheat and poppies.

Erato (Gr.)-- *See same under* DRESS.

SYMBOLS (cont.)

Eros (Gr.); Cupid (Ro.)--He is sometimes represented with eyes covered because of the blindness of his actions. *See also* Cupid.

Evato (Gr.)--Carried a lyre.

Hecate (Gr.)--A three-headed goddess with six arms which carried a torch or a spear and torch.

Heracles (Gr.); Hercules (Ro.)--Represented with a club in his hand and a lion-skin over his shoulder.

Hermes (Gr.); Mercury (Ro.)--Represented as a slightly draped, beardless youth with winged shoes (talaria) fastened to his ankles, a winged cap (petasos) on his head, and carrying a caduceus.

Hippolyta (Gr.)--Associated with a girdle given her by Ares, and coveted by Admeta, daughter of King Eurystheus, who sent Hercules in quest of it.

Janus (Ro.)--God of doorways. His insignia was a key which opened and closed the door; also, he carried a stick to drive away those who had no right to cross the threshold.

Jupiter (Ro.); Zeus (Gr.)--The Greeks conceived him as riding in his thun-der-car, wearing a breastplate or shield of storm-cloud, and lashing his enemies with lightning.

Maenades (Gr.)--Woman attendants of Bacchus, pictured as dancing and singing, and waving in the air a staff (*thyrus*) entwined with ivy and surmounted by a pine cone.

Mars (Ro.); Ares (Gr.)--His emblems: the spear and burning torch.

Medusa (Gr.)--Pictured with claws of bronze, serpents for hands, and snaky hair.

Melpomene (Gr.)--Muse of Tragedy, holding a tragic mask.

Minerva (Ro.)-- *See* Athena.

Neptune (Ro.); Poseidon (Gr.)--His symbol of power, the trident, or

Neptune (cont.)–three-pronged spear, with which he could shatter rocks, control storms and shake the earth.

Nike (Gr.)–Goddess of Victory; winged and wearing a wreath and palm branch.

Orpheus (Gr.)–Famous as a musician; his symbol was the lyre.

Pan (Gr.); Faunus (Ro.)–His invention, the syrinx, or "Pan's pipes."

Plenty (Gr.)–The goddess of Plenty adopted the Cornucopia as her symbol.

Pluto (Glass.); Hades (Gr.)–He carried the cornucopia, symbol of inexhaustible riches.

Portumnus (Ro.)–Represented as riding on a dolphin.

Proserpina (Gr.)–Goddess of spring, she bore a cornucopia and revisited the earth at recurring seasons.

Satyrs (Gr.)–They appeared as bearded creatures with snub noses, goat's ears and horse's tails. Later they resembled youths with sprouting horns.

Selene (Gr.)–Goddess of the moon; her weapons, the bow and arrow; her emblem, the crescent.

Silvanus (Ro.)–A rural deity, represented as a cheerful old man holding a shepherd's pipe, pine-cone-crowned, and carrying a branch or a gardener's knife.

Tersichore (Gr. and Ro.)–The Muse of dance and song. Her symbol: the cithara (a form of lyre).

Thalia (Gr.)–The Muse of comedy. She carried the shepherd's staff and the comic mask.

Themis (Gr.)–Goddess of justice. She is represented as woman of grave countenance and austere features. Her attribute is a pair of scales.

SYMBOLS (cont.)

Victoria (Ro.); Nike (Gr.)--Goddess of victory; personified with wings and carrying a wreath and palm branch.

Vulcan (Ro.); Hephaestus (Gr.)--Blacksmith of the gods; his symbol, a forge. He was sometimes represented as a vigorous man equpped with hammer and tongs.

SYRINX

Pan (Gr.); Faunus (Ro.)--He invented the syrinx from a tuft of reeds. Also called "Pan's pipes."

Syrinx (Gr.)--She ran from Pan, and at the bank of a stream became a bunch of reeds. Pan broke them into unequal lengths, fastened them together and fashioned the "syrinx" musical instrument in her honor.

T

TAIL

Cacus (Gr.)--A giant who stole some of Hercules cattle and dragged them backwards into his cave by the tail to make their tracks misleading.

TALKATIVE

Echo (Gr.)--A talkative nymph whose chatter displeased Juno, and prompted the goddess to condemn her to the loss of her voice, except for the purpose of replying.

TARTARUS *See also* HADES

Cronus (Gr.)--The only one of Gaea's Titan sons to block Uranus when he tried to thrust her younger children, the Hecatonchires, into Tartarus.

TARTARUS (cont.)

Danaïdes (Gr.)--For slaying their husbands on their wedding night, these fifty (all but one) daughters of Danaüs were condemned to spend eternity in Tartarus, trying to fill with water a vessel full of holes.

Proserpina (Gr.)--She was carried off by Pluto. The river Cyane tried to oppose him until Pluto struck the bank with his trident to open the earth and let him go on to Tartarus.

Tantalus (Gr.)--King of Phrygia, consigned to Tartarus for betraying some secrets of the gods. When he tried to reach for some fruit overhead, the winds whirled them beyond his reach.

TASKS *See also* LABORS

Jason (Gr.)--At Colchis, he had to perform certain tasks set up by Aeëtes, to obtain the Golden Fleece.

TEACHER *See also* TUTOR

Bacchus (Gr.)--Taught people the cultivation of the vine.

Chiron (Gr.)--A centaur who raised Aesculapias, and was the teacher of Achilles and Jason.

Linus (Gr.)--Music teacher of Hercules, and killed by him with a lute.

Silenus (Gr.)--The jovial teacher of young Bacchus.

TEARS *See also* GRIEF; MOURNING

Heliades (Gr.)--As they mourned for their brother, Phaëthon, they were changed into poplar trees. Their tears became amber.

Hymen (Gr.)--At the wedding of Orpheus and Eurydice, he conveyed no happy omens, since his torch smoked and brought tears to the eyes of all those present.

Niobe (Gr.)--Zeus changed her into stone, yet her tears continue to flow.

Niobe (cont.)--She remains on her native mountain, a mass of rock from which a trickling stream flows, a tribute to her never-ending grief over the loss of all her children.

TEETH

Cadmus (Gr.)--During his adventures he killed a dragon sacred to Mars, and had to serve penance to the god for eight years. Minerva told him to take the dragon's teeth and sow them in the earth. These sprouted into armed men who fought one another until only five were left. These five became the ancestors of the Thebans.

Graeae, The (Gr.)--These were hoary witches, sentinels for the Gorgons. They had only one tooth, and one eye which they handed from one to the other.

Jason (Gr.)--One of his tasks was to sow a dragon's teeth and destroy the crop of armed men that sprang up.

TEMPER

Neptune (Ro.); Poseidon (Gr.)--Some of his sons, especially those born of mortal mothers, had his same impetuous and ungovernable temper.

TEMPERANCE

Diana (Ro.); Artemis (Gr.)--A patroness of temperance.

Orthia (Gr.); Diana (Ro.)--A patroness of temperance in all things, and guardian of civil rights.

TEMPEST

Leander (Gr.)--During one of his nightly swims across the Hellespont to visit Hero, he was caught in a tempest and drowned. Hero, in despair, threw herself into the sea.

TEMPLE

Diana (Ro.); Artemis (Gr.)–Her temple was in Tauris.

Erechtheus (Gr.)–He was brought up by Minerva in her temple. He was the builder of the temple Erechtheus in Athens.

Herostratus (Gr.)--He wanted to immortalize himself by setting fire to the Temple of Ephesus, one of the wonders of the world, around 356 B.C.

Janus (Ro.)--His temple in the Forum had doors facing east for the beginning and west for the ending of the day.

Pylades (Gr.)--He and his friend, Orestes, were directed once to a temple of the Tauri in Scythia. There they found a barbarous people sacrificing all strangers to the goddess Diana. They were bound and carried to the altar, only to find that the priestess of Diana was no other than Orestes' sister, Iphigenia. The three escaped with the statue of Diana, and returned to Mycenae.

Triptolemus (Gr.)--After she had cured him of a fever, she took him in her chariot through all countries of the earth, and taught him the use of the plow, and rewards labor can win from the soil. Later he imparted to mankind the knowledge of agriculture. When he was older, Triptolemus built a temple to Ceres, and established worship of the goddess under the name, Eleusion mysteries, which in splendor and solemnity surpassed all other religious celebrations in Greece.

Vesta (Ro.); Hestia (Gr.)--Goddess of the hearth and its fire. From her altars other gods obtained their fires. Her temple was the oldest in Rome, and here a sacred fire was kept religiously alive by six virgin priestesses called Vestals.

TERROR

Deimos (Gr.)--The personification of terror or dread.

Deino (Gr.)--One of the hoary witches, the three Graeae, known as "the Terrifier."

Minotaur (con't)--to Crete until the artificer, Daedalus, constructed a

302

TERROR (cont.)

Minotaur (cont.)--labyrinth for it.

Pan (Gr.)-- *See same under* PANIC.

TERRIBLE

Furies, The (Gr.)--The goddesses of vengeance, also called the Dirae, meaning the terrible ones.

THEBES

Aëdon (Gr.)--Queen of Thebes. Envious of Niobe's having so many children, she tried to kill the oldest, but by mistake slew her own son.

Alcmaeon (Gr.)--He became the leader of the Epigoni against Thebes. After destroying the city, he returned to Argos. *See same under* MOTHER.

Alcmene (Gr.)--Although she was married to the mortal, Alcaeus, she had a son by Jupiter in Thebes. He became the mighty Hercules, national hero of Greece.

Cadmus (Gr.)--Apollo told him to follow a cow until she stopped, and there to build a city, and to call it Thebes.

Capaneus (Gr.)--From Argos, he was an ally in the enterprise against Thebes. Jupiter killed him with a thunderbolt.

Creon (Gr.)--He was made a regent of Thebes for Etocles and Polynices, the two sons of Oedipus.

Peigonus (Gr.)--One of the sons of the Seven against Thebes heroes. Thirty years after their fathers' defeat, with Alcmaeon as leader, they conquered and destroyed the city.

Harmonia (Gr.)--Wife of Cadmus; an ancestress of the unquiet dynasty of Thebes.

Kings of Thebes (Gr.)--Some of them were Amphion; Amphitryon;

Kings of Thebes (cont.)--Cadmus; Eteocles; Labducus; Laiüs; Lycus; Nycteus; Oedipus; Polynices.

Menoeceus (Gr.)--A soothsayer said victory would fall to Thebes if Menoeceus became a voluntary victim. He threw his life away in the first encounter.

Oedipus (Gr.)--After he grew up he returned to Thebes, and rid the city of the monster called the Sphinx. The grateful Thebans were so grateful they made him their king.

Seven against Thebes (Gr.)--These were seven heroes who aided Polynices to recover his throne. They were: Adrastus, Amphiaraüs, Capaneus, Hippomedon (or Eteocles), Polynices, Parthenopaeus and Tydeus.

Sphinx, The (Gr.)--A monster that infested the city of Thebes until Oedipus came along and guessed her riddle. She was so mortified that she cast herself from a rock and perished.

Thersander (Gr.)--Son of Polynices, who influenced Eriphyle to join in the war against Thebes.

THESSALY

Thessaly (Gr.)--Some of its kings were: Admetus, Ceyx, Deucalion and Pierus.

THIEVES

Cacus (Gr.)--A giant who stole some of Hercules' cattle. *See same under* STEALING.

Cercopes (Gr.)--Thievish gnomes who were captured by Hercules, after they stole some of his weapons.

Hermes (Gr.); Mercury (Ro.)--The god of cunning, theft and trickery, and a dangerous foe.

THIRST *See* WATER

THREAD

Arachne (Gr.)--Minerva transformed her into a spider forever spinning the thread by which she was suspended.

Ariadne (Gr.)--She led Theseus out of the labyrinth of Daedalus by a thread.

Damocles (Gr.)--King Dionysius seated him at a royal banquet with a sword hung over his head suspended by a hair, to show him the uneasy fate of kings.

Labyrinth (Gr.)--It was built to contain the monster, the Minotaur. Theseus went in to kill it, and used the thread Ariadne gave him to retrace his path.

THRONE See also KING

Eteocles (Gr.)--He refused to share the throne of Thebes with his brother, Polynices, which led to the expedition of the Seven against Thebes.

THUNDER *See also* LIGHTNING; STORMS

Amphiaraüs (Gr.)--Jupiter launched a thunderbolt which opened the ground and swallowed him and his chariot.

Athena (Gr.); Minerva (Ro.)--Goddess of the thundercloud.

Capaneus (Gr.)-- *See same under* THEBES.

Cyclopes (Gr.)--A race of men of gigantic size in Sicily, who forged the thunderbolts for Jupiter.

Jupiter (Ro.)--He rode in his thunder-car, wearing a breastplate or shield of storm-cloud, and lashing his enemies with lightning.

Minerva (Ro.)--Goddess of the storms and of the rushing thunderbolt.

Phaëton (Gr.)--After a wild ride across the heavens in Apollo's (his father's) chariot, he overcame the earth with heat, and Jupiter had to stop him by hurling a lightning bolt at him. He fell like a shooting star into the great river Eridanus.

Salmoneus (Gr.)--A Titan who presumed to vie with Jupiter by building a bridge of brass over which he drove his chariot to make sounds like thunder. Jupiter struck him with a real thunderbolt to teach him the difference between mortal weapons and divine.

Zeus (Gr.); Jupiter (Ro.)--He was the thunderer; the wielder of the thunderbolt.

TIME

Chronos (Gr.)--The god of Time; a power which destroys whatever it has brought into existence.

TITAN

Coeus (Gr.)--A Titan; husband of Phoebe.

Cronus (Gr.); Saturn (Ro.)--Lord of Heaven and Earth, called "the Crafty."

Dione (Gr.)--Goddess of women and marriage; a female Titan.

Gaea (Gr.)--Mother Earth; wife of Uranus; from their union came the Titans, and others.

Hyperion (Gr.)--A Titan; father of Helios, the sun-god.

Iapetus (Gr.)--Instigator of hatred and strife. He warred with Cronus and other Titans against the sovereignty of Jupiter.

Jupiter (Ro.)--Overcame the Titans by blinding them.

Mnemosyne (Gr.)--A Titaness; goddess of memory; mother of the nine M Muses, by Jupiter.

Neptune (Ro.); Poseidon (Gr.)--After the overthrow of the Titans, he was made god of the sea and of all waters.

Oceanus (Gr.)--Oldest of the Titans; the only one to side with Jupiter.

Ophion (Gr.)--One of the Titans; husband of Eurynome. They ruled over heaven before the age of Saturn.

Phoebe (Gr.)--A Titaness; mother of Latona.

Prometheus (Gr.)--Son of the Titan, Iapetus and Clymene. He stole fire from heaven for the use of man.

Rhea (Ro.); Cybele (Gr.)--A Titaness, issued from the marriage of Gaea and Uranus. Wife of Cronus, she gave birth to six gods.

Salmoneus (Gr.)--A Titan who presumed to vie with Jupiter by building a bridge of brass to make sounds of thunder with his chariot.

Tartarus (Gr.)--An abyss below Hades where Zeus confined the Titans. It was in charge of Pluto, and his wife, Persephone.

Tethys (Gr.)--One of the more important Titans; wife and sister of Oceanus. They were foster parents of Juno.

Thea (Gr.)--An important Titan.

Themis (Gr.)--Among the prominent Titans; daughter of Uranus.

Titans, The (Gr.)--They personified the mighty conclusions, such as volcanic eruptions and earthquakes of the physical world. Being instigators of hatred and strife, they played a quarrelsome part in mythical history.

Uranus (Gr.)--He personified heaven; husband of Gaea, and father of the Titans.

The history of the Titans was recorded by Homer in the *Iliad* and *Odyssey* in the 9th century. And by Hesiod, the Greek poet, in the 8th century.

TOMB *See also* SACRIFICE

Memnon (Gr.)--King of the Aethiopians. He fought bravely in the Trojan War. Killed by Achilles. The Aethiopians raised a tomb in his honor in the grove of the Nymphs, and Jupiter made him immortal.

Patroclus (Gr.)--In the Trojan War, he was mortally wounded by the spear of Hector, for which Achilles, in revenge, dragged Hector's body behind his chariot twice around the tomb of Patroclus.

TONGUE

Philomela (Gr.)--She became the second wife of King Tereus, after he had tired of her sister, Procne, and plucked out her tongue to insure her silence.

Procne (Gr.)-- *See* Philomela.

Tereus (Gr.)--King of Thrace. One day, in revenge, his wives, Philomela and Procne, killed his son, Itylus, and served him as food to his father.

TORCH

Demeter (Gr.); Ceres (Ro.)--She is depicted as holding a torch, ears of corn, wheat and poppies.

Hecate (Gr.)--A three-headed goddess, with six arms which carried a torch or a spear and torch.

Hero (Gr.)--Each night she placed a torch in a tower by the sea to guide Leander in his nightly swim across the Hellespont.

Lucifer (Ro.); Phosphor (Gr.)--The morning star; son of Aurora and Cephalus. By his torch this brilliant star heralded the coming of his goddess mother, Aurora.

Hymen (Gr.)--The god of marriage, who attended the wedding of Orpheus and Eurydice, and brought no happy omen, since his torch smoked and brought tears to the eyes of all present.

TORCH (cont.)

Mars (Ro.); Ares (Gr.)--His emblems are the spear and the burning torch.

Philoctetes (Gr.)--A close friend of Hercules. After the hero had been poisoned by his wife, he built his own funeral pile, rested his head on his club, spread a lion's skin over his body, and asked Philoctetes to apply the torch.

Poeas (Gr.)--Father of Philoctetes, who helped his son apply the torch to Hercules' funeral pile.

TORMENT *See also* PUNISHMENT

Aloadae (Gr.)--Two sons of Iphimedia and Neptune, who, at the age of nine, tried to dethrone the immortals. For their presumption, Jupiter struck them with his lightning, and they atoned in Hades by being bound to a pillar and forced to listen to the perpetual hooting of a screech owl.

Mezentius (Gr.)--King of the Etruscans, who invented unheard-of torments to gratify his vengeance. One was his fastening the dead to the living, face to face, leaving the victims to die in the dreadful embrace.

TRAGEDY

Melpomene (Gr.)--Muse of Tragedy. She holds a tragic mask.

TRAITOR

Antigone (Gr.)-- *See same under* FUNERAL.

Polynices (Gr.)--He fled Thebes to secure the aid of Adrastus, king of Argos, against his brother, Eteocles, who refused to share the throne with him.

TRANSFORMED *See* CHANGE OF FORM

TRAVELERS

Nessus (Gr.)--He carried travelers across a river for a stated fee. He was a centaur.

Periphetes (Gr.)--A ferocious savage always armed with a club. All travelers stood in terror of his violence, except the young hero, Theseus, who felled him with many blows.

Procrustes (Gr.)--Called "The Stretcher" he tied all travelers to his iron bedstead, and stretched them to make them fit, or lopped off their limbs if they were too long.

Sciron (Gr.)--A giant who kept watch on a cliff. He forced travelers to look at his feet, then kicked them into the waters below.

Sphinx, The (Gr.)--A monster with the body of a lion, and the upper torso of a woman. She arrested all travelers to ask them a riddle.

TREACHERY

Furies, The (Gr.)--The three goddesses of vengeance, who visited earth often, to punish treachery, murder, perjury, etc.

Scylla (Gr.)--Her father, King Nisus had a purple lock of hair on his head, upon which depended his life and fortune. When Scylla clipped and gave it to Minos, this enemy recoiled from the treacherous gift.

TREASURE

Dido (Gr.)--Queen of Carthage. When her husband, a man of immense wealth, was put to death, she and numerous followers escaped from Tyre carrying with them his treasures to a site which became Carthage.

Hermes (Gr.); Mercury (Ro.)--He was a god of science, trickery, luck and treasure trove.

Minyas (Gr.)-- *See same under* RICH.

Pygmalion (Gr.)--Brother of Dido, and covetous of the wealth of her

TREASURE (cont.)

Pygmalion (cont.)--husband, Sichaeus, had him put to death.

Sichaeus (Gr.)--He owned great treasures.

TREE *See also* CHANGE IN FORM

Aphrodite (Gr.); Venus (Ro.)--The myrtle and apple trees were sacred to her.

Aristaeus (Gr.)--Protector of the vine and olive.

Atlas (Gr.)--When Perseus and the Gorgon's head changed him to stone, his hair became forests.

Baucis (Gr.)--The gods granted her and her husband, Philemon, a wish that they die at the same hour. Accordingly, after they reached a great age, a leafy crown grew over their heads, and bark closed over their mouths. They became an oak and a linden, standing side by side.

Cyparissus (Gr.)--A boy who begged to mourn forever over the loss of his pet stag. Apollo changed him into a cypress tree, which with its dark foliage has continued to be associated with mourning.

Daphne (Gr.)--When she ran from Apollo she appealed to a woodland divinity for help, and was transformed into a laurel tree.

Daphnis (Gr.)--An ideal shepherd, whose father was Hermes, and his mother, a nymph. She laid him as an infant in a laurel grove, where he was brought up by nymphs and shepherds.

Diana (Ro.); Artemis (Gr.)--The cypress tree was sacred to her.

Dryads (Gr.)--Wood-nymphs. Each nymph's life began and ended with a particular tree.

Dryope (Gr.)--A friend of wood-nymphs who changed into a lotus tree. *See same under* NYMPHS.

Erysichthon (Gr.)--With his ax he violated a grove sacred to Ceres. For this, Famine gave him a raging hunger, which caused him to devour

311

Erysichthon (cont.)--his own limbs.

Giants, The (Gr.)--A race of monsters akin to men more than the Titans. They armed themselves with rocks and the trunks of trees.

Heliades (Gr.)--Daughters of Helios, who were changed into popular trees as they morned for their brother, Phaëton. Their tears turned amber.

Hesperides (Gr.)--The four nymphs who helped guard the orchard of the golden apples.

Lotis (Gr.)-- *See* Dryope.

Melampus (Gr.)--Before his house stood an oak tree which held a serpent's nest. The serpents licked his ears one day and taught him the language of birds and creeping things.

Minerva (Ro.)--She created the olive tree, and it was sacred to her.

Myrrha (Gr.)--Due to some slight, Venus changed her into a myrtle tree.

Oracles (Gr. and Ro.)--Their responses were sometimes given by the rustling of oak trees in the wind, interpreted by the priests.

Philemon (Gr.)-- *See* Baucis.

Phyllis (Gr.)--A Thracian princess, who, after she hanged herself was transformed by the gods into an almond tree, serving as an ideal maiden for pastoral poetry.

Protesilaüs (Gr.)--The nymphs planted elm trees around his grave, which flourished until they were high enough to command a view of Troy, then they withered away to give room for fresh twigs to spring from the roots.

Pyramus (Gr.)--He arranged to meet Thisbe at the foot of a white mulberry tree. A lion approaching with blood on its mouth made Thisbe think he had been killed, and she fled. He arrived and saw her torn veil and the lion's footprints and thought she had been slain. Impulsively he threw himself on his own sword. His blood on the mulberries tinged them red, and thenceforth the mulberry tree

TREE (cont.)

Pyramus (cont.)--produced nothing but purplish red berries.

Python (Gr.)--In commemoration of Apollo's conquest of this enormous serpent, he organized the Pythian games, in which the victors were crowned with a wreath of beech leaves.

Rhoecus (Gr.)--This youth saved a tree from falling, and was rewarded by the dryad of that oak tree with her love.

Tantalus (Gr.)--In Tartarus he was doomed to stand in a pool of water level with his chin, but parched with thirst. Trees laden with fruit leaned toward him, but when he tried to pick them the winds whirled them high above his reach.

Zeus (Gr.)--The loftiest trees and grandest mountains were dear to him.

TRIBUTE

Minotaur, The (Gr.)--Because his son, Androgeüs, had been killed while trying to conquer this bull-headed, man-bodied monster, King Minos II, imposed a penalty upon the Athenians. Each year they were required to send a tribute of seven youths and seven maidens from Athens to Crete to feed this monster.

TRICKERY See also CUNNING

Acetes (Gr.)--A fisherman who found the young Bacchus on the island of Dia, and promised to sail with him to Naxos. When Bacchus discovered they were heading for Egypt instead, he caused ivy to twine around their oars to stop them mid-ocean. Then he changed the crew into dolphins, leaving only Acetes to pilot him to Naxos.

Hermes (Gr.); Mercury (Ro.)--He was a god of cunning, trickery and theft.

Mercury (Ro.)-- See also Hermes. His cunning rendered him a dangerous foe, for he could well play the trickster.

Nisus (Gr.)-- See Scylla under TREACHERY.

TRIDENT

Amymone (Gr.)--One of the Danaïds, who was pursued by a satyr. Hearing her cry, Neptune dispatched the satyr and made love to the maiden himself. Boring the earth with his trident he called forth a spring that still bears her name.

Neptune (Ro.); Poseidon (Gr.)--His symbol of power was the trident, or three-pronged spear. When some of Aeneas's ships were wrecked by Juno, he pried them loose from rocks along the shore with his trident.

Pluto (Class.)--He struck a river bank with his trident, to open the way back to Hades.

TROY

Aeneas (Gr.)--A Trojan prince who fought to save Troy. He carried his father, Anchises, on his shoulders from the burning city.

Agenor (Gr.)--One of the bravest of the Trojan warriors.

Andromache (Gr.)--After the sack of Troy, she was carried off, to be the wife of Neoptolemus.

Cresua (Gr.)--Wife of Aeneas; mother of Ascanius; lost from them during their flight from the burning city of Troy.

Deïphobus (Gr.)--One of the leading warriors at the siege of Troy, where he was killed by Menelaüs.

Diomede (Gr.)--In one combat of the Trojan War he wounded Mars; in another, he felled Aeneas with a stone. It was he who entered Troy with Ulysses and carried off the celebrated statue of Minerva (the Palladium), which supposedly was protecting the city.

Erichthonius (Gr.)--Minerva brought him up in her temple. He was an Athenian hero; father of Tros, in the royal line of Troy.

Euryalus (Gr.)--A distinguished young Trojan soldier.

Helen (Gr.)--Paris persuaded her to elope with him to Troy. Her husband, King Menelaus, of Sparta, pursued them, enlisted many famous

Helen (cont.)--warriors and started the Trojan War, which lasted nine years. After the fall of Troy, she returned to her husband.

Hesione (Gr.)--Daughter of Laomedon of Troy. *See* Laomedon *under* RENEGE. When Neptune sent a sea monster to ravage the land, the was offered by her father to satiate its appetite.

Iliad (Gr.)--An ancient epic poem by Homer, describing events connected with the siege of Troy.

Ilus (Gr.)--Son of Tros, the founder of Troy; grandfather of Priam.

Laomedon (Gr.)--Founder and King of Troy. When he started to build walls around the city he was aided by Neptune and Apollo, then refused to pay the wages agreed upon. It was this that prompted Neptune to ravage the land and to send a sea monster.

Memnon (Gr.)--King of the Aethiopians, who led his people into the Trojan War. He fought bravely, killed Antilochus, son of Nestor, and held the Greeks at bay until Achilles appeared and killed him.

Menelaüs (Gr.)-- *See* Helen.

Pandarus (Gr.)--One of the Trojans, who, after the Greeks claimed victory, broke the truce by shooting an arrow at Menlaüs. A two-day battle resulted.

Penthesilea (Gr.)--A queen of the Amazons who brought momentary success to the sinking cause of Troy. She was slain by Achilles.

Philoctetes (Gr.)--He was with his friend Hercules, during the Grecian expedition against Troy. Wounded by a poisoned arrow, he was carried to the Isle of Lemnos to recover.

Priam (Gr.)--King of Troy. He was old when the siege of his city began. He lived to see the wooden horse smuggled into the gates, and to see Troy burned to the ground.

Sarpedon (Gr.)--One of the principal leaders in the Trojan War against the Greeks. He was slain by Patroclus.

TROY (cont.)

Teucer (Gr.)--Telamon refused to receive him on his return from Troy, for although Teucer was the best archer of the Greeks, he had failed to avenge the death of his stepbrother, Ajax.

Teucri, The (Gr.)--The Trojans; followers of Teucer.

Trojan War (Gr.)--It lasted nine years, since Zeus held the victory in the balance. It was finally won by the Greeks, after they succeeded in smuggling the wooden horse through the gates. Gods and goddesses on the Trojan side were: Aphrodite, Ares and Apollo. On the Grecian side: Athena, Hera and Poseidon.

Tros (Gr.)--Son of Erichthonius of Troy, who named the city after him.

Troy (Gr.)--In ancient times it was called Ilium, or Ilion. It is the site of nine super-imposed ruined cities in N.W. Asia Minor. The seventh stratum, a Phrygian city of *circa* 1200 B.C., was the scene of the *Iliad.*

Tydeus (Gr.)--Father of Diomede, he was prominent in the Trojan War.

Ulysses (Gr.)--He was in the Trojan War from the beginning to end. His own kingdom was Ithaca.

TRUMPETER

Triton (Gr.)--Son of Amphitrite and Neptune. By a blast on his sea-shell he could stir or calm the waves.

Tritons, The (Gr.)--Followers of Triton, son of Neptune; hoarse trumpeters of the deep who blew on long conch shells.

TRUTH

Nereus (Gr.)--A genial old man of the sea, distinguished for his knowledge, and love of truth and justice.

Orpheus (Gr.)--He taught mysterious truths concerning the origin of things and the immortality of the soul.

TURTLE (TORTOISE)

Aphrodite (Gr.; Venus (Ro.)--Sacred to her were rams, hares, dolphins, and tortoises.

Sciron (Gr.)--A giant who kept watch on a cliff, and kicked travelers into the waters below, where an enormous turtle swallowed them. Theseus came along and fed Sciron to this turtle.

TUTOR *See also* TEACHER

Iacchus (Gr.)--His tutor was the jovial Silenus, oldest of the Satyrs.

Silenus (Gr.)--Tutor of the young Iacchus (Bacchus), and probably an indulgent preceptor. He was generally tipsy.

TWILIGHT

Hermes (Gr.); Mercury (Ro.)--He was the god of twilight.

TWINS

Apollo (Gr.)--Son of Latona and Jupiter; the twin brother of Diana.

Death (Gr.); Thanatos (Gr.)--The twin brother of Sleep.

Dioscuri (Gr.)--Castor and Pollux. Jupiter rewarded their attachment (although they were half-brothers), by placing them among the stars as Gemini, the Twins.

Hypnos (Gr.)--He had a twin brother, Thanatos (Death), who with him was represented as a winged god. He was the god of sleep.

Idas (Gr.)--The inseparable companion of his brother, Lynceus.

UNDER WORLD *See also* HADES; LOWER WORLD

Cerberus (Gr.)--A three-headed dog, which guarded the gate to the Under World.

Dis (Ro.); Pluto (Gr.)--An Under World god whose worship was introduced into Rome at the time of the struggle with Carthage.

Hecate (Gr.)--A three-headed goddess, combining the characters of moon goddess, earth goddess and Under World goddess.

Pirithoüs (Gr.)-- *See* Theseus.

Pluto (Class.); Hades (Gr.)--During the council of the gods, his brother, Jupiter, assigned him the government of the Under World, dark, unseen, mysterious, where the spirits of the dead should dwell, and of Tartarus, for the fallen Titans.

Semnae (Gr.)--These were the three Furies, who attended Proserpina, Queen of the Under World. They visited the earth sometimes, to punish murder, treacher, etc., and to avenge the ghosts of those who had died violent deaths.

Sisyphus (Gr.)--For disclosing a secret of Jupiter, he was condemned to the Under World, to roll a huge stone endlessly uphill.

Theseus (Gr.)--He accompanied his friend, Pirithoüs, to the Under World, to help him kidnap the queen, Proserpina. Pluto seized both men and chained them to an enchanted rock at his palace gate, where they remained until Hercules arrived. Theseus was liberated, but Pirithoüs was left to his fate. Theseus was one of the few mortals, beside Aeneas, Hercules, Orpheus and Ulysses, who visited the Under World and returned.

Tiresias (Gr.)--He became a prophet in the Under World.

UNIVERSE

Pan (Gr.); Faunus (Ro.)--His name signified *all.* He came to be considered

UNIVERSE (cont.)

Pan (cont.)--a symbol of the universe; a personification of nature; also a representative of all the Greek gods, and of paganism itself.

Zeus (Gr.); Jupiter (Ro.)--Chosen Sovereign of the World by the council of gods. He was the supreme ruler of the Universe, wisest of the divinities, and the most glorious (his name signifying radiant light of heaven).

UNREQUITED *See* LOVE UNREQUITED

USURPER

Creon (Gr.)--He was made a regent of Thebes for Eteocles and Polynices, the two sons of Oedipus, who with Creon's urging, had thrust their father into exile.

Eteocles (Gr.)--After he and his brother, Polynices, sent their father, Oedipus, into exile, they agreed to share the throne of Thebes alternately. Eteocles reneged. Finally, they fought and felled each other.

Lycus (Gr.)--Usurping King of Thebes, who took his niece, Antiope, from her protector, King Epopeus, and treated her with extreme cruelty.

Pelias (Gr.)--The usurping King of Iolcus. He sent Jason in search of the Golden Fleece to keep him from the throne.

Polyphontes (Gr.)--After leading a revolt against Cresphontes, King of Messenia, he assumed the throne, and took the queen, Merope, for his wife.

V

VALLEY

Stymphalus (Gr.)--A valley which harbored the man-eating Stymphalian birds. They had cruel beaks and sharp talons. It was Hercules' fifth Labor to destroy them.

VASE *See* Pandora *under* BOX

VEGETATION

Aloadae (Gr.)-- *See* Otus.

Attis (Gr.)--A Phrygian god of vegetation and young life. He was a coun-
terpart of the Semitic Adonis.

Earth Goddess (Gr.); Gaea (Gr.)--An ancient goddess of flowers or of
blooming vegetation.

Hyacinthus (Gr.)--The personification of the blooming vegetation of
spring, which withers under the heats of summer.

Iacchus (Gr.); Bacchus (Gr.)--The god of wine, and especially the god of
animal life and vegetation.

Otus (Gr.)--He and his brother, Ephialtes, sons of Neptune and Iphimedia
were giants renowned for their strength, stature and courage. They
represented the unregulated forces of vegetation.

VENGEANCE *See also* AVENGE; MURDER; RETRIBUTION

Atreus (Gr.)--King of Mycena. In family feuding, he and his brother,
Thyestes, killed a third brother, Chrysippus. Later, Atreus killed
three sons of his faithless brother, Thyestes, and in further vengeance, caused him to eat the flesh of his own children at a banquet of
feigned reconciliation. One of Thyestes other sons, Aegisthus, then
killed Atreus.

Furies, The (Gr.)--The three goddesses of vengeance: Alecto, Megaera and
Tisiphone.

Harpies (Gr.)--Foul creatures with the heads and bosoms of women, and
the wings, tail, legs, and claws of birds. They snatched up and carried off the souls of the dead, or executed divine vengeance by seizing or defiling the food of their victims.

Ibycus (Gr.)--A poet, beloved of Apollo. When he was attacked and killed
by two robbers, the Greeks demanded vengeance for his death.

Mezentius (Gr.)--King of the Etruscans, who invented unheard of torments to gratify his vengeance.

Nemesis (Gr.)--An ancient goddess, who personified retributive justive, and represented the righteous anger and vengeance of the gods.

Niobe (Gr.)--Her pride in her fourteen children caused her to boast her superiority over the goddess, Latona, who had but two. In vengeance, these two, Apollo and Artemis, killed thirteen of the children, and Zeus changed Niobe into stone.

Polyphonte (Gr.)--A victim of the vengeance of Venus, he was turned into an owl.

Sisyphus (Gr.)--When he told of witnessing Jupiter's intrigue with Aegina, the vengeance of the gods fell upon him, and he was condemned to eternal punishment in Hades.

Theseus (Gr.)--He brought vengeance on his own son.

Thyestes (Gr.)-- *See* Atreus.

Venus (Ro.); Aphrodite (Gr.)--Goddess of love and beauty, but she did not fail to heap her vengeance upon those who dishonored her rites or defied her power.

Vulcan (Ro.); Hephaestus (Gr.)--One of the great gods; glorious, good-natured; a god of strong arms, but he could be cunning, even vengeful when the emergency demanded. He was more feared than courted.

VESSEL

Danaides (Gr.)--For killing their husbands on their wedding night, they were condemned to spend eternity in Hades, trying to fill a vessel full of holes with water.

VICTORY

Nike (Gr.)–The goddess of Victory.

Apollo (Gr.)--In commemoration of his illustrious conquest of the enormous serpent, Python, he organized the Pythian games, and sang for the first time, the *Paean*, the song of victory.

Victoria (Ro.)--*Same as* Nike (Gr.).

VIGOR

Artemis (Gr.)--*See same under* VIRGIN.

Hermes (Gr.); Mercury (Ro.)--He was beautiful and ever in the prime of young vigor.

VINE *See also* GRAPE; WINE

Aristaeus (Gr.)--He was the protector of vine and olive.

Priapus (Ro.)–Protector of the life of vineyards and gardens.

VIOLATED

Erysichthon (Gr.)--A despiser of the gods, he violated with an ax a grove sacred to Ceres.

VIOLENCE

Eurytion (Gr.)--A centaur, who became intoxicated at the marriage feast of Hippodamia and Pirithoüs, and threatened violence to the bride.

Periphetes (Gr.)--Son of Vulcan; a ferocious savage always armed with a club. All stood in terror of his violence, except Theseus, who killed him with many blows.

VIRGIN

Artemis (Gr.)--Diana (Ro.)--A virgin goddess; the ideal of modesty, grace

VIRGIN (cont.)

Artemis (cont.)--and maidenly vigor.

Astraea (Gr.)--Goddess of innocence and purity. She was placed among the stars as Virgo, the virgin.

Athena (Gr.); Minerva (Ro.)--The virgin goddess, who sprang from the brain of Jove agleam with the panoply of war.

Camilla (Gr.)--A virgin huntress and warrior, with deeds of valor unsurpassed. She was killed, unobserved, by Aruns.

Glaucus (Gr.)-- See Scylla.

Minerva (Ro.); Athena (Gr.)--A virgin goddess of gentle, fair and thoughtful aspect.

Parthenos (Gr.)--The Virgin; a title of Athena, and sometimes applied to Artemis and Hera.

Psyche (Gr.)--When Venus found her altar deserted, while men paid their vows to this virgin, she became jealous.

Scylla (Gr.)--Glaucus became infatuated with this fair virgin, but she rejected him. In desperation Glaucus asked the enchantress, Circe, for help, but she only changed her into a hideous monster made of serpents and barking dogs.

VIRTUE

Rhadamanthus (Gr.)--His life was not eventful, but he trained Hercules in wisdom and virtue.

VOICE

Echo (Gr.)-- See same under TALKATIVE.

Hermes (Gr.); Mercury (Ro.)--He was in the prime of young vigor, sweet-voiced, and had the power of persuasion by eloquence.

VOLCANO

Hephaestus (Gr.); Vulcan (Ro.)--He was the god of fire, especially of volcanic eruption and incendiary flame.

Typhon (Gr.)--A monster who disputed the reign of Jupiter. He had a hundred dragon-heads, from whose eyes shot fire. To this day he grumbles and hisses, and thrusts his tongue upward through a fiery volcano, breathing out hot winds, scorching trees and men.

VOLUPTUOUSNESS

Semiramis (Gr.)--Queen of Babylonia; noted for her great wisdom, beauty and voluptuousness.

VOTIVE

Erysichthon (Gr.)--He cut down an oak tree which had had many votive tablets hung on it by mortals grateful to the nymph of the tree, and around which Dryads had often danced.

VOYAGER

Castor (Gr.)--He and his inseparable half-brother, Pollux, made all expeditions in common. During a voyage to Colchis, they survived a storm, and when stars appeared on their heads they came to be honored as the patrons of voyagers.

Pollux (Gr.)-- *See* Castor.

VULTURE *See also* LIVER

Mars (Ro.); Ares (Gr.)--His favorite bird was the vulture.

W

WALL

Amphion (Gr.)--King of Thebes. He was so skillful a musician that when

WALL (cont.)

Amphion (cont.)--he played his lyre, stones moved of their own accord and took their places in the wall he was building to fortify the city.

Cybele (Ro.); Rhea (Gr.)--Mother of the gods; protectress of cities. She wore a turreted crown like the wall of a city.

Laomedon (Gr.)--Founder and King of Troy. Playing on his lyre, Apollo aided Neptune in building the walls of Troy for Laomedon.

WAND *See also* CADUCEUS; STAFF

Mercury (Ro.); Hermes (Gr.)--He bore a wand possessed of magical power over sleeping, dreams and waking. With the aid of this wand, Mercury put to sleep the hundred eyes of the monster, Ärgus, then killed him.

WANDERING

Dionysus (Gr.); Bacchus (Gr.)--Juno struck him with madness, and sent him wandering to many parts of the earth. In Phrygia, the goddess, Rhea, cured him, and taught him her religious rites, after which he set out through Asia, teaching people the cultivation of the vine.

Epaphus (Gr.)--Son of Io, by Zeus. Born in Egypt after the wanderings of his mother.

Hercules (Ro.)-- *See same under* LABORS.

Latona (Ro.)--Mother of Apollo and Diana, by Jupiter, for which the ire of Juno was never appeased. Due to her persecutions, Latona wandered from land to land, trying to escape.

Odysseus (Gr.); Ulysses (Gr.)--Hero of the *Odyssey,* which records his wanderings from the time he left Troy until he reached his own kingdom of Ithaca, over a period of ten years.

Orestes (Gr.)--When he was trying to avenge his father's murder, the Furies drove him frantic from land to land.

Pylades (Gr.)--He accompanied his friend, Orestes, during his wanderings.

Telemachus (Gr.)--He spent many years searching for his wandering father Ulysses.

Ulysses (Gr.)--In his wanderings between Troy and his own kingdom, Ithaca, he spent ten years.

WAR *See also* MURDER; TROY

Ares (Gr.); Mars (Ro.)--The war god. He usually fought on foot, but sometimes from a chariot.

Athena (Gr.); Minerva (Ro.)--The virgin goddess, sprang from the brain of Jove agleam with the panoply of war.

Bellona (Gr.)--A goddess personifying war; associated with Mars.

Enyalus (Gr.)--A god of war; an epithet of Mars, meaning the horrible. Identified with Ares.

Hecate (Gr.)--A three-headed goddess, who gave aid in war and athletic contests.

Helen (Gr.)--Paris eloped with her, and this triggered the Trojan War.

Jupiter (Ro.)--He won the war against the Titans by blinding them.

Mars (Ro.); Ares (Gr.)--In typifying the chances of war, he was not always successful. Minerva and Juno brought him grief more than once.

Minerva (Ro.); Athena (Gr.)--Goddess of war, rejoicing in martial music and protecting the war horse and the warship. She favored only defensive warfare, and had no sympathy with Mars' savage love of violence and bloodshed.

Phoenix (Gr.)--He educated Achilles in eloquence and the arts of war.

Quirinus (Ro.)--An ancient god of war.

Erichthoneus (Gr.)--A special ward of Minerva, who brought him up in her temple.

WARRIOR *See also* ARMY; CHIEFTAIN

Agenor (Gr.)--One of the bravest Trojan warriors.

Amphitryon (Gr.)--Warrior; King of Thebes; husband of Alcmene, and commonly known as the mortal father of Hercules.

Aruns (Gr.)--An Etruscan warrior, who, during battle, threw a javelin at the virgin warrior Camilla, and fatally wounded her. To avenge her, Diana had one of her nymphs kill Aruns with a secret arrow. He died ignobly and unknown.

Calaïs (Gr.)--A winged warrior who was on the Argonautic expedition, and served well in an encounter with those monstrous birds, the Harpies.

Calchas (Gr.)-- *Same as* Colchis; a soothsayer and prophet who accompanied the Greeks during the Trojan War. He told them that if the Trojans took possession of the wooden horse they would triumph over the Greeks. At one point Neptune assumed the form of Calchis to inspire the Greeks to force the Trojans to give way.

Camilla (Gr.)--The virgin warrior, whose deeds of valor surpassed those of the bravest.

Deïphobus (Gr.)--One of the leading warriors at the battle of Troy.

Idomeneus (Gr.)--One of the great Greek chieftains; King of Crete; leader of the Cretans against Troy.

Machaon (Gr.)--Son of Aesculapius; a brave warrior, and surgeon who proved of high value to the Greeks during the Trojan War.

Pygmies (Gr.)--An army of little warriors who found Hercules asleep, and were about to attack as if he were a city. He awoke, laughed, wrapped some of them in his lion's skin, and carried them back to King Eurystheus.

Turnus (Gr.)--Chief of the Italian tribe, the Rutuli. He killed Pallas, whom Aeneas avenged by thrusting his sword through Turnus.

Zetes (Gr.)--A winged warrior, who with his brother, Calaïs, won an encounter with the Harpies.

WATER *See also* BROOK; FOUNTIAN; OCEAN; SEA; SPRING; STREAM

Amphitrite (Gr.)--One of the Nereids; wife of Neptune, and with him founder of the yonger dynasty of the waters.

Arethusa (Gr.)-- *See same under* NYMPHS.

Charybdis (Gr.)--A whirlpool off the Sicilian coast. *See same under* WHIRLPOOL.

Clytie (Gr.)--A water-nymph in love with Apollo. *See same under* FLOWERS.

Cyrene (Gr.)--A water-nymph; loved by Apollo.

Dagon (Gr.)--The fish-god who swam nightly through subterranean waters, and appeared again at daybreak.

Danaïdes (Gr.)-- *See same under* VESSEL.

Fontus (Gr.)--God of flowing waters, of spring, brooks, and of healing. Son of Juturna.

Juturna (Ro.)--A water-nymph; goddess of springs and brooks, whose pool in the Forum was sacred.

Latona (Ro.)--Goddess of darkness. Persecuted by Juno, she wandered from land to land. In Lycia, weary and parched with thirst, she was about to drink from a pond of clear water, when the rustics forbade her by wading in to stir up the mud with their feet.

Naiads (Gr. and Ro.)--These were nymphs who lived in, guarded and gave life and perpetuity to rivers, lakes, streams, and fountains of fresh

WATER (cont.)

Naiads (cont.)--water, and kept them sacred.

Narcissus (Gr.)--Seeing that he was so conceited, Nemesis caused him to fall in love with his own reflection in the water. He talked to it, languished and pined for it until he died.

Neptune (Ro.); Poseidon (Gr.)--God of the sea and of all waters, being given this control after the overthrow of the Titans. Becoming dissatisfied with conditions in the world, he and his brother, Jupiter, swept away the race of men by a deluge.

Nereus (Gr.)--He was a genial old man of the sea, who lived with his wife, Doris, and their fifty mermaid daughters, in a great shining cave below the waters.

Pontus (Gr.)--God of the deep sea or the waterways; the father of Nereus, by Mother Earth.

Poseidon (Gr.); Neptune (Ro.)--God of the kingdom of the sea; founder of the younger dynasty of the waters.

Tantalus (Gr.)--In Tartarus, he was doomed to stand in a pool of water level with his chin, parched with thirst, but never permitted to drink.

Triton (Gr.)--Trumpeter of the Ocean. By a blast on his sea-shell he could stir or calm the waves.

WAYFARERS *See* SHIP; WANDERING

WAX

Cupid (Ro.); Eros (Gr.)--He visited Psyche only at night, warning her never to try to see him. One night she lit a candle to look at him, and when a drop of burning wax fell on him he vanished at once.

Daedalus (Gr.)--When he and his son, Icarus, were imprisoned by King Minos, he constructed wings made of feathers, fastened on with wax. *See same under* WINGS.

Sirens, The (Gr.)--In order to successfully pass the island of the Sirens, Ulysses stopped the ears of his seamen with wax, and had himself bound to the mast.

WEALTH *See also* RICH

Croesus (Gr.)--King of Lydia, renowned for his vast wealth. He lost his empire in a war with the King of Persia.

Dido (Gr.)-- *See same under* TREASURE.

Plutus (Gr.)--God of wealth.

Sichaeus (Gr.)--King of Tyre, a man of immense wealth, put to death by the covetous Pygmalion.

WEAPON *See slao* ARROWS; LIGHTNING; MURDER

Selene (Gr.)--An ancient goddess of the moon; her weapons, the bow and arrow.

WEAVING

Arachne (Gr.)--A Lydian princess who challenged Minerva to a weaving contest. Losing to the goddess so humiliated her that she hanged herself, and Minerva transformed her into a spider.

Athena (Gr.); Minerva (Ro.)--The virgin goddess, who presided over the useful and ornamental arts; in those of women, spinning, weaving and needlework.

Clotho (Gr.)--Youngest of the three Fates; she who wound the wool around the spindle.

Ergane (Athena) (Gr.)--Patroness of the arts, especially weaving.

Horae (Gr.)--Three goddesses of the hours, season and orderliness. They attended Venus, twining garlands and weaving robes for her, assisted by the Graces.

Laërtes (Gr.)--King of Ithaca; father of Ulysses, for whom Penelope insisted she was weaving a robe, saying she would choose a suitor when it was done. At night, she ravelled the work she had done during the day.

Penelope (Gr.)--Wife of Ulysses. *See also* Laërtes.

Procne (Gr.)--After her husband, Tereus, plucked out her tongue, she wove her story to her sister by means of a web.

330

WEDDING *See also* NUPTIALS

Danaïdes (Gr.)-- *See same under* HUSBANDS.

Golden Apples, The (Gr.)--Gaea had given these to Hera as a wedding present.

Hesperides (Gr.)--Four nymphs who, with the aid of the dragon, Ladon, guarded the garden where grew the tree of the Golden Apples. It had sprung up to grace the wedding of Hera and Jupiter.

Hymen (Gr.)--The god of marriage; personification of the wedding feast and the leader of the nuptial chorus. His torch smoked at the wedding of Orpheus and Eurydice, and brought tears to the eyes of all present.

Hypermnesta (Gr.)--The only one of the daughters of Danaüs, who would not slay her husband on their wedding night.

Lynceus (Gr.)--He escaped being slain on his wedding night, by Hypermnesta.

Vulcan (Ro.); Hephaestus (Gr.)--He gave Harmonia a necklace of unsurpassed brilliance for her wedding to Cadmus.

WELFARE

Penates (Ro.)--Gods of the household; the welfare and prosperity of the family.

WELL

Daphnis (Gr.)--He was struck blind by a Naiad, and when he called on his father, Mercury, for aid, the god transported him to heaven and caused a well to gush forth on the spot from which he ascended. Here the Sicilians offer yearly sacrifice in his honor.

WELL-INTENTIONED *See* INTENTIONED

WHEEL

Ixion (Gr.)--King of Lapithae, who, because he aspired to the love of a goddess (Hera), was sent to Hades and bound to an endlessly re-

WHEEL (cont.)

Ixion (cont.)--volving wheel.

Myrtilus (Gr.)--A charioteer, who was bribed by Hippodamia to remove a bolt from her father's chariot wheel, to allow her suitor, Pelops, to win the race.

WHIRLPOOL

Charybdis (Gr.)--A whirlpool off the Sicilian coast. Three times a day water rushed into the frightful chasm, to be three times disgorged. With the monster, Scylla, along the cliff, she guarded the strait of Messina.

WHIRLWIND

Niobe (Gr.)--After Zeus changed her into stone, her tears over the loss of her children continued to flow, even after she was borne by a whirlwind to her native mountain.

WHITE *See also* PALENESS

Andromache (Gr.)--Daughter of Eëtion, she was known as "The white-armed."

WILD *See* BULL; MADNESS

WIND *See also* BREEZE

Aeolus (Gr.)--Sometimes called Hippotades, he was king of the winds with a palace on the precipitous Isle of Aelia. Here, with six sons and and six daughters, he kept eternal carouse. He confined the winds in a cavern, and let them loose as he saw fit.

Aquilo (Gr.)--The north wind; synonymous with Boreas.

Ares (Gr.); Mars (Ro.)--The offspring of the North Wind and a Fury.

Aura (Gr.)-- *See* BREEZE.

Auster (Gr.); Notus (Gr.)--God the south wind.

Boreas (Gr.)--God of the north wind. He acted out his true character, seized the nymph Orithyia, and carried her off.

Eos (Gr.); Aurora (Ro.)--See BREEZE.

Eurus (Gr.)--God of the southeast wind.

Halcyone (Gr.)--After her husband was drowned in a shipwreck, she threw herself into the sea. The gods out of compassion, changed her into a kingfisher. Since that time, Jove has forbidden the winds to blow a week before and a week after the winter solstice. It is then that Halcyone broods over her nest, and the way is safe for seafarers.

Harpies (Gr.)--Personification of devastating winds.

Memnon (Gr.)--After his death in the Trojan War, the Winds conveyed his body to the banks of the river Aesepus in Mysia.

Midas (Gr.)--Breezes passing over reeds in a meadow caused them to whisper the secret of Midas's ears.

Notus (Gr.)--The south wind. Same as Auster.

Typhon (Gr.)--A monster with a hundred dragon-heads, who finally descended to Tartarus. To this day, he grumbles, hisses, and thrusts his tongue upward through a fiery volcano, breathing out hot winds, scorching trees and men. It was he who helped Aeolus and Boreas, and other winds to toss the ocean and to upset the ships of Aeneas.

Ulysses (Gr.)--At the island of Aeolus, he was given a leather bag containing such winds that might be hurtful and dangerous, allowing the winds outside to blow his ships toward his own country. Once while Ulysses slept, his crew became curious about the mysterious bag, and loosened the string. Immediately the winds rushed out, drove them far from their course, and back to the island they had just left. They were obliged to labor over their course once more with oars.

Zephyrus (Gr.)--The west wind; most gentle of all sylvan deities. It was he who carried Psyche to a flowery dale, fast by a palace, where Cupid came to visit her each night.

Zetes (Gr.)-- Son of Boreas.

WINE

Bacchus (Gr.); Dionysus (Gr.)--The god of wine. He represented the vital strength of everything that grows, and the power of the joyful life.

Dionysus (Gr.)-- *Same as* Bacchus. A deity of earth.

Iacchus (Gr.)-- *Same as* Bacchus. He was the only one who could persuade Vulcan to free Juno from a throne to which Vulcan had chained her in the depths of the ocean. He did so by drenching Vulcan with wine and conducting him personally to Olympus.

Philemon (Gr.)--While he and his wife, Baucis, were offering wine to Jupiter and Mercury in disguise, they were astonished to see that the wine renewed itself in the pitcher as fast as it was poured.

WINGS

Calaïs (Gr.)--A winged warrior who accompanied the Argonauts, and served well in an encounter with the Harpies.

Ceres (Ro.); Demeter (Gr.)--She drove a chariot drawn by winged dragons.

Daedalus (Gr.)--An artificer, who while in prison, constructed wings made of feathers, fastened on with wax. With his son, Icarus, he escaped, and dedicated his wings to the temple of Apollo. His son flew too near the sun, which melted the wax and caused him to drop into the sea, now named Icarian Sea.

Epimetheus (Gr.)--Brother of Prometheus, who was committed to provide all beings with properties necessary for their preservation: claws to some, wings and shells to others.

Erysichthon (Gr.)--Because he cut an oak tree to the ground the Dryads invoked punishment on him, by having Famine enfold him in her wings. Unable to fill the demands of his hunger, he devoured his own limbs.

Gryphons (Gr.)--They had the head and wings of an eagle; served as guardians of gold.

Hermes (Gr.); Mercury (Ro.)--He was a slightly draped youth with winged shoes, fastened to his ankles, a winged cap on his head, and carrying a wand.

334

WINGS (cont.)

Hypnos (Gr.)--The god of sleep. He and his twin brother, Thanatos, were represented as winged gods.

Icarus (Gr.)-- *See* Daedalus.

Marpessa (Gr.)--She was carried off by the strong man Idas, assisted by Poseidon, who gave him a winged chariot.

Medusa (Gr.)--She was a Gorgon, who had been laying the countryside to waste. Perseus was sent to conquer her. By borrowing Hades' helmet, which made him invisible, and Minerva's winged shoes, pouch and shield, and Mercury's knife, he was able to approach her and to cut off her head. One glimpse of this head turned beholders to stone. From Medusa's body sprang the winged horse, Pegasus.

Mercury (Ro.)-- *See* Hermes. His caduceus (wand) of wood or gold, was twined with snakes, and surmounted by wings.

Neptune (Ro.); Poseidon (Gr.)--He gave Idas a winged chariot with which to carry off Marpessa.

Nike (Gr.); Victoria (Ro.)--The goddess of victory, winged and carrying a wreath and a palm branch.

Pegasus (Gr.)--The winged horse which sprang from the body of Medusa. Minerva gave Bellerophon a magic, golden bridle, and when he put it on Pegasus, the steed sped through the air, found the monster, Chimaera, thus enabling the hero to gain an easy victory.

Pelops (Gr.)--He obtained winged steeds from Neptune, and won the race for the hand of Hippodamia.

Thanatos (Gr.)--A winged god. *See* Hypnos.

Victory (Ro.)-- *See* Nike.

Zetes (Gr.)--A winged warrior, who, with his brother, Calaïs, won an encounter with the Harpies.

WISDOM

Alcinoüs (Gr.)--A wise, just and beloved king of the Phaeacians in Scheria.

Hercules (Ro.); Alcides (Gr.)–He was trained in wisdom and virtue by Rhadmanthus.

Minerva (Ro.); Athena (Gr.)--Goddess of wisdom, skill and contemplation.

Priam (Gr.)--King of Troy; a wise ruler, strengthening his state by good government.

Rhadamanthus (Gr.)-- See Hercules.

Semiramis (Gr.)--Queen of Babylonia; noted for her great wisdom, beauty and voluptuousness.

Vulcan (Ro.); Hephaestur (Gr.)--A good-natured god, loved and honored among men as the founder of wise customs.

Zeus (Gr.); Jupiter (Ro.)--Sovereign of the World; the supreme ruler of the Universe; wisest and msot glorious of the divinities.

WISH

Baucis (Gr.)--She and her husband, Philemon, wished to be taken from life at the same hour. They were changed into oak and linden trees, standing side by side.

Cadmus (Gr.)--Became king of the Enchelians. One day in weariness he remarked: "If the serpent is so highly regarded by the gods, I wish I were one myself." As if in answer, he began to change form. His wife, Harmonia, shared his fate, and they both became serpents.

Harmonia (Gr.)– See Cadmus.

WITCH

Graeae, The (Gr.)–These were three hoary witches, known as the Gray Women, who served as sentinels for the Gorgons. They were daughters of Phorsys, a sea deity. They had only one eye among them, which they handed from one to the other, and only one tooth. They were: Deino--The Terrifier; Enyo--The Shaker, and Pephredo--The Horrifier.

Hecate (Gr.)--A three-headed goddess, who represented darkness, terrors,

WITCH (cont.)

Hecate (cont.)--magic and witchcraft.

WIVES

Aërope (Gr.)--Wife of Atreus, King of Mycenae.

Aethra (Gr.)--Wife of Aegeus; mother of Theseus.

Aglaia (Gr.)--Wife of Vulcan; one of the three Graces.

Alcestis (Gr.)--Wife of King Admetus, for whose life she substituted her own.

Alcmene (Gr.)--Wife of the mortal, Alcaeus, but mother of Hercules by Jupiter.

Althaea (Gr.)--Wife of Oeneus; mother of Meleager.

Andromache (Gr.)--Noblest of women in the *Iliad;* married to Hector, after whose death she was carried off to be the wife of Neoptolemus, and to bear him three sons. After he cast her aside, she married Helenus, brother of Hector, and still later, she returned to Asia Minor.

Andromeda (Gr.)--An Ethiopian maiden, whom Perseus rescued from a horrible sea-monster, then married. They had three sons, one of whom was Electryon.

Antiope (Gr.)--Queen of the Amazons; later the wife of Theseus.

Aphrodite (Gr.)--The wife of Vulcan, in one account; of Ares, in another. She made Pymalion's statue of Galathea come to life.

Ariadne (Gr.)--Deserted by Theseus, she married Bacchus. He gave her a crown studded with stars as a wedding present, and when she died, he threw it into the heavens where it can still be seen as Corona, or Adriadne's crown.

Atlas (Gr.)--He was married four times, and fathered three classes of nymphs:
    1. Pleione bore him the Pleides
    2. Aethra, the Hyades
    3. Hesperis, the Hesperides.
His fourth wife, Sterope I, became the mother of Maia, and the

337

WIVES (cont.)

Atlas (cont.)--grandmother of Mercury.

Baucis (Gr.)--An old Phrygian peasant woman, married to Philemon.

Callirrhoe (Gr.)--An ocean nymph; wife of Chrysaor. Or (b)--Wife of Alcmaeon.

Clymene (Gr.)--Wife of Apollo, and by him the mother of the Heliades. Also, she was the mother of Atlas and Prometheus, by Iapetus.

Clytemnestra (Gr.)--Wife of Agamemnon. Becoming enamored of Aegisthus, she was false to her husband, and successfully planned his destruction.

Cybele (Ro.)--Wife of Cronus.

Dejanira (Gr.)--Wife of Hercules. Jealous of his attention to Iole, she caused his death by means of a poisoned robe.

Dido (Gr.)--Married to Sichaeus, a man of immense wealth.

Dirce (Gr.)--The second wife of Lycus, who doomed Antiope to die by being dragged behind a bull.

Doris (Gr.)--Wife of the genial old man of the sea, Nereus, and mother of fifty Nereïds.

Eriphyle (Gr.)--Wife of Amphiaraüs. She was bribed by Polynices with the necklace of Harmonia.

Eurydice (Gr.)--Married to Orpheus.

Gaea (Gr.)--Wife of Uranus.

Halcyone (Gr.)--Wife of Ceyx, King of Trachis in Thessaly.

Harmonia (Gr.)--Wife of Cadmus. Vulcan gave her a brilliant necklace for a wedding present, which brought a curse on the house of Cadmus for several generations.

Hebe (Gr.)--Wife of King Priam.

Helen (Gr.)--Wife of Menelaüs, who eloped with Paris, and became the immediate cause of the Trojan War.

338

Hemba (Gr.)--*Same as* Hecuba.

Hera (Gr.)--Wife of Zeus; champion of wives.

Hermione (Gr.)--Married first to Neoptolemus, and later, to Orestes.

Hesione (Gr.)--Wife of Telamon.

Hippodamia (Gr.)--Wife of Pelops.

Hypermnestra (Gr.)--Married Lynceus, but refused to slay him on their wedding night, as her sisters had their husbands on their wedding night.

Ino (Gr.)--Second wife of Athamas.

Iphimedia (Gr.)--Her mortal husband; Aloeus. Mistress of Neptune.

Jocasta (Gr.)--Wife of Laïus, King of Thebes; mother of Oedipus.

Juno (Ro.); Hera (Gr.)--Wife of Jupiter, and extremely jealous of his many mistresses.

Juturna (Ro.)--Wife of Janus, and the mother of Fontus.

Laodamia (Gr.)--Wife of Protesilaüs.

Lavinia (Gr.)--Married to Aeneas; mother of Iulus.

Leda (Gr.)--Wife of Tyndareus, and mother of Castor and Clytemnestra.

Medea (Gr.)--Married to Jason; later to King Aegeus.

Merope (Gr.)--She was vested with mortality in consequence of her marriage with the mortal, Sisyphus, King of Corinth.

Myrrha (Gr.)--Wife of the Cinyras; mother of Adonis.

Nephele (Gr.)--Wife of Athamas; mother of Phrixus and Helle.

Niobe (Gr.)--Wife of Amphion, King of Thebes, by whom she had seven sons and seven daughters.

Orithyia (Gr.)--Married Boreas. Their children, Calaïs and Zetes.

Pasiphaē (Gr.)--Wife of King Minos II. Neptune caused her to have a passion for the Cretan Bull.

Penelope (Gr.)--Married to Ulysses, and faithful to him during his twenty-year absence.

Phaedra (Gr.)--Second wife of Theseus.

Philomela (Gr.)--Second wife of Tereus, King of Thrace.

Procne (Gr.)--First wife of King Tereus, who tired of her and plucked out her tongue.

Procris (Gr.)--Married to the young huntsman, Cephalus.

Proserpina (Gr.)--Wife of Pluto, ruler of Hades.

Psyche (Gr.)--Wife of Cupid.

Pyrrha (Gr.)--Wife of Deucalion.

Rhea (Gr.); Cybele (Ro.)--Wife of Cronus; mother of six gods.

Tethys (Gr.)--Wife and sister of Oceanus.

Themisto (Gr.)--Third wife of Athamas.

Venus (Ro.)--Wife of Vulcan.

WOLF

Apollo (Gr.); Lycius (Gr.)--Among his many names was Lycius, the wolf-god, or the golden god of light.

WOMEN

Dione (Gr.)--A female Titan; goddess of women and marriage. To her the cow was sacred.

Hera (Gr.); Juno (Ro.)--Goddess of woman's life; champion of wives and mothers.

Juno (Ro.); Hera (Gr.)--Guardian of women, she was the type of matronly virtues and dignity.

Phaon (Gr.)–A ferryman on a boat between Lesbos and Chios. Aphrodite gave him a salve possessing magic properties of youth. When he used it, the women of Lesbos went wild for love of him.

WOO

Pomona (Ro.)–A Hamadryad, who spurned offers of love made by innumerable Fauns and Satyrs. Finally, Vertumnus wooed her in many disguises: as a haymaker, fisherman, soldier, etc., and won her as a comely youth.

Tyro (Gr.)--A princess, loved by Enipeus, and wooed by Neptune in the guise of Enipeus.

WOODEN HORSE *See also* TROY

Colchas (Gr.)--A soothsayer who accompanied the Greeks during the Trojan War. Neptune assumed his form to raise the morale of the Greek warriors to such a pitch they forced the Trojans to give way.

Epeus (Gr.)--He was the builder of the wooden horse at Troy.

Laocoön (Gr.)--A priest of Apollo, who warned the Trojans that the wooden horse might be a fraud perpetrated by the Greeks. He hurled a spear at the side of the horse, and its reverberating sound made him suspicious, but the act incurred the enmity of Athena. She sent two immense sea serpents to wind their coils around Laocoön and his two sons to strangle them todeath.

Priam (Gr.)--King of Troy. He had been a wise ruler. He was old when the siege of Troy began, and he lived to see the wooden horse sumggled into the city, and to see Troy burned to the ground.

Sinon (Gr.)--A clever Greek left behind when the rest of his countrymen sailed away from Troy, and left the wooden horse outside the gates of the city. Taken captive by the Trojans, he assured them that the wooden horse was a propitiary offering to Minerva; that it had been made large for the express purpose of preventing its being carried into the city. With triumphal song, the Trojans pushed the horse through the gates and celebrated to the close of day. In the night, Sinon loosened the bolts and let the heroes out. They set the city on fire, slaughtered the people, and completely subdued Troy, thus ending the nine-year siege.

WOODS *See also* TREE

Clytie (Gr.)--A wood-nymph in love with Apollo, unrequited. She became a sun-flower, turning on its stem to follow the journeying sun.

Dyrads (Gr.)--Wood-nymphs. Each nymph's life begins and ends with a particular tree.

Dryope (Gr.)--A playmate of the wood-nymphs, beloved by Apollo. *See same under* NYMPHS.

Echo (Gr.)--A talkative, beautiful Oread, fond of woods and hills; a favorite of Diana. By her chatter she displeased Juno, who caused her to lose her voice, except for the purpose of replying.

Hamadryads (Gr.)--These were Dryads, female wood-nymphs, and of the lesser gods of earth.

Pan (Gr.); Faunus (Ro.)--God of woods and fields.

WORLD

Jupiter (Ro.); Zeus (Gr.)--He was chosen Sovereign of the World by the council of the gods, after the reign of Uranus, and his son, Cronus.

WORMS *See* Melampus *under* PROPHET

WORSHIP

Egeria (Ro.)--Associated with Carmenta, leader of the fountain-nymphs. The Roman King Numa received instructions from Egeria, concering the forms of worship which he introduced.

Iacchus (Gr.); Bacchus (Gr.)--He had many followers. After introducing his worship through Asia, he returned to Greece to do the same, but in spite of cries of Baccanals which could be heard everywhere, his own cousin, Pentheus, opposed him and forbade the rites. It was only after the death of Pentheus that the new worship of Bacchus was free to be established in Greece.

Pan (Gr.); Faunus (Ro.)--His name, which signified *all*, came to be considered a symbol of the universe, and a personification of nature; also a representative of all the Greek gods and of paganism itself.

WORSHIP (cont.)

Pentheus (Gr.)-- *See* Iacchus.

Persephone (Gr.); Proserpina (Ro.)--Her worship was connected with that of her husband Pluto.

Saturn (Ro.)--An ancient deity of seeds and sowing. The worship of Saturn was conformed in 217 B.C., to that of the Greek Cronus, from whom his images were made.

WOUND *See also* ARROWS

Ancaeus (Gr.)-- *See same under* HERO.

Aruns (Gr.)--An Etruscan warrior who inflicted a fatal wound in the virgin warrior, Camilla. Diana avenged her by having one of her nymphs shoot a secret arrow at Aruns. He died ignobly and unknown.

Diomede (Gr.)--During the Trojan War he wounded Mars; felled Pandarus with his spear, and crushed Aeneas with a stone. He, himself had been wounded by Pandarus.

Erysichthon (Gr.)--He wounded an oak tree, which seemed to shudder and groan as he chopped. For this, Famine enfolded him, and caused him finally to devour himself.

Hecatonchires (Gr.)--Uranus feared these offspring, and tried to destroy them, until Cronus, one of his Titan offspring, grievously wounded him with an iron sickle.

Hector (Gr.)--He was wounded and forced out of one combat of the Trojan War by Alex. Later, he mortally wounded Patroclus. This brought Achilles into the fight, and after Hector circled the city three times, he wounded him in the neck with his spear. In further vengeance, Achilles dragged his body with a cord tied to his chariot, back and forth in front of the gates of Troy.

Hyacinthus (Gr.)--One day he was playing quoits with Apollo when the god flung a discus high and far which struck him in the forehead. Apollo tried in vain to stanch the wound.

Hydra (Gr.)--A water-serpent with nine heads, anyone of which when cut off would grow two, unless the wound were cauterized.

Machaon (Gr.)--Son of Aesculapias, who, having inherited his father's

343

Machaon (cont.)--art, cured Philoctetes of a wound inflicted by one of Hercules' poisoned arrows. In the Trojan War, he was wounded by an arrow from the bow of Paris.

Megaera (Gr.)--One of the three Furies, born of the blood of the wounded Uranus.

Mezentius (Gr.)--In the war between the Trojans and the Etruscans, he was wounded in the thigh by Aeneas.

Oenone (Gr.)--A nymph whom the young Paris had married, and abondoned for the fatal beauty of Helen. When Paris was wounded during the Trojan War, he went to her for comfort, but she thought of the wrongs she had suffered, and refused to heal the wound.

Paris (Gr.)--He was wounded by an arrow of Hercules.

Patroclus (Gr.)-- *See* Hector.

Philoctetes (Gr.)-- *See* Machaon.

Telephus (Gr.)--He was wounded in the thigh by the spear of Achilles, but cured by the rust of that spear.

Tisiphone (Gr.)--One of the three Furies who sprang from the blood of the wounded Uranus. Her sisters were Alecto and Megaera.

Uranus (Gr.)-- *See* Hecatonchires.

WRATH

Juno (Ro.); Hera (Gr.)--She, the wife of Jupiter, was fearful in her wrath, and all of his misteresses had to endure in one way or another, her fury and vengeance.

WREATH

Megaera (Gr.)--One of the three Furies whose heads were wreathed with serpents.

Python (Gr.)--In commemoration of Apollo's conquest of this enormous serpent, he organized the Pythian games, in which the victors were crowned with a wreath of beech leaves.

WRESTLER

Acheloüs (Gr.)–A river-god who found he was no match for Hercules in the wrestler's art. Acheloüss, who could change form, tried to glide away as a serpent, but Hercules clasped him and choked him until he assumed a new shape, that of a bull. Hercules then dragged his head to the ground and rent one horn away. The Naiads consecrated it, filled it with flowers and named it Cornucopia.

Antaeus (Gr.)--A giant wrestler. *See more about same under* LABORS.

Gaea (Gr.)--By Poseidon, she was the mother of the giant wrestler, Antaeus.

Hercules (Ro.)-- *See* Acheloüs; Anteus.

Y

YEAR

Janus (Ro.)--The god of doors, and of beginnings, especially of good beginnings which insure good endings. He was also the god of the opening year.

YOUTH

Aeson (Gr.)–After he had reached old age, the sorceress, Medea, restored him to the vigor of youth.

Coroebus (Gr.)–A noble youth who killed a monster that for a season had been destroying the children.

Cumaean Sibyl (Gr.)--Apollo tried to win her, and promised her any gift in his power to bestow. She pointed to a pile of sand and asked to live as many years as there were grains of sand in the heap. But she forgot to ask for youth, and had to look forward to centuries of time with the burdens of old age.

Endymion (Gr.)--A youth of great beauty, loved by Diana. *See same under* MOON.

Ganymede (Gr.)–A handsome Trojan boy, who succeeded Hebe as cup-bearer to the gods.

Hebe (Gr.)--She poured nectar for the gods in Olympus. She became the wife of the deified Hercules, and was believed to have the power of restoring youth. She was youth personified as a goddess.

Hermes (Gr.); Mercury (Ro.)--He was represented as a young, vigorous, beardless man with winged shoes, and a winged cap. He was the god of youth.

Hyacinthus (Gr.)--He was killed in his youth by a discus thrown by his friend, Apollo.

Hymen (Gr.)–A beautiful youth of divine descent; the god of marriage.

Juventas (Ro.)– *The same as* Hebe, *which see.*

Lausus (Gr.)--Son of the cruel Mezentius; a generous youth worthy of a better sire.

Linus (Gr.)--The beautiful son of Psamathe and Apollo; a legendary musician. In his youth he was torn to pieces by vicious dogs.

Medea (Gr.)-- *See* Aeson.

Menoceus (Gr.)--In the exploit, the Seven against Thebes, this heroic youth threw away his life in the first encounter.

Minos II (Gr.)--King of Crete. Because he had lost his son, Androgeüs, to the Marathonian bull, he required a penalty of the Athenians: To send a tribute of seven youths and seven maidens from Athens to Crete each year to feed the monster.

Orthia (Gr.); Diana (Ro.)--Protectress of youth.

Persephone (Gr.)--Goddess of death; cruel unyielding, inimical to youth, life and hope.

Phaedra (Gr.)--Wife of Theseus, she became enamored of his son, Hippolytus, who was young like herself. He repulsed her, however, and she hung herself.

Phaon (Gr.)--Aphrodite gave this ferryman a salve which possessed magical properties of youth and beauty. His use of it set the women of Lesbos wild for him.

Phoebus (Gr.); Apollo (Gr.)--A pure and just god; the ideal of fair and

Phoebus (cont.)--manly youth.

Pyramus (Gr.)--The handsomest youth in Babylonia, in love with the
young Thisbe. Each committed suicide believing the other to be
dead.

Rhoecus (Gr.)--This youth saved a tree from falling, and was rewarded
with the love of the dryad of the oak.

Satyrs (Gr.)--Dieties of the woods and fields, appearing early as youths
with sprouting horns.

Tithonus (Gr.)--Aurora fell in love with him, and asked Jupiter to grant
him immortality, but forgot to have youth joined in the gift. He
grew old and she lost interest. Finally, she turned him into a grasshopper.

Vertumnus (Gr.)--He wooed Pomona in many guises, and won her as a
comely youth.

AN INDEX OF THE NAMES OF
THE GODS AND HEROES

Cross-Referenced by Their Associations

A

Abas (Gr.) *See* *Offspring*

Abderus (Gr.) *Horse*

Absyrtus (Gr.) *Murder*

Acamus (Gr.) *Princess Box*

Acastus (Gr.) *Kings*

Acestes (Gr.) *Kings*
Sicily

Acetes (Gr.) *Pilot*
Trickery

Achates (Gr.) *Friendship*

Achelous (Gr.)
Athletics   *Horn*
Bull   *River*
Change in From   *Serpent*
Cornucopia   *Wrestler*

Acheron   *River*

Achilles (Gr.)
Ankle   *Hero*

Arrow   *Infant*
Chariot   *Murder*
Heel

Acis (Gr.)
Blood Trans-   *Offspring*
formed   *Rock*
Love   *Stream*
Naiads

Acrisius (Gr.)
Box   *Oracle*
Discus   *Prophecy*
Feet   *Sea*
Games

Actaeon (Gr.)   *Hunter*
                     Offspring

Admeta (Gr.)   *Girdle*

Admetus (Gr.)   *Animal*
                     Fates
                     Kings

Adonis (Gr.)
Boar   *Personification*
Love   *Shepherd*

349

Index

Antigone (Gr.)
   Funeral   Traitor
   Offspring

Antilochus (Gr.) Bravery
                 Hero

Antiope (Gr.)
   Abduction   Queens
   Amazon   Shepherd
   Bull   Wives
   Cruelty

Aphareus (Gr.)   Kings
                 Places

Aphrodite (Gr.)
   Animal   Sea
   Beauty   Sea Animals
   Flowers   Statue
   Goddesses   Tree
   Love   Turtle
   Plants   Wives
   Queens

Aphrodite Porne Love

Apollo (Gr.)
   Arrow   Nymphs
   Athletics   Offspring
   Chariot   Oracle
   Cruelty   Plague
   Death   Poetry
   Gods   Priestess
   Healing   Punishment
   Herds   Revenge
   Laws   Serpent
   Light   Shepherds
   Love   Sun
   Lyre   Symbols
   Mistress   Twins
   Mouse   Victory

356

357

363

Hippomenes (Gr.)
Apples, Golden
Change in Form   *Penance*
Happiness   *Races*

Horae, The (Gr.)
Attendant   *Hours*
Cloud   *Offspring*
Gate   *Olympus*
Goddesses   *Seasons*
Horae   *Weaving*

Hunt, Calydonian Boar (Gr.)
Boar   *Hunt*

Hyacinthus (Gr.)
Blood, Transformed
Companion   *Springtime*
Flowers   *Vegetation*
Games   *Wound*
Personification   *Youth*

Hyades (Gr.)
Heaven   *Nymphs*
Hyades   *Offspring*
Nurse   *Stars*

Hyale (Gr.)
Attendant   *Nymphs*

Hydra (Gr.)
Head   *Slain*
Marsh   *Swamp*
Monster   *Wound*
Serpent

Hygeia (Gr.)
Goddesses
Health   *Personification*

Hylas (Gr.)
Argonaut   *Expedition*
Blessed   *Nymphs*
Companion   *Springs*
Drowned

Hyllus (Gr.)   *Invasion*

Hymen (Gr.)
Feast   *Tears*
Gods   *Torch*
Marriage   *Wedding*
Offspring   *Youth*
Personification

Hyperion (Gr.)
Beauty
Sun   *Titan*

Hypermnestra (Gr.)
Wedding   *Wives*

Hypnos (Gr.)
Dreams   *Solace*
Gods   *Twins*
Sleep   *Wings*

I

Iacchus (Gr.); Bacchus (Gr.)
Animal   *Sea*
Gods   *Tutor*
Guardian   *Vegetation*
Offspring   *Wine*
Satyr   *Worship*

Iapetus (Gr.)
Hatred
Sovereign   *Titan*

374

376

378

380

Index

Prometheus (Gr.)

Art	Man
Birds	Offspring
Captive	Punishment
Creator	Rock
Cunning	Titan
Fire	
Liver	

Proserpina (Ro.); Persephone (Gr.)

Animal	Offspring
Attendant	Spring
Carried Off	Springtime
Chariot	Symbols
Corn	Tartarus
Cornucopia	Wives
Cruelty	
Food	
Giant	
Goddesses	
Hades	

Protesilaus (Gr.)

Death	Sacrifice
Hero	Ship
Lower World	Slain
Nymphs	Tree

Proteus (Gr.)

Age, Old	Change in Form
Altar	Funeral
Beasts	Gods
Bee	Prophet
Bull	Sea
Captive	

Psamanthe (Gr.) Mountain

Psyche (Gr.)

Beauty	Lower World
Box	Oracle
Heaven	Sleep
Immortality	Virgin
Jealous	Wives
Love	

Psychopompus (Gr.)

Ghost	Guide
Gods	Hades

Pygmalion (Gr.)

Covetous	
Life	Statue
Sculpture	Treasure

Pylades (Gr.)

Altar	Sacrifice
Friendship	Temple
Offspring	Wandering

Pylos (Gr.) Places

Pyramus (Gr.)

Blood, Trans-	Plants
formed	Suicide
Buried	Tree
Fruits	Youth
Lion	
Love	

Pyrrha (Gr.)

Offspring	Stone
Race	Wives

Pyrrhus (Gr.)

Offspring	Spear

Pythia (Gr.) Priestess

Index

396